T0319933

HISPANIC ENTREPRENEURS IN THE 2000s

HISPANIC ENTREPRENEURS IN THE 2000s

An Economic Profile and Policy Implications

Alberto Dávila
and Marie T. Mora

Stanford Economics and Finance
An Imprint of Stanford University Press
Stanford, California

Stanford University Press
Stanford, California

Special discounts for bulk quantities of titles in the Stanford Economics and Finance imprint are available to corporations, professional associations, and other organiza-tions. For details and discount information, contact the special sales department of Stanford University Press. Tel: (650) 736-1782, Fax: (650) 736-1784

Printed in the United States of America on acid-free, archival-quality paper

Library of Congress Cataloging-in-Publication Data

Dávila, Alberto E., author.
    Hispanic entrepreneurs in the 2000s : an economic profile and policy implications / Alberto Dávila and Marie T. Mora.
        pages cm
    Includes bibliographical references and index.
    ISBN 978-0-8047-7793-3 (cloth : alk. paper)
    1. Hispanic American businesspeople.   2. Hispanic American business enter-prises.   3. Entrepreneurship—United States.   I. Mora, Marie T., author.   II. Title.
    HD2358.5.U6D384 2013
    338.0089′68073—dc23

                                                            2013010528

    ISBN 978-0-8047-8801-4 (electronic)

Typeset by Newgen in 10/14 Minion

Acknowledgments

THIS BOOK WOULD NOT HAVE BEEN POSSIBLE WITHOUT THE help and support of several of our colleagues. In particular, we would like to express our sincere appreciation to Barbara Robles and the anonymous reviewers of our manuscript for their valuable comments and suggestions. We also thank Mark Hugo López, Rakesh Kochhar, and Sibin Wu for their insights regarding our initial proposal. Moreover, we thank the American Society of Hispanic Economists for providing us the opportunity to present some of this material in their conference sessions during the past couple of years, as well as the Board of Governors of the Federal Reserve System, the Federal Reserve Bank of Atlanta, and the Ewing Marion Kauffman Foundation for allowing us to participate in the conference "Small Business and Entrepreneurship during an Economic Recovery" in November 2011. A special acknowledgment goes to Margo Beth Fleming for her suggestions and help throughout this process, starting in the summer of 2009 at the Western Economic Association International annual meetings, when she first reached out to us with the confidence that we would successfully complete this manuscript. Finally, we would like to thank the graduate students here at the University of Texas–Pan American who provided useful research assistance at various stages of this manuscript, especially Sergio Garcia, Juan Guerrero, Nese Nasif, Xu Sun, and Lu Xu.

Contents

Figures and Tables

Figures

Tables

Preface

IN THE FIRST DECADE OF THE 2000s, MORE THAN HALF OF THE population growth in the United States was a product of the country's increasing Hispanic population. The decade started with 35.3 million and ended with 50.5 million individuals of Hispanic origin. And while one in eight Americans was of Hispanic ethnicity in 2000, this share had risen to one in six by 2010. Among many of the consequences of this population growth is the significant increase in the number of Hispanic business owners during this time. This observation is unsurprising (given that the larger base of this ethnic group helped generate more self-employment), but this population growth also brought with it an increasing demand for Hispanic products that, arguably, created more entrepreneurial opportunities for Hispanics. Consider this: more than 2.3 million Hispanic-owned businesses in the United States generated $350.7 billion in sales in 2007 alone.

Scholars such as us have found this phenomenon relatively unexplored by the popular press and in the academic literature. Over the past several years, we have participated at conferences, delivered papers, and served as discussants in a variety of academic venues to delve more into this issue. In one conference, the annual meeting of the Western Economic Association International in Vancouver, British Columbia, we presented a paper in an American Society of Hispanic Economists session titled "Changes in the Entrepreneurial Earnings of U.S. and Foreign-Born Mexican American Men: 2000–2007" in the summer of 2009. There we had the opportunity to chat with Margo Crouppen (now Fleming), a representative of Stanford University Press, on the importance of learning more about Hispanic entrepreneurship in the United States. She invited us to propose a book on this topic (which we did), and after several iterations and reviews, this book is the result of this effort.

We note that working on this book brought many challenges as we took on a relatively new topic. One stylistic challenge was to write this book with as few tables and methodological jargon as possible. From an academic perspective, many of these challenges, as other scholars writing on entrepreneurship topics have found, are data driven. Alicia Robb, an economist with the Kauffman Foundation, specifically mentioned this concern in the conference "Small Business and Entrepreneurship during an Economic Recovery," hosted by the Federal Reserve Board of Governors on November 9, 2011. To be sure, surveys on entrepreneurs in the United States abound, but many of these present conflicting evidence, lack time continuity, and have sampling issues.

That said, we use a variety of data sets here that provide new insights to the study of Hispanic entrepreneurs, particularly in the first decade of the 2000s. Our empirical analyses highlight the recently released microdata from the 2007 Survey of Business Owners. Also, because of our interest in learning more about the self-employment experiences of Hispanic subpopulations (i.e., partitioned by gender, national affiliation, region, and occupation), we rely heavily on annual microdata from the American Community Survey. Existing longitudinal data, such as the National Longitudinal Survey of Youth, do not have adequate sample sizes or cover the time period required to accomplish the intended objectives of this book. One convenient methodological tool that we adopt from the labor economics literature is synthetic-cohort analysis, to empirically analyze the business-cycle effects on Hispanic entrepreneurial outcomes.

With these data and methodological challenges come also definitional ones. For example, what does *entrepreneur* mean? According to *Merriam-Webster Dictionary* the term comes from the old French *entreprendre* ("to undertake"), defined as "one who organizes, manages, and assumes the risks of a business enterprise." Moreover, the dictionary defines *self-employed* as "earning income directly from one's own business, trade, or profession rather than as a specified salary or wages from an employer." The self-employed could proxy for the entrepreneur. The crux of the matter becomes what constitutes a business enterprise. Can this business enterprise comprise only an individual, or does it require paid employees as well? We note that some of the surveys we use here are more specific than others in answering this question.

Another definitional issue relates to the interpretation of entrepreneurial success. A quick answer to this issue simply invokes financial success, but a broader response should entail measures of entrepreneurial goals and targets. For example, in 2004, Mike Simpson, Nicki Tuck, and Sarah Bellamy, in a series of interviews of small business owner-managers in Sheffield, England, classified businesses into four categories of entrepreneurial success: (1) the empire builder, an entrepreneur who measures success in terms of financial success; (2) the happiness seeker (as the category suggests), who simply wants to be happy at work; (3) the vision developer, who seeks achievement and recognition in the marketplace; and (4) the challenge achiever, who strives for a personal sense of achievement and recognition. From a labor economics perspective, these research efforts recognize the hedonic aspects and preferences of individuals beyond the simple assumption that business owners seek to maximize income.

It is worth noting that sociologist Zulema Valdez in a 2011 study discusses how business "success" differs across race, class, and gender. In particular, she states:

> White middle class and male entrepreneurs garner the greatest rewards in enterprise. Middle class Latino/a men lag far behind their white counterparts in earnings; however, they earn significantly more than lower class Latino/a men and women, the latter group regardless of class. The lower earnings among Latina entrepreneurs are associated with their lack of market and social capital resources relative to Latino/a men, and highlight the significant role that gender plays in shaping Latino/a inequality. (p. 159)

She notes also that "the earnings of lower-class Latinos are likely to fall short of their economic expectations, leading them to rearticulate a meaning of success that captures *relative* economic success" (p. 107).

As is the case with much research, however, we must make assumptions throughout this book to tell our story. We (for the most part) call an entrepreneur a self-employed individual or a business owner and measure entrepreneurial success in terms of financial outcomes. But, yes, we realize that this approach might be simplistic. In this regard, we can only state that we attempt to move forward the argument (and in some cases the debate) of the experiences of Hispanic entrepreneurs at the turn of the 2000s. We believe that our account contributes, at a minimum, to empirical insights into the labor markets of an increasingly important population that might serve as fodder for future research on this matter.

HISPANIC ENTREPRENEURS IN THE 2000s

1 A Macro View of Hispanic Self-Employment in the 2000s

HISPANICS REPRESENTED ONE OUT OF EVERY SIX PEOPLE in the United States in 2010, up from one out of eight a decade earlier. Arguably, this Hispanic population growth was the catalyst for the sharp increase in the number of Hispanic business owners in the 2000s. For example, the most recent version of the Survey of Business Owners (SBO) reports that the number of Hispanic-owned businesses increased by 43.7 percent, from 1.6 million to 2.3 million firms, between 2002 and 2007, tripling the 14.5 percent growth in the number of businesses owned by non-Hispanics.

Figure 1.1 illustrates the rise in Hispanic entrepreneurship in the 2000s.[1] The representation of Hispanics among the self-employed aged 25–64 increased by 58.5 percent, from 8.2 percent to 13.0 percent, between 2000 and 2010 (see Panel A). This increase outstripped the 36.4 percent growth among Hispanics workers in general during this time. While Hispanics remained underrepresented in the self-employment sector, these changes served to reduce the extent of the underrepresentation of this population by the end of the decade.

A closer examination of the self-employed indicates that the disproportionate growth of Hispanics in the entrepreneurial sector stemmed from their rising presence in the U.S. workforce and from the strengthening of entrepreneurial tendencies within the Hispanic population. Indeed, our estimates reveal that Hispanic self-employment rates significantly increased from 7.9 percent in 2000 to 9.1 percent in 2010, rising almost every year during the

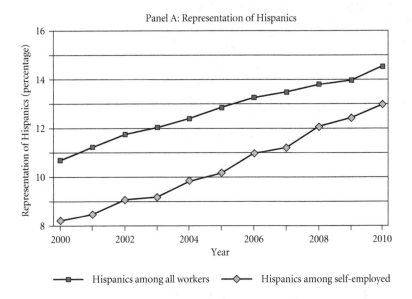

Panel A: Representation of Hispanics

Hispanics among all workers ■ Hispanics among self-employed ◆

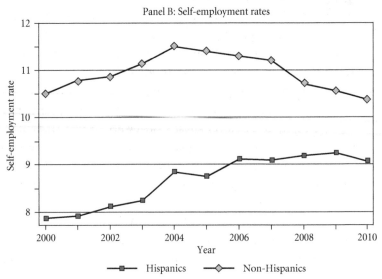

Panel B: Self-employment rates

■ Hispanics ◆ Non-Hispanics

FIGURE 1.1 Representation of Hispanics in the workforce and Hispanic and non-Hispanic self-employment rates, 2000–10

SOURCE: Authors' estimates using PUMS and ACS data in the IPUMS.
NOTES: The sample includes workers between the ages of twenty-five and sixty-four not living in group quarters.

decade. In contrast, despite increasing in the early 2000s, the self-employment rates of non-Hispanic workers declined over the time frame. Hispanics particularly narrowed their self-employment gap vis-à-vis non-Hispanics in the second half of the decade.

We provide in this chapter an overview of these changing entrepreneurial tendencies among the Hispanic population, which will set the stage for more detailed topics discussed later in the book. This chapter also presents information on the heterogeneity of the Hispanic population, such that one-size-fits-all policies affecting Hispanics overall could have disparate implications for specific Hispanic groups.

Hispanic Self-Employment and Macroeconomic Conditions

The first ten years of the new millennium witnessed historically sharp variations in the business cycle. This decade provided entrepreneurial opportunities, but it also brought with it significant challenges for entrepreneurs. To begin exploring this issue, we consider changes in the business cycle measured by annual economic growth rates (i.e., the percentage change in real gross domestic product). While U.S. economic growth slowed from 4.1 percent in 2000 to 1.1 percent in 2001, it mostly recovered from this slowdown over the following few years, as the economy expanded by 3.5 percent in 2004. After 2004, the U.S. economy began to slow down, and eventually it hit an economic recession in 2008 (or the Great Recession, which technically started in December 2007). The economy shrank by 0.3 percent in 2008, and despite the fact that the Great Recession officially ended in June 2009, throughout 2009 the economy contracted by another 3.5 percent. By 2010, economic output rebounded, growing at an annualized rate of 3.0 percent.

With few exceptions, the self-employment rates of non-Hispanic workers moved with economic growth. As the economy grew, in general so did non-Hispanic self-employment rates. When the economy slowed down, the entrepreneurial tendencies of non-Hispanic workers fell (although they kept falling in 2010, despite the recovery). Through 2005, the self-employment rates of Hispanics changed in a similar fashion as those of non-Hispanics. In much of the second half of the decade, however, Hispanic entrepreneurial tendencies moved in the opposite direction from those of non-Hispanics. The Hispanic self-employment rate peaked at 9.3 percent in 2009, and while it declined to 9.1 percent in 2010, it remained higher than at the height of the business cycle.

What might explain the resilience of Hispanic self-employment rates in the face of a slowing economy in the second part of the decade? An answer to this question involves an understanding of the factors that influence the self-employment decision and self-employment survival. From an individual perspective, research on the factors related to business ownership points to the relative returns to entrepreneurial employment, human capital, credit access from institutions and families (including family experience in self-employment), and preferences for business ownership. The group perspective points to the importance of labor-market discrimination and social capital in leading to the entrepreneurship decision.

The self-employment decision has also been cast in terms of occupation and industry, as well as spatial differentials. For example, economists Magnus Lofstrom and Chunbei Wang, in a 2009 study of the self-employment patterns of Mexican Americans, noted the importance of recognizing potential issues related to heterogeneity in business ownership across industries, such as differences in the "human and financial capital intensiveness" among ethnic groups, which might lead to different barriers to entry across industries. Economists Timothy Bates and Alicia Robb (2008) further reported that minority neighborhoods do not offer the same business opportunities as the broader regional marketplace; they concluded that the housing market in minority neighborhoods is associated with reduced business viability.

Of course, these are but some of the myriad issues related to business ownership and survival in the entrepreneurship literature. The purpose of the foregoing discussion is to provide initial context; we delve more deeply into the literature on these (and other) issues throughout this book.

For now, consider the impact of the economic slowdown in the 2000s on the labor market for Hispanics. Panel A in Figure 1.2 shows the unemployment rates of the Hispanic and non-Hispanic civilian population between 2000 and 2010, based on our estimates from data from the U.S. Bureau of Labor Statistics. The unemployment rates of Hispanics exceeded those of non-Hispanics in every year shown, although they tended to move together. For example, the unemployment rates for both groups rose steadily between 2000 and 2003, and then declined through the middle years of this period. After reaching a trough of 5.2 percent in 2006, the Hispanic unemployment rate increased sharply thereafter, increasing by 2.4 times to 12.5 percent in 2010. This result indicates that the Great Recession negatively affected employment

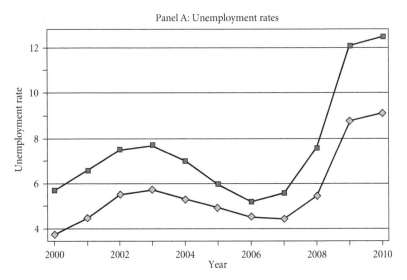

Panel A: Unemployment rates

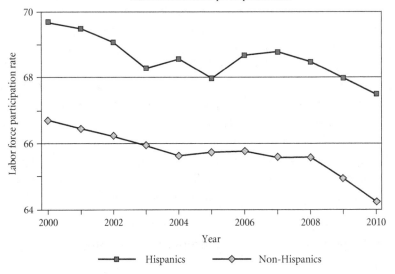

FIGURE 1.2 Unemployment and labor-force participation rates among Hispanics and non-Hispanics, 2000–10

SOURCE: Authors' estimates using data from the U.S. Bureau of Labor Statistics.
NOTE: The sample includes noninstitutionalized civilians aged sixteen and older.

opportunities in general, but disproportionately so for Hispanics than for the workforce overall.

Panel B in Figure 1.2 contains the labor-force participation rates (LF-PRs) of both groups. The LFPRs show that Hispanics were more likely to be in the labor force than non-Hispanics, and the gap remained fairly steady throughout the decade. In 2000, the LFPR for Hispanics of 69.7 percent was three percentage points higher than that for non-Hispanics. In 2010, the LFPR for Hispanics had fallen to 67.5 percent, and that of non-Hispanics reached 64.2 percent; for both groups, these were the lowest LFPRs in the entire decade.

Except during the Great Recession, the self-employment rates of non-Hispanics appear in lockstep with their unemployment rates. Namely, until 2008, self-employment rates for non-Hispanics tended to increase when unemployment rates for non-Hispanics were rising, and they fell when unemployment rates for non-Hispanics declined. For Hispanics, however, self-employment tended to increase when unemployment rates for Hispanics were rising in the first and last part of the decade (except in 2010), but they also increased in the middle of the decade (except for 2005)—a time when unemployment rates for Hispanics were falling.

Self-employment activities in the Hispanic population throughout the decade thus did not appear to be solely driven by cyclical conditions in the labor market. In the following chapter, we provide a more detailed discussion of whether Hispanics and non-Hispanics were pushed into self-employment at certain times because of a dearth of job prospects or whether the growing self-employment rates reflected increasing business opportunities that pulled them into the entrepreneurial sector. The remainder of this chapter explores other macroeconomic facets of Hispanic entrepreneurship.

The Representation of Microentrepreneurs Among Hispanic Business Owners

The foregoing discussion suggests a general increase in self-employment rates among Hispanics during the first decade of the 2000s. Indeed, during the economic expansion as well as through the slowdown and recession, Hispanic participation in entrepreneurial activities intensified. While these trends indicate that Hispanic entrepreneurs were creating jobs for themselves, how did they fare in terms of creating jobs for other workers?

Using SBO data from 2002 and 2007, Hispanic-owned businesses created on net four hundred thousand new jobs, as their total number of paid employees increased from 1.5 million to 1.9 million workers. Non-Hispanic-owned businesses added more than six hundred thousand jobs over the five-year period. This information indicates that Hispanic-owned enterprises disproportionately contributed to the creation of new paid-employment positions between 2002 and 2007. At the same time, the growth in the number of jobs created by Hispanics was smaller than the overall growth in the number of Hispanic-owned businesses, such that the average number of paid employees per firm declined (from about 1 worker to 0.8 workers per firm). The average number of workers per non-Hispanic-owned businesses also fell during this time (from 2.6 to 2.3), but by a slightly smaller proportion. As such, the expansion in Hispanic entrepreneurship in the first decade of the millennium occurred mainly at the level of very small firms.

Another way to investigate these patterns is to consider the share of microentrepreneurs among Hispanic entrepreneurs. We define *microentrepreneurs* as those businesses that have fewer than ten paid employees. We thus turn to the Public Use Microdata Sample (PUMS) of the 2007 SBO. (A comparable version of the 2002 SBO does not exist.) As described in Appendix A, the 2007 SBO PUMS (released by the U.S. Census Bureau in August 2012) contains detailed demographic, socioeconomic, and business-related characteristics based on the 2007 SBO questionnaire. In these data, nearly all (98.1 percent) Hispanic-owned firms had fewer than ten employees; this share was slightly higher than the 95.4 percent of businesses owned by non-Hispanics that had fewer than ten workers. These numbers are high partly because the vast majority of firms, particularly those owned by Hispanics, did not have employees: employer firms represented about one in ten (11.1 percent) of Hispanic-owned businesses and one in five (79.1 percent) of other businesses. When focusing exclusively on employers, microentrepreneurs were slightly overrepresented among Hispanics in 2007, as 82.6 percent had fewer than ten employees, compared to 77.9 percent among their non-Hispanic peers.

Moreover, turning to an alternative data set (the Current Population Survey, or CPS) that contains information on the number of employees working for the self-employed, we find that in every year between 2000 and 2010, microentrepreneurs represented higher shares of self-employed Hispanics than non-Hispanics, although the gap did not remain constant. Consider

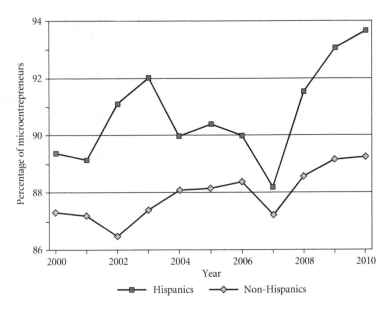

FIGURE 1.3 Representation of microentrepreneurs among self-employed Hispanics and non-Hispanics, 2000–10

SOURCE: Authors' estimates using CPS data in the IPUMS-CPS for microentrepreneurship (defined as having fewer than ten employees).

NOTES: The sample includes self-employed workers between the ages of twenty-five and sixty-four. The year is the year in which the individual was a microentrepreneur (the year prior to the CPS survey); see Appendix A.

Figure 1.3, which presents these shares. Between 2001 and 2003, the increase in self-employment among Hispanics occurred with a rising incidence of microentrepreneurship. Perhaps more Hispanics perceived lucrative business opportunities in the small-business sector during the economic expansion, thus leading to more Hispanic-owned microenterprises. Rates of Hispanic microentrepreneurs among the self-employed fell between 2005 and 2007, when the economy was slowing down.

With the onset of the Great Recession, the representation of microentrepreneurs among both self-employed Hispanics and non-Hispanics increased (although more sharply for Hispanics), thus resulting in the highest microentrepreneurship rates for the decade (93.7 percent for Hispanics and 89.3 percent for non-Hispanics) in 2010. In general, these results indicate that the rapidly growing population of Hispanic entrepreneurs affected microenterprises in the first decade of the 2000s. Hispanic entrepreneurial growth appears to have had a positive impact on job creation, but mostly at the scale of smaller firms, especially at the end of the decade. Later in this book, we return to the issue of microentrepreneurship by exploring gender- and immigrant-related variations in the shares of microentrepreneurs.

Another aspect related to firm size concerns the share of incorporated versus other types of businesses. Incorporated businesses tend to be larger than unincorporated firms with respect to several dimensions, including number of employees, sales, assets, and profits.[2] Using data from the Public Use Microdata Sample of the 2000 decennial census as well as from the 2001–10 American Community Surveys (ACS), we estimate that Hispanic-owned businesses had lower shares of incorporated firms in every year in the first decade of the 2000s than firms owned by non-Hispanics. The highest rate of incorporated firms for Hispanics occurred in 2000 (at 28 percent). This was also the year when the gap in this rate between Hispanics and non-Hispanics was narrowest.

Furthermore, changes in the ratio of Hispanic-owned incorporated versus unincorporated firms did not mirror such changes among other businesses overall. The incorporated share among Hispanics fell sharply in 2001; reached its lowest level (21.4 percent) in 2002; and began climbing until 2005, when it reached 26.8 percent. After that year, there was a general decline in the share of incorporated firms among Hispanic entrepreneurs, such that the decade ended with 23.3 percent of self-employed Hispanics operating incorporated firms. For non-Hispanics, with few exceptions, their shares of incorporated businesses rose throughout the decade (from 32.3 percent in 2000 to 36.4 percent in 2010). Combined with the declining incorporated shares among Hispanic entrepreneurs after 2005, such changes led to a widening of the difference between Hispanics and non-Hispanics in these shares in the second part of the decade. These changes again point to the notion that the rising self-employment rates of Hispanics during the economic slowdown and subsequent recession led to an increase in smaller-scale Hispanic-owned businesses.

Industry and Geographic Region

Industry. An additional question relates to whether the growth in Hispanic-owned businesses occurred evenly across the industrial spectrum in the

2000s, or whether it remained concentrated in particular industries. Such information is important to consider given the sensitivity of certain industries (e.g., construction) to macroeconomic events, while others (e.g., personal services) tend to be more insulated. It is also important to consider the cost of entering these industries, as suggested by the Lofstrom and Wang study mentioned earlier.

Focusing on 2000, Hispanic representation among entrepreneurs in transportation and warehousing, and to a lesser extent in construction, was higher than among entrepreneurs in general, and this representation was smaller in professional services industries. However, given the rapid growth in the number of Hispanic entrepreneurs in these industries during the decade, Hispanic overrepresentation among entrepreneurs in transportation and warehousing, as well as construction, increased. By 2010, Hispanics accounted for 13.0 percent of entrepreneurs overall, but Hispanic business owners represented 16.8 percent of those in transportation and warehousing, 16.0 percent in construction, and 12.9 percent in professional services.

The case of construction warrants particular attention. As Timothy Bates noted in his 2011 article on minority entrepreneurship, "Construction (absent discriminatory barriers) offers MBEs [minority business enterprises] major advantages lacking in many other industries. Lack of advanced education credentials and large financial investment are not usually a barrier to entry" (p. 245). In the first part of the decade when the housing bubble started, the presence of Hispanic entrepreneurs rose in this industry despite a decline in their self-employment rate between 2000 and 2002—a time when non-Hispanic self-employment was rising in the industry. In fact, Hispanic self-employment in construction in 2002 was at its lowest rate (at 14.0 percent) for the decade. This suggests that the sheer numbers of Hispanics in the industry, and not an intensification of their entrepreneurial tendencies, enhanced their representation in the industry in the first few years of the housing bubble.

As housing prices continued to escalate, Hispanic self-employment rates in construction increased, even as they tapered off among non-Hispanics. The decline in the housing sector led to a temporary decline in the Hispanic construction self-employment rate (to 15.0 percent) in 2007. However, Hispanic self-employment rates rose at a faster pace during the correction of the housing market (reaching their highest rate in the decade in 2010, at 18.5 percent) than they had when the housing bubble was growing. This was not the case for non-Hispanics, as their self-employment rates in construction fell after 2007. This information indicates that construction became an increasingly important industry for Hispanic entrepreneurs during and after the Great Recession.

The growing participation of Hispanics in the construction industry after 2002 seems to partly explain the overall rising self-employment rates for Hispanics during the economic slowdown and into the recession. Given that housing prices did not start falling until 2006, and that Hispanic entrepreneurs became increasingly likely to work in construction between 2002 and 2006, the housing market appears to be a stronger predictor of Hispanic entrepreneurship than overall economic growth in the first decade of the millennium.

Geography.   Geographic location also is a predictor for the increased entrepreneurial tendencies of Hispanics. Urban economists, such as Edward L. Glaeser in 2009, have written on the importance of local and socioeconomic conditions (including customer base, industrial composition, and costs) in stimulating entrepreneurship. An important socioeconomic factor relating geography to Hispanic entrepreneurship is immigration. (The previously mentioned study by Bates and Robb also illustrates the importance of accounting for the spatial dimension, even at the level of neighborhoods, when studying the business formation patterns of minorities).

Immigrants, who represented two-thirds of all self-employed Hispanics aged 25–64 in 2000, are arguably relatively mobile. In fact, while Hispanics have traditionally been concentrated primarily in the Southwest and Florida, Hispanic populations (particularly immigrants) moved into many nontraditional geographic areas in the first decade of the millennium. As highlighted in a 2011 Pew Hispanic Center report by Jeffrey Passel, D'Vera Cohn, and Mark Hugo López, the Hispanic population growth rate between 2000 and 2010 was higher in the South and the Midwest than almost anywhere else in the United States.

Recent SBO data indicate substantial variation in regional growth in Hispanic self-employment across the nation. Four of the five states with the greatest change in the number of Hispanic-owned firms between 2002 and 2007 were located in the South: Arkansas, North Carolina, Tennessee, and South Carolina. Ranking third, with a growth rate of 106.8 percent (to 22,797 firms), Pennsylvania was the only non-Southern state in the top five in terms of Hispanic business growth.

Our estimates reveal that, in every region, Hispanics increased their presence among entrepreneurs, but the growth was uneven across regions. The

Pacific region had the highest presence of Hispanics among entrepreneurs in every year between 2000 and 2010, reaching 22.3 percent in 2010. Nevertheless, despite representing a smaller share of the self-employed nationally, the growth of the share of Hispanics during the decade was stronger in four other geographic areas (New England, North Central, South Atlantic, and South Central—defined in Appendix A). Moreover, while Mountain and South Central states had similar shares of Hispanics among the self-employed in 2000 (10.1 percent and 10.3 percent, respectively), Hispanics represented a greater share of the self-employed in South Central states (at 17.2 percent) than in Mountain states (13.8 percent) in 2010. Middle Atlantic and South Atlantic states also had a similar presence of Hispanics in the entrepreneurial sector in 2000 (7.7 percent and 7.6 percent, respectively), but the disproportionate growth of Hispanic entrepreneurs in the South Atlantic region caused their share among the self-employed to rise to 13.3 percent (close to their presence in Mountain states) by 2010, thus exceeding their presence (10.6 percent) in Middle Atlantic states.

In summary, this information suggests that while Hispanic entrepreneurial activities strengthened in all regions of the United States in the 2000s, the intensity appears to be sensitive to geographic location. Given the heterogeneity of the Hispanic population, however, we next consider differences in the entrepreneurial tendencies of specific Hispanic groups; such differences could explain some of the regional differences in Hispanic entrepreneurship observed thus far.

Hispanic Diversity

Mexican-origin populations (including U.S.-born Mexican Americans) represent the largest Hispanic ethnic subgroup. In a 2010 Census brief, Sharon Ennis, Merarys Ríos-Vargas, and Nora Albert estimated that the 31.8 million individuals who reported being Mexican or Mexican American accounted for 63 percent of all Hispanics living in the fifty states and District of Columbia, followed by Puerto Ricans (9.2 percent), Cubans (3.5 percent), Salvadorans (3.3 percent), Dominicans (2.8 percent), and Guatemalans (2.1 percent), with the remainder reporting other smaller Hispanic subgroups.

In terms of Hispanic business owners in the SBO, Mexican Americans (a population that includes Mexican immigrants) owned one million firms in 2007, such that they represented the largest Hispanic subgroup; however, their representation (of 45.8 percent) was smaller than their share of the overall population. Puerto Ricans, too, were underrepresented, as they held 157,000 (6.9 percent) of Hispanic-owned firms. In contrast, Cubans owned 251,000 (11.1 percent) of all Hispanic-owned businesses, more than triple their overall population share.

As in the overall Hispanic population, with the exception of Puerto Ricans, the increasing presence of these Hispanic subgroups in the business sector was driven by more than their overall population growth. Their self-employment rates were higher in 2010 than in 2000, indicating an intensification of their entrepreneurial tendencies during the decade. Among the four largest Hispanic subgroups, in every year in the decade, Cubans had the highest self-employment rates, followed by Salvadorans, then Mexican Americans, and finally Puerto Ricans.

The highs for the self-employment rates of Hispanic subgroups occurred at different times in the decade. The rates increased (albeit slightly, relative to the other groups) almost every year among Mexican Americans, such that they reached their highest rate (at 8.7 percent) in 2009—the year in which the most recent recession ended. Even with a slight decline the following year, Mexican Americans had their second highest self-employment rate of the decade in 2010.

Over the same time period, Cubans reached their highest self-employment rate in 2006 (15.4 percent), at the beginning of the housing crisis. In 2007, 2009, and 2010, their self-employment rates fell, such that they ended the decade with the lowest self-employment rate since 2003. Among Salvadorans, the self-employment rate reached its highest level for the decade in 2002 (at 10.7 percent), and then its lowest level (8.5 percent) the following year. In a large part of the decade, Salvadoran and Cuban self-employment rates moved together, although for Salvadorans, the 2010 rate exceeded that of 2009 because of a rebound that year. The self-employment rates of Puerto Ricans remained fairly steady between 2000 and 2003, and then rose in 2004 to their highest point in the decade (at 6.2 percent). This self-employment rate tapered slightly the following year and was again generally stable until 2008, after which time it declined for the remainder of the decade.

Concluding Remarks

This overview of Hispanic entrepreneurship in the first decade of the 2000s highlights the differences that existed in self-employment across regions, industries, and ethnic subgroups. In addition, the chapter makes note of the importance of the business cycle during this time for studying Hispanic entrepreneurship, particularly as it relates to the study of the self-employment patterns of Hispanics in the periods before, during, and after the Great Recession. In what follows, we focus our attention on the earnings of Hispanic entrepreneurs over this business cycle, and with this information we build on our analyses to include immigrants, education, and gender issues.

2 Entrepreneurial Earnings of Hispanics in the 2000s

SELF-EMPLOYMENT PROVIDED AN INCREASINGLY IMPORTANT source of jobs as well as economic opportunity for Hispanics in the 2000s. Self-employment rates among Hispanics were higher in 2010 than in 2000, and this trend might appear, at first glance, to bode well for Hispanics' economic progress. Such an assessment, however, should consider at least two related questions. First, were these groups pushed into self-employment in the 2000s because of a dearth in job prospects, or did the trends reflect increasing business opportunities that pulled the ethnic Hispanic populations into the entrepreneurial sector? As Timothy Bates discusses in his 2011 study on minority entrepreneurship:

> Barriers limiting the range of opportunities for wage and salary work have often *pushed* minorities toward embracing self-employment, even among individuals who preferred to work as employees. Alternatively, many preferred to own their own business ventures and chose to give up paid employment when attractive opportunities became available; in this sense, they were *pulled* into small business ownership. The push/pull dynamic continually altering the size and scope of the minority business community is easily clarified by examining applicable constraints and opportunities in historical context. (p. 160)

Second, what was the relative impact of the increase in the number of entrepreneurs on the average "quality" (i.e., innate entrepreneurial talent plus acquired skills) of self-employed Hispanics? Arguably, if these entrepreneurs were pushed into self-employment and this process eroded the average talent and skills of Hispanic entrepreneurs, then an optimistic assessment based on the increasing self-employment rates of these demographic populations would not be warranted.

In this chapter, we outline relevant literature that sheds light on these issues and provides insight into our investigation of the impact of an increasing entrepreneurial base on the talent and skills of the self-employed. We further delve into these questions by analyzing the sales and profits of Hispanic-owned firms, as well as changes in the relative earnings of self-employed Hispanics during the first decade of the 2000s. We also consider how entrepreneurial earnings changed for the largest Hispanic ethnic subgroups and for workers in the construction industry versus other industries. Related changes along other demographic dimensions, such as immigration and gender, are explored later in the book.

Many of our analyses in this chapter (and subsequent ones) focus on two specific periods during the decade: 2002 to 2007 and 2007 to 2010. Although data availability necessitated part of this decision, these spans also correspond to specific periods in the business cycle. As discussed in the previous chapter, an economic recovery was under way in 2002 after a slowdown the year before, and economic growth remained positive through 2007. The 2002–7 period also was a time when the housing market boomed—an important driver of the construction industry, in which Hispanics actively participated. The 2007–10 period contains the Great Recession, which lasted from December 2007 until June 2009. Comparing 2007 with 2010 therefore allows us to observe how Hispanic entrepreneurs fared during the recession.

Conceptual Issues

Economists Kenneth Clark and Stephen Drinkwater show in a conceptual study from 1998 that when entrepreneurial talent distributes normally across a population, and when those with more talent are the first to choose self-employment, the overall average quality of entrepreneurs declines over time as additional individuals choose self-employment. All else being equal, this entry of new workers into the entrepreneurial sector subsequently dampens the average earnings of the self-employed in comparison with their salaried counterparts. A noteworthy point about this theoretical observation is that the decline in quality occurs independently of whether individuals are pulled or pushed into self-employment. Namely, during relative improvements in the entrepreneurial sector (which attract workers to self-employment), those who become self-employed come from a lower part of the entrepreneurial skill distribution than that of existing entrepreneurs. Individuals displaced from the wage and salary sector also, on average, have fewer entrepreneurial skills than those who are already self-employed.

The magnitude of the average decline in entrepreneurial quality resulting from entry into self-employment, however, depends on whether the entry into the entrepreneurship sector is related to factors of pull or push. For example, consider that the wage and salary sector has "talented" and "untalented" would-be entrepreneurs, where the average quality of the talented would-be entrepreneurs falls below that of existing entrepreneurs. In the case of expanding entrepreneurial opportunities, the talented prospective entrepreneurs join first; that is, they are pulled into self-employment. However, if workers are displaced from the wage and salary sector because of, say, increasing importance of observable skills (e.g., education) and unobservable skills (e.g., innate ability), the untalented would-be entrepreneurs move toward the self-employment sector. In this case, the push into self-employment drags the average quality of the entrepreneurial sector down more than the pull into self-employment does.

The caveat to this argument can be cast in terms of the so-called disadvantaged theory, as discussed by sociologist Ivan Light. This theory predicts that socioeconomic and demographic factors (e.g., discrimination, limited English-language fluency, relatively low levels of education) push individuals into self-employment because they have difficulty competing for paid-employment jobs. Yet if labor-market discrimination pushes workers into self-employment, those with the best entrepreneurial prospects would be the first to exit the paid-employment sector and become self-employed. For example, economists Pia Orrenius and Madeline Zavodny suggest in a 2009 study that after September 11, 2001, increased immigration enforcement may have negatively affected the employment prospects of Hispanics, not because of increasing returns to skills but because of the perception that some of these workers might not be legally working in the United States. In this case, we expect that after September 11, 2001, prospective Hispanic entrepreneurs with more talent left the wage and salary sector for self-employment.

In terms of potential earnings impacts, economic theory predicts that the earnings of the self-employed should decline with push factors, all else being equal, given the increase in the number of entrepreneurs and a decrease in their average quality. The net change in average earnings of the self-employed, however, becomes less clear in the presence of pull factors. While earnings should fall because of the decrease in the number and quality of entrepreneurs, the increase in the demand for entrepreneurs (which can occur when the demand for goods and services they provide rises) that attracted them into the entrepreneurial sector should increase earnings.

The foregoing discussion addresses potential changes in entrepreneurial quality given the choices of U.S.-born workers. The average quality of the pool of entrepreneurs can be further affected by immigrants who first choose to migrate to the United States and then select self-employment rather than paid employment. The topic of immigration and entrepreneurship is discussed in the following chapter.

Before moving to our empirical discussion, we want to be clear in stating that the push-pull framework informs individuals' potential entry into and exit from self-employment, but it is also marred by interpretations of how these processes affect entrepreneurs' earnings. Ultimately, the empirical results we present here can be interpreted in a host of ways within this conceptual framework. Indeed, Timothy Bates states in his 2011 article, "The push-versus-pull dynamic shaping minority venture behavior is widely recognized, yet this concept is nonetheless underutilized as an analytical tool" (p. 294).

Empirical Analysis of the Sales, Profits, and Earnings of Hispanic Entrepreneurs

In this section, we investigate some of the key financial outcomes achieved by Hispanic entrepreneurs, including sales, profits, and labor-market earnings during the first decade of the 2000s. As we mentioned in the preface, no single measure of the success of entrepreneurs exists. While nonfinancial rewards (e.g., satisfaction of being one's own boss) are part of this story, data availability generally limits analyses of entrepreneurial success to more tangible outcomes.

Sales Between 2002 and 2007. Recall from the previous chapter that, according to the Survey of Business Owners (SBO), the 43.7 percent growth in the number of Hispanic-owned businesses tripled the 14.5 percent growth in the number of other businesses in the United States between 2002 and 2007.[1] During this time, sales of Hispanic-owned firms also increased, rising (in nominal terms) by 10 percent, from $141,000 to $155,100 overall. This increase was not enough to keep up with the 14.4 percent rate of inflation during this time.

Despite rapid growth in the number of Hispanic-owned enterprises, it appears that such firms were, on average, more successful in 2002 than in 2007 with respect to the real value of sales per firm. But this may be driven by the growth in the number of microenterprises. Partitioning Hispanic-owned firms between employer and nonemployer enterprises provides some support for this notion. For example, average sales rose by 25 percent (from $899,600 to $1.12 million) for Hispanic-owned employer firms, but only by 13.9 percent (from $30,900 to $35,200) for Hispanic-owned nonemployer firms between 2002 and 2007. Even though the latter fell short of the inflation rate during this time, the gap was smaller than when considering Hispanic enterprises overall.

Furthermore, despite having lower average sales than their non-Hispanic counterparts, Hispanic entrepreneurs in general (particularly nonemployers) narrowed the gap with comparable non-Hispanics during this time. Average sales increased by 8.3 percent (from $409,400 to $443,100) among all non-Hispanic-owned businesses and by a mere 3 percent (from $43,900 to $45,200) among the non-Hispanic nonemployers during the five-year period. Only among employers did non-Hispanics gain ground against their Hispanic counterparts; their average sales rose by 32 percent (from $1.58 million to $2.08 million).

A Closer Examination of Sales in 2007.   Admittedly, focusing exclusively on sales per firm provides an incomplete picture of the relative success of Hispanic-owned businesses. One reason is that the distribution of sales tends to be skewed toward lower revenue levels. To illustrate, more than one-third (37.6 percent) of all Hispanic-owned firms in the 2007 SBO had sales of less than $10,000, and nearly two-thirds (63.6 percent) had sales of less than $25,000. Fewer than 15 percent of these firms had sales of $100,000 or more. As such, the average sales of $155,100 mentioned earlier do not reflect the "typical" Hispanic-owned business. Accounting for the shape of sales distributions therefore provides a more complete picture of the revenue outcomes of Hispanic-owned versus non-Hispanic-owned businesses.

One way to accomplish this is to analyze sales logarithmically. We note, however, that one shortcoming of this empirical strategy is that, as noted by Alejandro Portes and Min Zhou (1996), "the loglinear form fits the data better, but at the cost of obliterating substantively important information, namely the preponderance of the self-employed among positive outliers" (p. 219).

For this analysis, we use the Public Use Microdata Sample from the 2007 SBO (SBO PUMS). The natural logarithm of annual sales averaged $9.756 (approximately $17,300) among all Hispanic-owned firms and $10.141 (approximately $25,400) among other firms,[2] which represents a statistically significant sales gap of 38.5 percent between Hispanic- and non-Hispanic-owned enterprises. Despite the seeming magnitude, this is considerably smaller than the 185.7 percent gap estimated using the sales-per-firm figures of $155,100 versus $443,100 mentioned above. Moreover, when separating employers from nonemployer firms, those owned by Hispanics appeared to fare better (especially among nonemployer companies), at least in 2007. The sales gaps between Hispanic- and non-Hispanic-owned enterprises were 31.2 percent among employer firms and a statistically insignificant 3.5 percent among nonemployer firms.

Another potential problem with focusing on average sales (even when logarithmically transformed) is that they reflect a variety of business conditions and characteristics beyond the entrepreneurial talent of the owners. The rapid growth in the number (and presence) of Hispanic-owned businesses in the 2000s indicates that many of these businesses were new; newer firms tend to be smaller and to have fewer employees than more established ones. Recall from the previous chapter that there were disproportionately fewer employer Hispanic business owners than employer non-Hispanic business owners, and that among employers, Hispanics were more likely to be microentrepreneurs. It is therefore not surprising that average sales of Hispanic-owned firms were less than those of other firms.

To address this issue, we compare the natural logarithm of sales between Hispanic and non-Hispanic entrepreneurs, controlling for other observable characteristics identified in the literature as predictors of business outcomes, such as the traits of the owners (e.g., gender; birthplace: United States or abroad; education, age) and the firm (e.g., age, industry, whether it was a "home business," geographic location).[3] On the basis of this approach, we estimate that the sales of Hispanic-owned firms were, on average, 10 percent less than those of other comparable businesses in 2007. As such, much of the sales differential between Hispanic and non-Hispanic firms noted above can be explained by differences in observable characteristics between the two groups. Similarly, the magnitude of this sales differential decreases when employer and nonemployer firms are separated in this analysis. Compared to otherwise-similar non-Hispanic-owned businesses, Hispanic employers had 9.5 percent lower sales, and Hispanic firms without employees had a trivial 1.7 percent sales gap.

Sales and Profits in the Mid-2000s.   Of course, sales do not represent the earnings of entrepreneurs, as they do not account for business costs. Unfortunately, the SBO does not provide information to the public on profits. We therefore turn to data from the 2003 version (the most recent version) of the Survey of Small Business Finances (SSBF) to consider the sales and profits of firms in the 2004–5 period (for more information, see Appendix A). This nationally representative data set focuses on a smaller set of businesses than those in the SBO, as it contains for-profit, nonfinancial, nonfarm, nonsubsidiary business enterprises that had fewer than five hundred employees and were in operation at the end of 2003. The 2007 SBO, in contrast, contains a sample of most firms in operation in 2007 identified through a combination of tax returns and data from other economic census reports.

As noted by Bates (2011), firms in the SSBF "represent an older, more established, larger-scale subset of the nation's small business community" (p. 219). It is therefore not surprising that nonemployer firms (which tend to be relatively small) represent the vast majority of businesses in the 2007 SBO (four out of five) but only a small share (one out of four) of those in the 2003 SSBF. It follows that the two data sets are not necessarily directly comparable, which readers should bear in mind throughout this book.

In the SSBF, average sales and profits for the mid-2000s were $776,200 and $136,100, respectively, among Hispanic-owned small firms, and $1,055,400 and $172,900, respectively, among other small businesses. While both metrics were lower for Hispanic-owned businesses than for non-Hispanic businesses, there are three points that should be made. First, the difference in average profits between the two groups was not statistically significant at conventional levels (though average sales differed), which suggests that Hispanic-owned small firms were not faring worse with respect to their profits than other small businesses, as the numbers might initially imply. Second, the average profit margin of Hispanic-owned small businesses of 17.5 percent ($136,100 divided by $776,200) slightly exceeded the average profit margin of 16.4 percent ($172,900 divided by $1,055,400) of other small enterprises. Finally, when controlling for other characteristics that are likely related to sales and profits, such as the owners' education and age of the firm (see Appendix B), neither the sales nor the profits of Hispanic-owned small enterprises significantly differed from those of their otherwise-similar non-Hispanic counterparts in this particular data set.

We also considered whether Hispanic-owned firms differed from firms owned by non-Hispanics with respect to the likelihood of profits achieving two different benchmarks: breaking even and reaching at least $10,000. Having positive profits matters because of the long-term implications for a firm's stability. The $10,000 benchmark has been identified in a series of studies by economists Robert Fairlie and Alicia Robb as a key measure of a firm's success.[4] Approximately three-quarters of both groups were breaking even, and 60 percent recorded profits of $10,000 or more in the mid-2000s. When taking into account other observable characteristics of owners and firms related to profits, both groups continued to be similar with respect to achieving these profit targets.

Earnings of the Self-Employed Between 2002 and 2007.   We use the American Community Survey (ACS) to explore the earnings of the self-employed relative to workers in the paid-employment sector during the 2000s. In these data, self-employment earnings refer to business income net of expenses. Self-employed Hispanics between the ages of twenty-five and sixty-four earned an average of $33,000 ($21.94 per hour) in 2002, compared to the $27,200 ($16.10 per hour) earned by other Hispanic workers. Five years later, the average earnings of both groups had increased (in nominal terms) to $36,400 ($23.69 per hour) for Hispanic entrepreneurs, relative to $31,100 ($18.45 per hour) for Hispanic paid employees.

These numbers reveal several interesting points. First, the increase in annual self-employment earnings nearly matched the 10 percent increase in sales of Hispanic-owned businesses in the SBO, which suggests some comparability in changes in Hispanic entrepreneurs' self-employment income and sales. Second, the earnings (both annual and hourly) of self-employed Hispanics did not keep up with the inflation rate (of 14.4 percent) over the five-year period, whereas the earnings of Hispanics in the paid-employment sector did. Finally, the seeming earnings advantage of Hispanic entrepreneurs over their paid-employee counterparts narrowed slightly during the five years, consistent with the disproportionate growth in the number of self-employed Hispanics. This general observation parallels the conceptual argument presented above that regardless of the reason (push or pull) for entering the entrepreneurial sector, relative self-employment earnings should fall, all else being equal.

These comparisons, however, relate to differences in the level of average earnings. Many labor economists tend to analyze differences with respect to the natural logarithm of earnings instead of their actual values because outliers in the upper tails of earnings distributions tend to skew the distributions.[5] Of specific interest here, when focusing on natural logarithms, self-employed Hispanics earned less on an annual and hourly basis than did other Hispanic workers in both years. Indeed, using this measure, compared to Hispanics in paid-employment jobs, the annual labor-market income of Hispanic entrepreneurs was 18.8 percent less in 2002 and 22.5 percent less in 2007. The fact that Hispanic entrepreneurs have lower average earnings (when expressed in natural logs) than their fellow ethnics in the paid-employment sector matches the literature on entrepreneurs in general. We henceforth refer to this gap as a self-employment earnings penalty.

The Effects of Observables Versus Unobservables on Hispanics' Self-Employment Earnings Between 2002 and 2007. The foregoing discussion of the push-pull framework suggests that relative changes in the Hispanic entrepreneurs' observed human capital levels and other characteristics, as well as unobserved factors, can affect their relative earnings. More meaningful estimates of entrepreneurs' income with respect to those accrued by other workers should account for differences in observable characteristics.

Figure 2.1 presents a simple visualization of these estimates in the first decade of the 2000s. The lines labeled "Unadjusted" refer to the percentage differences in annual earnings (in terms of natural logs) between entrepreneurs and paid-employment workers, without accounting for observable socioeconomic and demographic characteristics. The "Adjusted" lines show the percentage differences in earnings between self-employed and salaried workers when controlling for observable socioeconomic and demographic characteristics, industry, and geographic region (see Appendix B). For purposes of comparison, we also present these numbers for non-Hispanics.

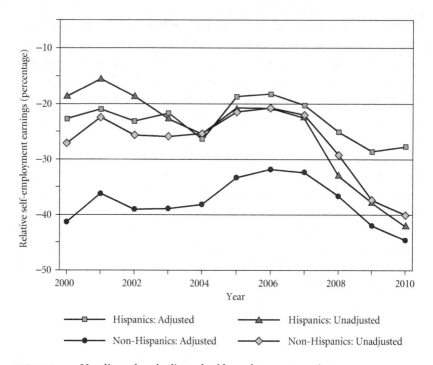

FIGURE 2.1 Unadjusted and adjusted self-employment earnings penalties for Hispanic and non-Hispanic workers, 2000–10

SOURCE: Authors' estimates using PUMS and ACS data in the IPUMS.

NOTES: Earnings penalties are defined on the basis of the relative earnings of the self-employed versus workers in the paid-employment sector. The "unadjusted" earnings penalties show the "raw" penalties, while the "adjusted" penalties show the penalties when controlling for observable characteristics. The sample includes workers between the ages of twenty-five and sixty-four not living in group quarters. For estimation details, see Appendix B.

Between 2000 and 2002, the adjusted penalties were greater than unadjusted penalties for Hispanics. This means that differences in unobservable characteristics between Hispanic entrepreneurs and Hispanic workers in the paid-employment sector exacerbated the self-employment penalty. For example, in 2002, the adjusted earnings penalty of 21.7 percent for self-employed Hispanics was 2.9 percentage points larger than the "raw" 18.8 percent penalty mentioned above, which means that when accounting for observable characteristics, Hispanic entrepreneurs were faring worse than expected with respect to their relative earnings.

Despite worsening in 2004, both the unadjusted and the adjusted earnings penalties shrank in magnitude after that year, reaching their smallest levels in the decade in 2006 (with an adjusted penalty of 18.3 percent)—the peak of the housing bubble. While the characteristics-adjusted earnings account for the industry in which the entrepreneurs worked, later in this chapter, we explicitly consider whether this pattern occurred primarily in the construction sector.

The direct comparison between 2002 and 2007 in Figure 2.1 indicates that Hispanic entrepreneurs experienced a relative improvement in their adjusted earnings, even though their unadjusted relative earnings declined. It follows that changes in unobservable characteristics (e.g., better entrepreneurial quality) served to reduce part of the Hispanic self-employment penalties during this time. For example, these characteristics trimmed 2.2 percentage points off the total penalty in 2007 but had added 2.9 percentage points to the penalty five years earlier. This figure further shows that the self-employment penalties widened again in 2007 and continued to do so more sharply during the Great Recession.

These changes are consistent with predictions from the push-pull framework. During an expansionary economy when more opportunities exist for entrepreneurs, self-employment rates tend to rise, which could have the effect of dampening self-employment earnings. However, the pull forces might be strong enough to mitigate this potential negative effect, which seems to have been the case for Hispanic entrepreneurs during the mid-2000s. Along with increasing self-employment participation, their earnings improved relative to otherwise similar workers in the paid-employment sector. As the economy weakened, stronger push than pull conditions likely existed, which would have resulted in a deterioration of relative earnings of the self-employed.

Figure 2.1 also indicates the comparative advantage that Hispanics had over non-Hispanics in the self-employment sector when controlling for observable characteristics, as they had a smaller adjusted earnings penalty in each of the years shown. Arguably, the comparative advantages in self-employment may partly explain Hispanics' increasing tendency toward self-employment throughout the decade.

Decomposing Changes in Earnings Between 2002 and 2007.   At this point, we delve further into the change in the self-employment earnings penalty for Hispanics following an empirical technique developed in 1993 by Chinhui

Juhn, Kevin Murphy, and Brooks Pierce. The logic behind this technique revolves around tracking changes in labor-market income between two groups over time. This empirical methodology explains relative changes in four different factors: (1) observable characteristics, (2) returns to observable characteristics, (3) unobservable characteristics, and (4) returns to unobservable characteristics. In particular, the discussion above noted that the total (unadjusted) Hispanic self-employment penalty rose from 18.8 percent in 2002 to 22.5 percent in 2007. This indicates that, in a relative sense, Hispanic entrepreneurs lost a total of 3.7 percentage points in their earnings between these two years. The Juhn-Murphy-Pierce (henceforth JMP) technique can be used to untangle the components behind this change.

Figure 2.2 presents our JMP estimates for the 2002–7 period (for details, see Appendix B). The first column (labeled "Total Change") displays the 3.7-percentage-point loss in Hispanic entrepreneurs' relative earnings; the sum of the four remaining columns equals this loss. The first JMP component ("Obs. Char") tracks a change in observable skills and other characteristics between Hispanic entrepreneurs and their peers in the paid-employment sector. Our estimates suggest that this component alone would have caused the relative earnings of Hispanic entrepreneurs to deteriorate by 6.7 percent. This could mean that workers in the self-employment sector in 2007 had lower average observable skills (or that those in the paid-employment sector had higher observable skills) than in 2002.

The second component affecting relative earnings between these two groups involves a change in the relative returns to these observable characteristics over this time interval. To illustrate this point, let's say that Hispanic entrepreneurs lost one year in education over their paid-employment counterparts between 2002 and 2007, and that each year of education increased earnings by 4 percent. Without taking into account the changes in the returns to education over the period, the lower average education level of Hispanic entrepreneurs would have increased their earnings penalty by four percentage points. However, if the returns to schooling also increased during this time frame, say, to 6 percent, then a one-year loss of schooling, in relative terms, would exacerbate the earnings penalty by an additional two percentage points.

In terms of our JMP estimates, the returns to observable characteristics fell slightly between 2002 and 2007, providing a negligible improvement of one-tenth of a percentage point in relative earnings of Hispanic entrepre-

FIGURE 2.2 Illustration of the JMP components of the change in the relative earnings of self-employed Hispanics between 2002 and 2007

SOURCE: Authors' estimates using ACS data in the IPUMS.

NOTES: The sample includes workers between the ages of twenty-five and sixty-four not living in group quarters. The "total change" equals the sum of the four remaining columns. For estimation details, see Appendix B.
Obs. = observable; Unobs. = unobservable; Char. = characteristics.

neurs. In most of our JMP estimates, changes in the returns to observable characteristics are consistently small (as would be expected over short intervals), such that most of our discussion focuses on changes in the levels of observable versus unobservable characteristics over the intervals in question.

The other two JMP components parallel the first two, but in these cases, changes in earnings between workers in the self-employment and paid-employment sectors relate to changes in unobservable characteristics (e.g., motivation, ability, schooling quality) and in the returns on these characteristics. According to our estimates, the level of this unobserved quality increased between 2002 and 2007 in a relative sense for Hispanic entrepreneurs, thus offsetting the average self-employment penalty by 2.8 percentage points. Admittedly, while this finding seemingly runs counter to the push-pull conceptual framework discussed above (which predicts lower average skills as more workers turn to self-employment, regardless of the cause), we note that overall the average skills of Hispanic entrepreneurs fell. The fourth JMP component suggests a trivial change in the returns to unobservable skills, which also served to slightly reduce the self-employment penalty.

In all, these results indicate that changes in observable skills served to reduce the relative earnings of self-employed Hispanics between 2002 and 2007, but these earnings effects were somewhat mitigated by improvements in the levels of unobservable characteristics. Indeed, when controlling for observable characteristics, Hispanic entrepreneurs experienced improved relative earnings during this time. That Hispanic entrepreneurs' skills-adjusted self-employment earnings increased at a time when their self-employment rates were also rising suggests the presence of relatively strong conditions pulling Hispanics toward self-employment in the middle of the decade.

Decomposing Changes in Earnings Between 2007 and 2010.   We replicate the JMP analysis for the 2007–10 period. Consider first that during the Great Recession, the relative earnings, both unadjusted and adjusted, of Hispanic entrepreneurs declined, such that they reached their largest characteristic-adjusted penalty of the decade (at 28.6 percent) in 2009, as the Great Recession ended (see Figure 2.1). The recession essentially erased all gains Hispanic entrepreneurs had made earlier in the decade. While there was a modest improvement (to an adjusted penalty of 27.7 percent) in the following year, the relative self-employment earnings of Hispanics remained considerably lower than they were earlier in the decade.

Consider also, as mentioned in the previous chapter, that self-employment rates among Hispanics continued to rise during the Great Recession. As their relative entrepreneurial earnings declined during this time, it appears that push factors became prevalent. Namely, our findings suggest that an increasing share of Hispanics became self-employed during this economic downturn, to avoid becoming unemployed or having to drop out of the labor force, which would be consistent with the decline in their relative earnings.

The JMP results between 2007 and 2010, reported in Table 2.1, provide supporting evidence for this explanation. The total (unadjusted) entrepreneurial earnings penalty rose by 19.7 percentage points for Hispanics during this period. The largest component of this decline is attributable to a loss in the relative observable characteristics of this population (a twelve-percentage-

TABLE 2.1 JMP components of the change in the relative annual earnings of self-employed Hispanics between 2002–7 and 2007–10, by subgroup

Characteristic	All Hispanics	Mexican Americans	Cubans	Puerto Ricans	Salvadorans
SELF-EMPLOYMENT EARNINGS RELATIVE TO OTHER WORKERS					
2002	–18.80%	–21.23%	7.23%	–54.62%	–5.06%
2007	–22.48%	–21.02%	–7.66%	–37.63%	–22.05%
2010	–42.14%	–42.95%	–29.44%	–53.19%	–32.26%
PERCENTAGE-POINT CHANGE IN RELATIVE EARNINGS, 2002–7					
Total change	**–3.69**	**0.21**	**–14.89**	**16.99**	**–16.99**
Observable characteristics	–6.69	–4.77	–15.55	8.22	–14.26
Unobservable characteristics	2.82	4.02	0.13	8.03	3.38
Returns to observables	0.11	0.29	1.43	0.78	–6.28
Returns to unobservables	0.08	0.24	–0.90	–0.05	0.18
PERCENTAGE-POINT CHANGE IN RELATIVE EARNINGS, 2007–10					
Total change	**–19.65**	**–21.71**	**–29.44**	**–15.69**	**–10.21**
Observable characteristics	–11.95	–10.90	–16.71	–20.80	–0.24
Unobservable characteristics	–7.95	–10.75	–5.89	2.20	–0.09
Returns to observables	0.35	–0.43	–0.41	1.12	–10.55
Returns to unobservables	–0.50	0.36	1.23	1.71	0.68

SOURCE: Authors' estimates using ACS data in the IPUMS.

NOTES: The sample includes self-employed Hispanic workers between the ages of twenty-five and sixty-four not living in group quarters who reported labor-market earnings. For estimation details, see Appendix B.

point decline). The average unobservable quality of Hispanic entrepreneurs further contributed another eight percentage points to their relative earnings loss over the period.

Changes in returns on observable and unobservable characteristics were quite small between 2007 and 2010—the former contributing only a third of a percentage point to the relative earnings decline, which was more than off-set by the latter's effect of improving relative earnings by half a percentage point. Combined, the JMP findings suggest that as more Hispanics turned to self-employment during the recession, the average quality of entrepreneurs in terms of both observable and unobservable characteristics fell, thus resulting in a reduction in their relative earnings.

Sales and Earnings of Hispanic Ethnic Subpopulations

As noted in Chapter 1, distinct Hispanic populations exist in the United States who, because of geographic, industry, and cultural reasons, might have had different self-employment experiences during the foregoing two time periods. In this section, we replicate the earnings analyses from above by Hispanic subpopulation using SBO and ACS data for the 2002–7 time period and only ACS data for the 2007–10 period (given that SBO data are not available for these years). Neither the SBO PUMS nor the SSBF data identify Hispanic subpopulations.

Mexican American Entrepreneurs.   The SBO data between 2002 and 2007 show that the number of firms owned by Mexican Americans with paid employees grew by 33.5 percent (from 89,285 to 119,233 firms). For firms without employees, this growth rate was 49.8 percent (to nearly 612,000 firms). These firm creation rates parallel the increase in the self-employment numbers estimated using the ACS. With regard to sales per firm, firms with and without paid employees grew less dramatically over this time period (by 15.3 percent for the former and 17.7 percent, respectively), but both grew beyond the 14.4 percent inflation rate between 2002 and 2007. By 2007, sales per firm were $1.0 million for employers and $37,300 for nonemployers.

The ACS data for this time period give insight into the changing earnings penalty for this Hispanic subgroup. Somewhat consistent with their sales data, the total earnings penalty for self-employed Mexican Americans slightly improved (by two-tenths of a percentage point, to 21.0 percent) between 2002 and 2007. The flat change in relative earnings between these two years owes to a relative decline in the average quality of the observable characteristics of Hispanic entrepreneurs, which was offset by a relative increase in the unobservable characteristics of the group.

We note, however, that during this time period, the relatively robust business climate might have bolstered the earnings of self-employed Mexican Americans despite their increasing numbers in this sector. The JMP analysis bears out this possibility, as shown in Table 2.1. During the period of the Great Recession, business opportunities for the self-employed arguably declined, leading to a 21.7 percent increase in the self-employment penalty for Mexican American entrepreneurs. This sharp increase resulted from relative declines in average skills—both observed (contributing 10.9 percentage points to the penalty increase) and unobserved (contributing another 10.7 percentage points)—of self-employed Mexican Americans.

Cuban American Entrepreneurs.   There are some inconsistencies between the ACS and SBO data sets between 2002 and 2007 for self-employed Cuban Americans. According to our estimates using the ACS data, there were 115,000 self-employed Cuban Americans (of all ages) in 2002, and this number grew by 14.8 percent to 132,000 in 2007. In contrast, the SBO data indicate that there were 151,700 Cuban American entrepreneurs in 2002, compared to 251,000 in 2007 (an increase of 65.5 percent). Given that the SBO contains both employer and nonemployer firms, the discrepancy might pertain to nonemployer Cuban American firms. Employer firms owned by this Hispanic ethnic subgroup grew by 15.6 percent, which is roughly consistent with the growth rate in the ACS for the self-employed of this subgroup. Sales per Cuban-owned employer firms rose by a greater proportion (41.3 percent, to $1.6 million) during this time.

Moreover, the growth rate reported in the SBO for the number of nonemployer Cuban-owned firms between 2002 and 2007 was relatively high, at 76.7 percent (123,800 to 218,800), while average sales declined from $36,700 to $35,800 in the period, a decline compounded by the 14.4 percent inflation rate. While we remain agnostic about potential underreporting of self-employment among Cuban Americans in the ACS (or an overestimate of Cuban business owners in the 2007 SBO), the JMP analysis for this group between 2002 and 2007 might provide clues as to the decline in sales per firm of Cuban nonemployer firms. Indeed, the analysis reveals that the self-employment penalty for Cuban Americans increased by 14.9 percentage points, which reflects mostly a relative average decline in observable characteristics (see Table 2.1).

For the 2007–10 period, the earnings penalty deterioration for Cuban Americans became more pronounced. We estimate that the Cuban American self-employment penalty grew by 21.7 percentage points between 2007 and 2010. The growth of this penalty was aided by a decline in average quality of unobservable skills (5.9 percentage points) and a continued deterioration in average observable skills of this Hispanic subgroup (16.7 percentage points).

Puerto Rican Entrepreneurs. The ACS and the SBO data show that the number of businesses owned by Puerto Ricans grew between 2002 and 2007 (to 156,500 firms according to the SBO, for a 42.9 percent increase). Again, the base numbers for the self-employed differ between the ACS and the SBO. With regard to sales per firm, the SBO reveals minimal gains for Puerto Rican firms between 2002 and 2007 that failed to keep up with inflation; sales rose by 7.5 percent (to $870,600) among employer firms and 1.3 percent (to $28,700) among nonemployer firms over the five years.

Following the conceptual logic used for the other Hispanic ethnic subgroup entrepreneurs, we expected to observe an increase in the total self-employment earnings penalty for Puerto Ricans between 2002 and 2007. The JMP results, however, yield the opposite result. As Table 2.1 shows, self-employed Puerto Ricans gained with respect to relative earnings (17 percent) during this interval. Moreover, this improvement was primarily led by similar increases in both the relative observed and relative unobserved skills between the two years.

A possible explanation for this puzzling finding relates to a potential change in the ratio of island-born to mainland born Puerto Ricans in the U.S. labor force during the 2002–7 period. Data from the World Bank give some credence to this, as Puerto Rico's net migration rate (number of immigrants less number of emigrants) reached a thirty-year high in the middle of the first decade of the 2000s. Our estimates using the ACS are consistent with more recent arrivals from the island, as the average number of years since arrival to the U.S. mainland fell among Puerto Rican entrepreneurs (from 28.2 years in 2002 to 27.2 years in 2007). Yet we also find that the share of the island-born Puerto Ricans fell in this group, from 47.5 percent in 2002 to 40.5 percent in 2007.

The other JMP numbers in Table 2.1, those for the 2007 and 2010 interval, are also puzzling. While the self-employment earnings penalty increased for this Hispanic subgroup, as it did for the other subgroups, the increase occurred despite a decline in the number of Puerto Rican entrepreneurs during the period. The self-employment penalty increased in magnitude by 15.7 percentage points, buoyed by a relative decline in the observable skills of self-employed Puerto Ricans (which added 20.8 percentage points) that was somewhat mitigated by a relative improvement in the average unobservables of this group. As in the 2002–7 case, the predicted change (that an overall increase in average skill levels of the self-employed resulted from a decline in the number of self-employed Puerto Ricans) might have been confounded by a change in the ratio of island-born to mainland-born Puerto Ricans in the U.S. labor force during this period.

Salvadoran Entrepreneurs.   According to a 2011 study by the Pew Hispanic Center, there were 1.7 million Salvadoran immigrants living in the United States in 2009. This population represents the third-largest Hispanic-immigrant population in the United States. Because of the growing presence of this Hispanic ethnic subpopulation, we also conducted an earnings analysis for this group for the two time periods discussed above. (We cannot track their sales in the SBO, as the data do not specifically identify Salvadoran firm ownership.)

With regard to the JMP analysis for the 2002–7 period, Table 2.1 reveals that Salvadoran entrepreneurs' earnings penalty rose by 17.0 percentage points, mostly as a result of a decline in the average returns to observable skills for this group, and to a lesser extent, as a result of an increase in the returns to skills during this time. Over the 2007–10 interval, the penalty continued to rise (by another 10.2 percentage points). In this case, this increase was mostly driven by a deterioration in this Hispanic ethnic subpopulation's average level of unobservable skills rather than their observable characteristics.

Hispanics in Construction Versus Nonconstruction Industries

Recall from the previous chapter that some of the intensification in the entrepreneurial activities of Hispanics in the mid-2000s appeared to be related to the boom in the housing industry. Both SBO and ACS data back this up, as the number of Hispanic-owned construction businesses rose by 64.0 percent (from 212,500 to 340,800 firms in the SBO), of greater magnitude than Hispanic-owned enterprises in other industries (a 41.0 percent increase) between 2002 and 2007. Hispanic construction businesses also made greater gains over other industries in terms of sales per firm during this time, as observed in the SBO; average sales rose by 12.6 percent in construction and by 9.4 percent in nonconstruction industries. Note that while the increase in sales per firm for both groups did not keep up with the inflation rate, the average sales differential between construction and nonconstruction widened during this time.

Sales and Profits of Hispanic-Owned Firms in Construction Versus Other Industries.   Because average sales explain only part of the story of a business's success, we revisit the SBO PUMS and SSBF data to provide a deeper analysis of their sales than that which can be gained from simply comparing averages. We also consider the profits of construction versus nonconstruction Hispanic-owned firms. In the 2007 SBO PUMS, based on the natural logarithm of sales, Hispanic-owned businesses in construction generated 48.7 percent more in revenue than those in other industries when controlling for other observable characteristics (described in Appendix B); however, given the relatively large variances, this estimate lacks statistical significance at conventional levels.

When focusing exclusively on Hispanic employers, those in construction appeared to have a sales advantage over their peers in other industries, as their revenue was 62.9 percent higher (and statistically significant) when accounting for other owner- and business-level traits. For nonemployers, the seeming sales premium of 35.2 percent in construction was not statistically different from the sales generated by Hispanics in other industries.

In the SSBF, small firms owned by Hispanics had average sales and profits of $1.1 million and $287,700 in construction, and $759,000 and $123,200 in other industries, respectively, in the mid-2000s. Despite the differences in magnitudes, as with the sales observed in the SBO PUMS, neither outcome significantly varied between the two industry groups because of their large variances. Moreover, when controlling for other owner- and firm-level characteristics (discussed in Appendix B), the sales and the profits of Hispanic-owned small enterprises in construction were statistically similar to those in other industries.

In terms of breaking even, nearly three-quarters of Hispanic-owned small enterprises in construction in the SSBF had profits greater than zero in the mid-2000s, which was similar to the share of firms with positive profits in other industries. Almost two-thirds of small construction businesses with Hispanic owners had profits of $10,000 or more—a slightly higher proportion (but not significantly so) than the 58 percent of other Hispanic-owned small firms that achieved this profit benchmark. Similarly, when accounting for other observable characteristics related to profits, Hispanic-owned construction businesses were not more or less likely to break even or earn a minimum of $10,000 in profits than firms in other industries during this time period.

Construction and Nonconstruction Self-Employment Earnings. Even though the SBO and SSBF data indicated that sales (and profits in the case of the SBO) did not significantly differ on average between Hispanic-owned businesses in construction and nonconstruction industries, when analyzing the earnings of the self-employed, some industry differences emerge. As Figure 2.3 shows, Hispanic entrepreneurs in construction had considerably

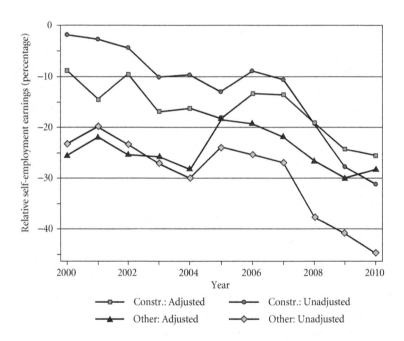

FIGURE 2.3 Unadjusted and adjusted self-employment earnings penalties for Hispanic and non-Hispanic workers in construction and nonconstruction industries, 2000–10

SOURCE: Authors' estimates using PUMS and ACS data in the IPUMS.

NOTES: Earnings penalties are defined on the basis of the relative earnings of the self-employed versus workers in the paid-employment sector. The "unadjusted" earnings penalties show the "raw" penalties, while the "adjusted" penalties show the penalties when controlling for observable characteristics. "Constr." refers to the construction industry, and "Other" refers to nonconstruction industries. The sample includes workers between the ages of twenty-five and sixty-four not living in group quarters. For estimation details, see Appendix B.

lower self-employment penalties than those in other industries earlier in the decade, in terms of both total penalties and characteristics-adjusted penalties. Still, this seeming advantage in construction dwindled by the end of the decade, especially with respect to adjusted penalties.

Turning to the specific time periods we have been discussing, in 2002, Hispanics on average earned 4.4 percent less in construction compared to their counterparts in the paid-employment sector, but 23.3 percent less in other industries. While this difference shrinks somewhat when controlling for other observable characteristics related to earnings (the adjusted self-employment penalty was 9.5 percent in construction versus 25.3 percent in nonconstruction), construction represented a relatively lucrative industry for Hispanic entrepreneurs in that year.

By 2007, the relative advantage of construction for Hispanics was narrower than it had been five years earlier because the total self-employment penalty had risen by 6.2 percentage points (to 10.6 percent), of greater magnitude than the 3.5-percentage-point loss in relative earnings that self-employed Hispanics accrued in other industries. An explanation for this larger relative loss in construction entrepreneurial income can be detected using the JMP approach. Indeed, we find that Hispanic construction business owners lost ground with respect to both observable and unobservable characteristics (with the former contributing 4.8 percentage points and the latter, 4.0 percentage points, to the total loss in relative self-employment earnings). The relative weakening of unobservables during this time is shown in Figure 2.1, through the decline in the adjusted self-employment earnings penalty between 2002 and 2007. Unlike the results for Hispanics in general discussed earlier, changes in the returns to observable characteristics offset part of the deterioration of the self-employment penalty in the sector. These returns likely reflect the increasingly lucrative nature of construction industry during this time, as the demand for construction-related goods and services had escalated.

In other industries, Hispanic business owners also lost ground during this period with respect to their average observable characteristics (which would have reduced their relative earnings by 7.3 percentage points). Nevertheless, they gained in terms of their unobservable traits, offsetting more than half of the earnings effect from the change in observable characteristics, even though their returns to both observed and unobserved characteristics remained steady.

After 2007, as with Hispanics in general, the relative earnings of Hispanic entrepreneurs in both construction and nonconstruction industries declined; in fact, their unadjusted relative earnings were lower in 2010 than any other point in the decade. Between 2007 and 2010, the average unadjusted self-employment penalty for Hispanics in construction rose by 20.6 percentage points (to 31.2 percent), of greater magnitude than the 17.8-percentage-point loss in relative entrepreneurial earnings in other industries. The JMP results indicate that Hispanic construction business owners continued to lose ground with respect to observable and unobservable characteristics, particularly the latter, with each contributing 8.2 and 11.2 percentage points, respectively, to the total penalty decline between 2007 and 2010. Changes in the returns to both observable and unobservable characteristics further added to the total decline, by slightly more than a percentage point (with the returns to unobservables accounting for more than half of this).

For Hispanics in nonconstruction industries, the largest component of the deterioration in relative self-employment earnings after 2007 was the change in observable characteristics (explaining 11.2 percentage points of the decline), followed by unobservable characteristics (contributing 7.1 percentage points) and then returns to observable characteristics (which explain only a third of a percentage point). The latter was more than offset by a relative improvement in entrepreneurial earnings of 0.7 percentage points, which was caused by a shift in the returns to unobservable characteristics.

In all, these industry findings follow the push-pull framework and findings discussed above, particularly for construction. The boom in the housing sector in the earlier part of decade attracted growing numbers of Hispanic entrepreneurs into the construction industry, which seems to have reduced their average quality (in terms of both observed and unobserved traits), thus dampening their relative earnings. However, the overall business conditions related to these pull factors—namely a growing demand for construction-related goods and services—helped offset part of this earnings-dampening effect. Once the housing bubble burst, the pull factors vanished, thereby leading to a corrosion of the relative earnings of self-employed Hispanic construction workers.

Concluding Remarks

In the first decade of the 2000s, self-employment provided an increasingly important means for Hispanic workers to earn a living. While Hispanic entrepreneurs earned less on average than their counterparts in the paid-employment sector, they fared better, in a relative sense, than their non-Hispanic counterparts when controlling for other observable characteristics (e.g., education, gender, immigration, industry, geographic region) related to labor-market income. This seeming relative earnings advantage of Hispanics versus non-Hispanics may partly explain the intensifying entrepreneurial tendencies of Hispanics.

That said, our results reveal that changes in the relative earnings of self-employed Hispanics during the 2000s appeared sensitive to macroeconomic conditions, which affected the reasons workers joined the entrepreneurial sector. A decline in the relative observable characteristics of self-employed Hispanics (with the exception of Puerto Ricans) served to reduce Hispanics' relative earnings between 2002 and 2007. However, this negative earnings effect was offset by improvements in their relative levels of unobservable characteristics, which indicates the potential existence of pull factors in their rising self-employment rates before the Great Recession. Our findings suggest that as the recession got under way, Hispanic self-employment rates continued to rise, because many sought self-employment as a means to avoid unemployment. This shift into self-employment seemed to dampen the average quality of Hispanic entrepreneurs in terms of both observable and unobservable characteristics, thus reducing Hispanics' relative earnings in the self-employment sector. In all, the Great Recession erased the earnings gains made by self-employed Hispanics earlier in the decade.

3   Hispanic-Immigrant Entrepreneurs

O NE OF THE MOST IMPORTANT TAKEAWAYS FROM THIS BOOK
is that Hispanic-immigrant entrepreneurs have added significant value to the U.S. economy in recent times. To add to this point, this
chapter continues the discussion of how immigration affected Hispanic entrepreneurship in the first decade of the 2000s. Of the businesses that reported
the birthplace of owners, we estimate that immigrants owned more than half
(55.8 percent) of Hispanic-owned businesses.[1] Moreover, the representation
of foreign-born Hispanics was higher among such firms established between
2000 and 2007 than among those formed before 1990 (58.4 percent versus
47.4 percent). As such, a large part of the story behind Hispanic entrepreneurship in the 2000s involved Hispanic immigrants.

Figure 3.1 provides additional evidence of the growing presence of Hispanic immigrants in the entrepreneurial sector, as their share among the self-
employed rose almost every year in the decade, including during the Great
Recession.[2] Indeed, the proportion of foreign-born Hispanics among all
self-employed workers increased by a larger magnitude (from 5.4 percent to
9.1 percent) than among other salaried workers (from 6.3 percent to 8.3 percent) between 2000 and 2010. The growing number of native-born Hispanic
workers in the self-employment sector was driven by population growth, as
their presence increased similarly between self-employed and salaried workers.

To provide insight into the characteristics of Hispanic-immigrant entrepreneurs, this chapter first explores differences in sales between firms owned

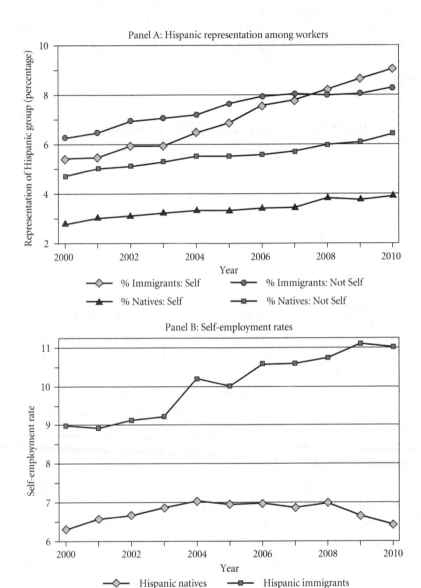

FIGURE 3.1 Representation of Hispanic immigrants and natives among self-employed and paid-employment workers, and their self-employment rates, 2000–10

SOURCE: Authors' estimates using PUMS and ACS data in the IPUMS.
NOTE: The sample includes workers between the ages of twenty-five and sixty-four not living in group quarters.

by foreign-born and U.S.-born Hispanics. We then consider how demographic characteristics, including ethnic origin, industry distributions, and the geographic concentrations of self-employed Hispanic immigrants changed in the first decade of the 2000s. Later in this chapter, we address the relationship between Hispanic-immigrant entrepreneurship and ethnic enclaves. We also consider issues pertaining to the self-selection of immigrant entrepreneurs, which culminates in an analysis of the earnings of self-employed Hispanic immigrants versus U.S. natives. Finally, the chapter concludes with a discussion of some of the economic impacts of Hispanic-immigrant entrepreneurs.

Sales and Other Characteristics of Hispanic-Immigrant- Versus Native-Owned Businesses

Among firms reporting the birthplace of owners in the 2007 SBO PUMS, we estimate that the average sales of businesses owned by foreign-born Hispanics ($257,000) were lower than those of U.S.-born Hispanics ($337,500), which suggests that immigrant-owned firms tend to lag behind their counterparts owned by U.S. natives. Yet when considering the average natural logarithm of sales, Hispanic immigrants appeared to fare better, as their revenue was 21.1 percent higher than that of their U.S.-born counterparts—a statistically significant difference. This implies that, as a result of the shape of the sales distribution, focusing on average revenue alone provides an incomplete picture of the success of immigrant- versus U.S. native-owned firms.[3]

When comparing Hispanic-owned employer versus nonemployer firms with information on the birthplace of owners, immigrants represented about one-fifth of both categories of firms in 2007. It follows that birthplace by itself does not appear to be a factor in predicting the likelihood of Hispanic-owned enterprises having paid employees. The relationship between birthplace and sales, however, differed for Hispanic employers and nonemployers. To illustrate, when exclusively considering employer firms (which accounted for one-fifth of both foreign- and U.S -born Hispanic-owned firms), those owned by immigrants had lower average sales than those owned by U.S. native Hispanics ($1.1 million versus $1.5 million); however, immigrants fared better than natives in this regard among nonemployer firms ($47,400 versus $39,700). Taking the natural logarithm of the sales, the differences are less extreme; Hispanic-immigrant-owned businesses had 6.1 percent lower revenue than their U.S.-born counterparts among employers, but nonemployer firms had 30.2 percent higher revenue.[4]

Some of these differences in birthplace and nativity may be attributable to the education level of the business owners. A more detailed discussion and analysis of education is provided in the following chapter, but consider that foreign-born Hispanic business owners had less formal education than their U.S.-born counterparts. In the SBO PUMS, 27.0 percent of Hispanic-immigrant firm owners did not have a high school diploma, and 20.1 percent did not have at least a four-year college degree, compared to 9.1 percent and 28.3 percent of Hispanic U.S. natives with these schooling levels. At the same time, gaps existed with respect to education for immigrants and natives between employers and nonemployers. Among Hispanic-owned employer firms in 2007, 17.1 percent of immigrants had not completed high school and 28.0 percent were college graduates, compared to 4.9 percent and 35.8 percent of natives who had these respective schooling levels. For Hispanic nonemployers, those without a high school diploma represented 29.2 percent of the foreign born and 10.2 percent of the U.S. born. In the same group, college graduates represented 18.1 percent of the foreign born and 26.4 percent of the U.S. born. As such, education alone is probably not the only reason for the different levels of success among Hispanic immigrants with respect to natives among employer versus nonemployer firms.

Industry distributions may be another factor in the immigrant-native revenue differentials. Compared to employer firms owned by U.S.-born Hispanics, the 2007 SBO PUMS reveals that those owned by immigrants had a higher share in the relatively lucrative trade industry (18.8 percent versus 14.0 percent). Nevertheless, they also had a higher share in the relatively low-revenue-producing industries of entertainment, recreation, and food services (14.3 percent versus 9.2 percent). In addition, immigrant employers accounted for a lower share than their native counterparts in professional services (17.5 percent versus 23.5 percent) and construction (14.3 percent versus 16.8 percent). In contrast, in 2007 the entertainment, recreation, and food services industries comprised a smaller segment of nonemployer businesses firms owned by Hispanic immigrants than by natives (14.3 percent versus 9.2 percent), while construction represented a larger segment of the former group (14.4 percent versus 11.6 percent). Trade and professional services were similarly represented between foreign-born and U.S.-born Hispanic nonemployers (10–11 percent for trade, and 24 percent for professional services).

Given these apparent differences between Hispanic-immigrant- and native-owned businesses, it is worth testing whether the immigrant-native sales gaps remain when controlling for other characteristics (including owner education level and age, firm age, industry, among other factors) likely related to sales. In conducting this analysis (described in Appendix B), we found that in 2007 businesses owned by Hispanic immigrants, regardless of being employers or not, had statistically similar sales to those businesses owned by their U.S.-born counterparts. It therefore appears that the differences in revenue along the lines of birthplace observed above can be explained by differences in characteristics of immigrant versus native Hispanic-owned companies.

Changes in the Demographic Characteristics of Self-Employed Hispanic Immigrants

The previous information points to several underlying differences between businesses owned by foreign-born versus U.S.-born Hispanics in 2007, just before the Great Recession started. We do not know whether such differences were relatively static during the decade. We therefore turn to ACS and PUMS data to explore the demographic and socioeconomic characteristics of self-employed Hispanic immigrants during the 2000s.

Specific Ethnic Origins of Hispanic-Immigrant Entrepreneurs. As with self-employed Hispanics in general, Mexican Americans represented the largest subgroup (more than half) of self-employed Hispanic immigrants and natives in the 2000s, slightly more so among the U.S. born. Table 3.1 shows that their representation in both birthplace groups rose as the decade progressed, and by a slightly larger magnitude among the U.S. born than the foreign born. Cubans were the second-largest ethnic subgroup among Hispanic-immigrant entrepreneurs before the Great Recession, followed by Salvadorans. However, these rankings had reversed by 2010. The smaller shares of both groups (particularly Salvadorans) among self-employed U.S. natives versus immigrants further indicate the relatively strong entrepreneurial propensities of the foreign born in these groups. Immigrants from Cuba and El Salvador likely migrated to the United States for different reasons (e.g., as refugees) than their Mexican and "other" Hispanic counterparts, who usually migrate to find work in the United States. We return to this point later in the chapter.

TABLE 3.1 Ethnic subgroup, industry, and geographic characteristics of self-employed and salaried Hispanics

Characteristic	Hispanic immigrants			Hispanic U.S. natives		
	2002 (%)	2007 (%)	2010 (%)	2002 (%)	2007 (%)	2010 (%)
ETHNIC SUBGROUP						
Mexican American	53.1	54.7	55.9	57.9	59.1	62.5
Cuban	8.7	6.9	6.4	4.0	4.4	5.3
Puerto Rican	0.4	0.2	0.4	15.8	17.4	14.3
Salvadoran	6.5	6.2	6.9	0.3	0.4	0.7
"Other" Hispanic	31.3	32.0	30.4	22.0	18.7	17.2
INDUSTRY						
Professional services	22.8	18.1	19.7	15.4	19.1	20.8
Construction	18.4	23.0	24.2	18.2	20.5	19.2
Transportation and warehousing	5.5	5.6	5.2	4.8	4.7	4.6
Other	53.3	53.3	50.9	61.6	55.7	54.9
GEOGRAPHIC REGION						
Pacific	36.3	34.1	33.1	32.3	28.1	30.6
South Atlantic	24.5	21.6	22.4	11.2	12.5	13.6
South Central	18.1	19.0	20.4	23.4	25.9	25.9
Middle Atlantic	9.4	11.7	10.9	10.2	8.3	8.6
Mountain	5.3	7.0	6.3	14.2	16.2	12.4
Other region	6.4	6.6	6.9	8.7	9.0	8.9

SOURCE: Authors' estimates using ACS data in the IPUMS.
NOTE: The sample includes self-employed Hispanic workers between the ages of twenty-five and sixty-four not living in group quarters.

Industry Distributions of Hispanic-Immigrant Entrepreneurs. The middle section of Table 3.1 reports that the industry composition of Hispanic-immigrant versus native entrepreneurs also changed during the business cycle of the first decade of the 2000s. The three specific industries shown in Table 3.1 (construction, professional services, and transportation and warehousing) are those in which self-employed Hispanics experienced the largest growth during the decade. One of the primary reasons for this increased concentration is the empirical observation that the foreign born disproportionately shifted into the construction sector (even after the housing bubble burst). That is, while construction accounted for less than one-fifth of self-employed Hispanic immigrants in 2002, it rose to 23 percent by 2007 and to nearly one-quarter by 2010. This increase was more than enough to offset the decline in the representation of Hispanic-immigrant entrepreneurs in the professional services industry between 2002 and 2010.

In contrast, the increased industry concentration of U.S.-born Hispanic entrepreneurs occurred because of their shift into the professional services sector, with construction playing a weaker role. Indeed, the proportion of self-employed Hispanic natives in professional services increased by more than five percentage points between 2002 and 2010, while this group's representation in construction only rose by one percentage point across this eight-year timespan. These changes indicate that, unlike what their foreign-born counterparts experienced, the Great Recession eroded the presence of the construction industry among U.S.-born Hispanic entrepreneurs. To the extent that pull factors exist with respect to self-employment, these changes suggest that Hispanic entrepreneurs sought out growth industries to increase their odds of success earlier in the decade. However, among self-employed Hispanic immigrants, the continued shift into the construction industry after 2007 may indicate the presence of push factors, as the industry contracted during the Great Recession.

Between 2002 and 2007, the three largest groups of foreign-born Hispanic entrepreneurs participated more in the construction industry than in the professional services sector. Representation in construction firms also rose between 2007 and 2010 (to more than a quarter) for Salvadorans and Cubans, and it stayed about the same (at a quarter) for Mexican immigrants.

Regional Distributions of Hispanic-Immigrant Entrepreneurs. The geographic dispersion of the Hispanic population that occurred in the 1980s and 1990s continued into the 2000s. Table 3.1 shows that this was also the case for Hispanic-immigrant entrepreneurs. Pacific states and the Atlantic region saw declines in the share of Hispanic immigrants among the self-employed between 2002 and 2010. The remaining major geographic regions showed gains among foreign-born Hispanic entrepreneurs, with the largest growth occurring in the South Central region.

In terms of specific ethnic groups, Mexican and particularly Salvadoran immigrant entrepreneurs had a pattern similar to that of Hispanic-immigrant entrepreneurs in general, although their losses were more acute (from 50 percent to 44 percent among Mexicans, and from more than 50 percent to 42 percent among Salvadorans between 2002 and 2010). Foreign-born Cuban entrepreneurs became more geographically concentrated after 2002 (even compared to their U.S.-born counterparts). Indeed, by 2010 nearly nine out of ten foreign-born Cuban entrepreneurs resided in the South Atlantic region, compared to two-thirds of self-employed U.S.-born Cubans.

Hispanic Enclaves and Immigrant Entrepreneurship

The foregoing discussion generally supports the view that the presence of Hispanic-immigrant entrepreneurs was quite fluid during the early 2000s across ethnic subgroups, industries, and U.S. regions. These patterns may reflect changes in economic opportunities but also the unique labor-market challenges that different Hispanic populations faced during that time. In subsequent chapters we discuss the important role of human capital (particularly education) and financial capital on entrepreneurial outcomes. We discuss here the issue of social capital and its importance in promoting self-employment in ethnic enclaves before we move to an empirical analysis of Hispanic-immigrant self-employment propensities in ethnic enclaves.

Existing literature both supports and questions the view that entrepreneurial opportunities improve for immigrants in areas with a large co-ethnic presence. A host of studies have found evidence that ethnically concentrated economies enhance self-employment probabilities for minorities, citing the comparative advantages of social capital for minority entrepreneurs (given their knowledge of the culture, language, and "tastes"), lower consumer discrimination, greater access to financial capital via ethnic networks, and the ability to tap into niche labor markets. Alternatively, ethnic enclaves might provide a relatively wide range of paid-employment and social networking opportunities for the foreign born, perhaps dampening their need to become self-employed. This point has been made by, among others, Alejandro Portes and Ruben Rumbaut, who stated in a 1996 study, "A tightly knit ethnic enclave is not . . . the only manifestation of immigrant entrepreneurship" (p. 22).

Indeed, social capital in the context of ethnic enclaves is an elusive concept, not only in terms of its definition, as Timothy Bates amply discusses in his 2011 study, but also in terms of its importance across different geographic areas. It is widely assumed that social capital is beneficial to ethnic entrepreneurs only in ethnic enclaves, but there is a fallacy in this assumption. For example, social capital might benefit the Mexican entrepreneur who owns a Mexican restaurant in a non-Hispanic white suburb (because the Mexican owner might be construed by the non-Hispanic white population in that area as a more "authentic" entrepreneur in this business venture), but this capital might not benefit the same entrepreneur in a Mexican neighborhood (with many other Mexican restaurants). However, a self-employed Mexican plumber might benefit more from working in a Mexican neighborhood than in a non-Hispanic white suburb.

Bates succinctly summarizes in his 2011 study what we know with regard to the importance of capital (human, financial, and social) and self-employment:

> Our present understanding is that viable minority-owned businesses are those run by skilled, experienced, often highly educated owners. Although financial capital requirements vary in different lines of business, success in most fields requires both sufficient investment to operate at an efficient scale and access to capital to exploit opportunities for further venture development.... Being embedded in supportive networks is widely viewed as a positive, but precisely how the social capital arising from one's network connections translates into greater business viability is not well established in a causal sense. (p. 287)

Did Hispanic enclaves, then, promote entrepreneurship among Hispanic immigrants in the first decade of the 2000s? To address this question, we explore the concentration of Hispanics in 2007 and 2010, defined here as the share of Hispanics in a metropolitan statistical area (MSA).[5] On average, this analysis reveals that Hispanic-immigrant entrepreneurs typically lived in communities with about one-third of their fellow co-ethnics. However, the average concentration fell between 2007 and 2010 (from 35.6 percent to 33.0 percent). It is of interest that this decline did not reflect a general shift in this concentration for foreign-born Hispanics in general, as the average Hispanic concentration rose by about two percentage points (to 30.2 percent) for those in the paid-employment sector (as it also did for self-employed Hispanic natives) during this time. Despite these changes, these concentrations were less than the ones for Hispanic-immigrant entrepreneurs in both years.

We note, too, that Hispanic immigrants in cities with a large Hispanic presence had significantly higher self-employment rates than Hispanic immigrants in areas with low Hispanic concentrations, particularly in 2007.

To illustrate, 13.9 percent of foreign-born Hispanics in MSAs with above-average Hispanic concentrations were self-employed in 2007, compared to 8.9 percent of Hispanic immigrants in other areas. By 2010, this difference had narrowed but remained significant, as Hispanic-immigrant self-employment rates in Hispanic-concentrated cities declined to 11.3 percent while primarily holding steady for other foreign-born Hispanic workers. For U.S.-born Hispanics, the self-employment rates were lower in areas with above-average shares of Hispanics in 2007 (6.7 percent versus 7.2 percent) than in areas with lower-than-average shares of Hispanics; three years later, the self-employment rates fell for both groups to 5.6 percent.

These estimates provide supporting evidence that ethnic enclaves enhanced the self-employment propensities of Hispanic immigrants, although to a lesser degree after the Great Recession. If ethnic enclaves serve to stimulate immigrant entrepreneurship, the weaker enclave effect among foreign-born Hispanics after the Great Recession can be interpreted as a deterioration of self-employment pull factors unique to this group. These findings might also reflect the adaptiveness of some foreign-born Hispanic entrepreneurs who migrated outside of enclaves during worsening economic conditions to tap into better opportunities elsewhere.

Another possibility could be that overall business conditions were specific to the industries or geographic areas in which the immigrant entrepreneurs lived, or to their skills, rather than enclave effects per se. We therefore take an additional approach (described in Appendix B) to studying self-employment rates among Hispanic immigrants (and for comparison purposes, their U.S.-born counterparts) that considers the effect of Hispanic enclaves while controlling for other observable characteristics—including education, industry, and region—related to the probability of being self-employed.

We find that each percentage-point increase in Hispanic concentration in a metropolitan area enhanced the chance of self-employment for Hispanic immigrants by 0.1 percentage points in 2007, the effect of which dropped to 0.03 percentage points in 2010. Hispanic enclaves, however, had virtually no impact on the self-employment tendencies of U.S.-born Hispanics in either year. The smaller enclave effect on immigrants' self-employment tendencies after the Great Recession supports what the average numbers showed: while ethnic enclaves played a role in Hispanic-immigrant entrepreneurship, the weakening economy mitigated the enclave effect.

When focusing on specific Hispanic subgroups, the concentration of Hispanics (regardless of Hispanic subgroup or birthplace) in an area enhanced the self-employment probabilities of Mexican, Cuban, and Salvadoran immigrants in 2007. Similar to the general case, three years later, these odds weakened for Mexicans and became statistically insignificant for Salvadorans. Only for Cuban immigrants did the relationship remain statistically unchanged during the Great Recession. One explanation might be the increase in the geographic concentration of self-employed Cuban immigrants in the South Atlantic region, which maintained a relatively high demand for these immigrant entrepreneurs.

Other results from this exercise indicate that the likelihood of being self-employed was similar between immigrant men and women in 2007, but by 2010, immigrant women were 1.3 percent less likely than their male counterparts to be self-employed. U.S-born Hispanic women had lower self-employment tendencies (by 1.5 percent) than U.S.-born Hispanic men in 2007, which further decreased (to 2.4 percent) in 2010. The issue of the intersection between gender and immigration is one that we explore in much more detail in Chapter 5.

A final point on ethnic enclaves pertains to the attention in some of the literature to the earnings of self-employed (and salaried) Hispanic immigrants and, more broadly, to Hispanics in enclaves. A recent example comes from Michael Bernabé Aguilera, who noted in a 2009 study, "Scholars within the ethnic enclave literature often claim that ethnic solidarity provides beneficial employment outcomes for employees. Ethnic solidarity implies that co-ethnic employers and supervisors provide special employment benefits to their co-ethnic workers because they are obligated to them over other workers" (p. 416). But he goes on to state, "Evidence also suggests that ethnic solidarity within ethnic enclaves can create special constraints for employers, which may outweigh the benefits of self-employment within an ethnic enclave" (p. 417). Using census data for Mexican and Cuban immigrant entrepreneurs in California and Texas (for the Mexican sample) and Florida (for the Cuban sample), Aguilera finds that Mexican immigrant entrepreneurs earn less in enclaves than their counterparts who do not live in enclaves. Aguilera interprets his findings as "contrary to the ethnic enclave hypothesis, which suggests that there are economic advantages associated with owning firms in ethnic enclaves" (p. 413).

This type of empirical analysis, however, raises more questions than it does answers. In particular, Aguilera's findings do not account for potential hedonic effects (Mexican immigrant entrepreneurs might value the proximity of their fellow co-ethnics, and thus accept lower earnings) and potential cost-of-living differentials between living in enclaves and other areas. Without data on these important dimensions, it is not possible to determine whether there is support for the ethnic enclave hypothesis.

Hispanic-Immigrant Entrepreneurial Talent— Conceptual Issues

Given that Hispanic-immigrant assimilation matters to policy and economic academic discussions, we consider the relationship between the returns to Hispanic-immigrant self-employment and immigrants' length of stay in the United States. This relationship arguably relates to the underlying entrepreneurial talents of the group. If immigrants have the same or more talent than native populations, then the process of economic assimilation ensures macroeconomic benefits to the United States as a whole.

We proceed with the idea of immigrant talent (or quality) in a systematic fashion by asking two related questions. First, does the United States receive the "best" or the "worst" from other countries? Second, how does this immigrant talent change the average entrepreneurial talent of Hispanic entrepreneurs in the United States?

Immigrant Quality and the Migration Decision.   The issue of the quality of immigrants has permeated U.S. policy debates for some time. For example, in the late 1800s and early 1900s, in response to the large waves of low-skill immigrants from Southern and Eastern Europe, Congress designed U.S. immigration policy, in some cases by overriding presidential vetoes, in favor of Northern and Western Europeans.[6]

During the past thirty years, social scientists have followed this inquiry to quantify the quality dimension of foreign-born immigrants. Economist Barry Chiswick has argued that people who emigrate have higher levels of motivation and energy than their host country's native counterparts, and that these unmeasurable characteristics positively relate to innate labor-market quality and outcomes. Using U.S. census data from 1970, he found in a 1978 study that the earnings of immigrants surpassed those of U.S. natives after approximately fifteen years of working in the United States. Chiswick's interpretation was that because in his sample the foreign born outperformed their U.S.-born counterparts, immigrants had a higher level of unobserved skills than U.S. natives.

Economist George Borjas, in contrast, subsequently made the case in a 1987 study that immigrant quality depends on the relative earnings dispersion between origin and host countries. According to his view, immigrants from countries with "tight" income distributions relative to that of the United States (e.g., countries with strong welfare states) have a higher set of observable and unobservable skills because they are attracted to the returns to relatively high skills in the United States (and vice versa). This conceptualization suggests that immigrants from countries such as Mexico with relatively high income inequality disproportionately send workers with low observable and unobservable skills to the United States. In the case of political refugees, such as Cubans and Salvadorans, as Borjas suggests, the immigrants from these countries might be the most talented (see his "refugee-sorting" scenario).

Borjas's empirical findings seemingly support this theory, as he used census data from 1970 and 1980 to synthetically track the economic performance of immigrant cohorts in the United States. This theory, however, has been challenged by other economists, particularly in the case of Mexican immigrants, with empirical evidence provided in two 2005 studies (one by Daniel Chiquiar and Gordon Hanson, and the other by Pia Orrenius and Madeline Zavodny) that suggests that relatively high-skilled Mexicans tend to emigrate to the United States because their skills tend to lower the broader social and economic costs of migration.

Immigrant Entrepreneurial Talent.   After arriving in the United States, immigrants also make decisions with respect to their labor-market activities. On the one hand, immigrant entrepreneurs appear to be more educated than their counterparts in the wage and salary sector. On the other hand, the push-pull framework discussed in the previous chapter raises the issue that minorities might become self-employed because of paid-employment discrimination; low skill levels; or in the case of immigrants, the fact that education, language, and other skills obtained abroad have lower value than those obtained in the United States. In the United States, the least assimilated immigrants are arguably the population group most likely to be pushed into self employment; some evidence from the 2000 study by sociologists Rebeca

Raijman and Marta Tienda points to "blocked mobility" as a reason for becoming self-employed.

It follows from this conceptual argument that if the least assimilated immigrants have a more difficult time obtaining employment than other immigrants (perhaps because of discrimination or because they lack the necessary skills), a greater portion of this group would become self-employed. This shift would therefore imply lower average quality among Hispanic-immigrant entrepreneurs with respect to those in the paid-employment sector, thus lowering the self-employment returns for this group.

Hispanic-Immigrant Talent—Empirical Tests

Observable Quality.   Our estimates indicate that before the Great Recession began, in the 2000s self-employed Hispanic immigrants between the ages of twenty-five and sixty-four had higher average levels of human capital than other foreign-born Hispanics, which suggests higher quality among foreign-born entrepreneurs (thus, stronger pull factors than push factors into self-employment). For example, in 2007, compared to their counterparts in the paid-employment sector, Hispanic-immigrant entrepreneurs on average had more education (10.6 versus 10.2 years), more potential work experience (27.1 versus 24.4 years), longer U.S. tenure (19.0 versus 17.2 years), and greater English-language fluency rates (53.5 versus 51.9 percent).

By 2010, the Great Recession, however, had led to narrowing human capital differentials between entrepreneurs and employees in terms of education (10.5 versus 10.4 years), work experience (27.5 versus 25.1 years), and U.S. tenure (19.7 versus 18.6 years); self-employed immigrants also had lower rates of English proficiency that year than their salaried counterparts (57.3 percent versus 59.1 percent). These changes suggest that the seeming human capital advantage of Hispanic-immigrant entrepreneurs versus other foreign-born Hispanics fell between 2007 and 2010, which is consistent with the development of push rather than pull factors into the self-employment sector. (More on the education of foreign-born versus U.S.-born Hispanic entrepreneurs is discussed in the following chapter.)

Alternatively, these changes could have been driven by macro-level characteristics related to relative labor demand. Recall the analysis of self-employment rates for 2007 and 2010 described earlier in this chapter, in which we held constant observable traits. Returning to those results, the likelihood of being self-employed was significantly enhanced by education, experience, and English-language fluency, but not by U.S. tenure. It turns out that several of the human capital effects did not significantly change between 2007 and 2010, which suggests a relative weakening of the seeming skill advantage that Hispanic-immigrant entrepreneurs had over their salaried counterparts after the Great Recession.

The exception to this result comes from the significant decline in the role of English-language fluency; whereas the foreign-born who did not speak English well were 1.3 percent less likely than otherwise similar immigrants to be self-employed shortly before the economic downturn began, they were only half a percentage point less likely by 2010. The waning importance of English proficiency as a predictor of self-employment fits with the conceptualization that the Great Recession generated self-employment push factors among Hispanic immigrants.

Unobserved Talent.   In the foregoing conceptual discussion, changes in immigrants' earnings, relative to those of U.S. natives, have been used in the empirical literature to assess the unobserved relative quality of immigrants. Our findings in the previous chapter showed that the Great Recession led to a deterioration in the average observable and unobservable skills of Hispanic entrepreneurs relative to wage and salary workers. Were Hispanic immigrants immune to these effects, or were they affected in a similar fashion as natives?

To address this question, we replicate these exercises only for Hispanic immigrants. In 2007, self-employed Hispanic immigrants earned 16.4 percent less than foreign-born employees in the paid-employment sector. Controlling for observable skills and other features to obtain adjusted relative self-employment earnings yields an almost identical estimate, which means that observables did little to explain immigrants' self-employment penalty that year. Three years later, similar to Hispanics in general, foreign-born Hispanics lost significant ground in terms of their relative earnings, as their penalty more than doubled to 35.0 percent. Observable characteristics contributed about eleven percentage points to this penalty, leaving an unexplained penalty of 24 percent. Therefore, the relative earnings of self-employed Hispanic immigrants appear to have fallen between 2007 and 2010 because of a decline in both their observable and unobservable characteristics in comparison with those in the paid-employment sector.

The JMP results substantiate this finding, as the total raw change in the self-employment penalty of 18.6 percentage points during this time stemmed mostly from a relative deterioration in observable characteristics. This indicates that only a trivial amount of the total decline in the relative earnings of self-employed Hispanic immigrants occurred because of changes in returns to skills, observable or otherwise. As such, these results point to a loss in the average quality of foreign-born Hispanic entrepreneurs between 2007 and 2010.

Nevertheless, a similar loss occurred among U.S.-born Hispanics. During this period, their self-employment earnings penalty increased by 19.0 percentage points (to 46.5 percent). The JMP results show that observable and unobservable characteristics accounted for much of this erosion in Hispanic natives' entrepreneurial earnings, with the former contributing 11.2 percentage points, and the latter 8.5 percentage points, to the total change. Arguably, then, these results point to comparable (if not slightly higher) declines in the relative self-employment quality of U.S.-born versus foreign-born Hispanics during the Great Recession. We return to this issue in Chapter 5, where we further explore gender-related differences with respect to immigrant and native earnings differentials among the self-employed.

Unobservables in a Cohort of Hispanic-Immigrant Entrepreneurs.   In his 1987 study of immigrant quality, Borjas conducted empirical tests by synthetically tracking cohorts in consecutive decennial censuses. We follow this empirical approach to identify the entrepreneurial talent of a cohort of Hispanic-immigrant entrepreneurs in 2002, 2007, and 2010. We note, however, that this type of test has the potential drawback that individuals can "migrate" into different labor-market roles over time (or return to their home countries), thus yielding a variation in the sample of the entrepreneurial pool of Hispanic immigrants over time. That said, shifts into and out of entrepreneurship are relevant to changes in the average quality (and hence earnings) of workers in the self-employment and paid-employment sectors. This analysis therefore allows us to observe changes in relative quality, reflected in changes in earnings, between 2002 and 2010 of a cohort of Hispanic-immigrant entrepreneurs who had arrived in the United States by 2002.

Specifically, our cohort contains Hispanics between the ages of twenty-five and fifty-six in 2002, thirty and sixty-one in 2007, and thirty-three and sixty-four in 2010, excluding immigrants who migrated to the United States after

2002. We further partitioned the immigrant cohort into two groups: one of recent immigrants, defined as those who arrived in the United States between 1997 and 2002, and the other containing those who had migrated before 1997. To account for underlying shifts in macroeconomic and business conditions, we use U.S.-born Hispanics in the same age cohort as a comparison group.

We then estimated the earnings differentials between the two Hispanic-immigrant groups and their U.S.-born counterparts in this synthetic cohort in the three years while controlling for the characteristics we have used in our previous earnings analyses. Our results indicate that in 2002, recently arrived self-employed Hispanic-immigrants earned on average 22.8 percent less than their U.S.-born counterparts.

Five years later, these immigrants earned wages statistically similar to those of Hispanic natives in the self-employment sector; this was also the case in 2010. It follows that Hispanic immigrants who arrived in the United States between 1997 and 2002 made greater progress than U.S.-born Hispanics with respect to improving their entrepreneurial earnings between 2002 and 2010, as they erased their initial immigrant earnings penalty in the self-employment sector. Moreover, the Great Recession did not appear to undo their relative gain. It follows that Hispanic immigrants new to the United States in 2002 seemingly advanced with respect to their underlying quality over the following eight years relative to U.S. natives in the self-employment sector.

When estimating the earnings differentials between Hispanic immigrants and the U.S. born for immigrants with longer tenure in the United States (i.e., those who migrated before 1997), we also find evidence of a relative improvement in quality achieved by the foreign born between 2002 and 2010. Self-employed Hispanic immigrants earned about the same as U.S. natives in 2002, and by 2007, they earned a 15.5 percent premium. Three years later, while their earnings premium in the self-employment sector had fallen to 7.6 percent, it still remained greater than their 2002 relative earnings.

Does this boost in the relative earnings of Hispanic-immigrant entrepreneurs simply reflect the influence of assimilation on labor-market income? Perhaps this earnings growth resulted solely from the income gains that immigrants tend to have as they become more assimilated and experienced in U.S. labor markets. Changes in the earnings differentials between immigrants and U.S. natives in the paid-employment sector, however, suggest this was not the case. In 2002, recent Hispanic immigrants earned an average of 15.1 percent less than U.S.-born Hispanics in the paid-employment sector. Despite an improvement in their relative labor-market earnings (likely tied to assimilation effects), unlike their self-employed counterparts, immigrant employees who migrated between 1997 and 2002 continued to earn considerably less (8.9 percent less in 2007, and 6.9 percent less in 2010) than their U.S.-born counterparts. The paid-employment earnings of immigrants who migrated before 1997 also rose with respect to those of Hispanic natives, from being the same as natives' wages in 2002 to being 3.5 percent higher in 2007 and 4.8 percent higher in 2010. Note, however, that their gain over the eight years was smaller than the one experienced by tenured immigrant entrepreneurs.

In terms of Hispanic ethnic subgroups, the empirical results also suggest that a relative earnings improvement occurred among tenured Mexican-immigrant entrepreneurs between 2002 and 2010. In particular, self-employed Mexican immigrants who had been in the United States for at least five years had earnings similar to those of their U.S.-born counterparts in 2002. Their relatively neutral earnings turned into a premium of 9.8 percent in 2007 and a premium of 13.3 percent in 2010, which reflects the relative quality of Mexican-immigrant entrepreneurs.

However, comparable improvements in the self-employment earnings of recent Mexican immigrants and Cuban immigrants, tenured or otherwise, did not develop during this time.[7] Mexican immigrants who migrated to the United States between 1997 and 2002 had similar wages as Mexican American natives in the self-employment sector in both 2002 and 2010, despite the development of a significant immigrant earnings penalty in 2007. Recently arrived Cuban entrepreneurs also received the same labor-market income as their U.S.-born counterparts in 2002, but eight years later, they earned about 46 percent less. Tenured Cuban-born immigrants and U.S.-born Cubans had virtually the same labor-market income in the self-employment sector in all three years.

In all, these findings provide evidence that Hispanic-immigrant entrepreneurs who were residing in the United States in 2002 had relatively high levels of unobservable skills, as their earnings, compared to those of their U.S.-born Hispanic equivalents, were higher on average after the Great Recession than they were eight years earlier. While the subgroup analysis points to potential differences associated with the specific country of origin and time of migration, from a policy perspective, our results give credence to views that have promoted flexible strategies to attract immigrant entrepreneurs, including those of Hispanic origin, to the United States. We discuss some of these policies later in the book, particularly in Chapter 8.

Starting to Understand the Economic Impact
of Hispanic-Immigrant Entrepreneurs

Much analysis and conceptualization are needed to fully address the economic impacts of Hispanic immigrants in the United States. But several points can be made with respect to entrepreneurial outcomes. Neoclassical theory would argue for the benefits of increased competition coming from additional entrepreneurial resources. An increase in the supply of Hispanic-immigrant entrepreneurs should lower the profits of some native entrepreneurs, all else being equal. (For example, consider the case of native owners of construction businesses who have had to compete with an increasing number of foreign-born Hispanics joining this industry in the 2000s.) That said, the general impact of Hispanic-immigrant entrepreneurs theoretically provides the economy with an increased array of products at competitive prices. Moreover, in a 2003 study Robert Fairlie and Bruce Meyer did not find evidence at the national level that U.S. natives went out of business as a result of competition with immigrants.

Another important facet of this discussion is that Hispanic-immigrant business owners create employment (at least for themselves) rather than competing for jobs with U.S. natives, which contributes to the economic development of the localities in which they reside. This economic development issue matters for policy debate. While data limitations prevent us from providing extended empirical analysis of this issue, we can provide insight into two key issues. The first relates to the considerable employment and payroll implications of Hispanic-immigrant-owned firms. On the basis of our estimates using the 2007 SBO PUMS, the 446,700 firms owned by foreign-born Hispanics hired an aggregate of 673,300 workers, and their payrolls totaled $17.5 billion. Given that some firms did not report owner birthplace, the actual number of workers hired by (as well as the payroll of) companies owned by Hispanic immigrants may be even higher. This indicates that the employment these businesses generated went beyond the jobs these entrepreneurs created for themselves.

An additional economic impact involves how foreign-born Hispanic entrepreneurs affect government coffers. Using the 2007 SBO PUMS, we estimate that businesses owned by Hispanic immigrants generated at least $6.63 billion in state sales taxes, slightly less than the $6.81 billion in state sales taxes generated by firms owned by U.S.-born Hispanics.[8] It should be noted again that because some businesses did not report owner birthplace, these figures understate the total sales-tax revenue generated by all Hispanic-owned enterprises (which we estimate at $20.2 billion). They also likely understate total sales-tax revenue because some municipalities have sales taxes in addition to state sales tax.

Furthermore, using Current Population Survey (CPS) IPUMS data, we estimate that in 2007, self-employed Hispanic immigrants contributed another $6.56 billion to federal and state coffers on the basis of taxes paid on their labor-market income (net of tax credits). Specifically, our estimates indicate that they paid $2.09 billion in federal income taxes, $3.83 billion in Federal Insurance Contributions Act (FICA) taxes, and $639 million in state income taxes that year. On a per-person basis, the average foreign-born self-employed Hispanic generated $6,148 in income and FICA tax revenue (split across $1,961 in federal income taxes, $3,588 in FICA taxes, and another $599 in state income taxes), net of tax credits. Combined, this information indicates that businesses owned by Hispanic immigrants generated at least $13.2 billion in tax revenue based on state sales, income, and FICA taxes in 2007 alone.

We do not have data to estimate how the Great Recession affected state sales-tax revenue generated by Hispanic-owned enterprises, because the most recent SBO is from 2007, but we do observe a sharp decline in the income taxes they paid using the CPS IPUMS. To illustrate, in 2010, the income and FICA taxes paid by self-employed Hispanic immigrants had fallen to $5.16 billion—a loss of more than one-fifth of the total income and FICA tax revenue they had generated just two years earlier. At the same time, in absolute and relative terms, this loss was smaller than that for self-employed U.S.-born Hispanics (whose income and FICA taxes fell from $5.84 billion in 2007 to $4.07 billion in 2009). Moreover, on the basis of aggregated income and FICA taxes, Hispanic-immigrant entrepreneurs contributed more each year than did their U.S.-native counterparts to government and state coffers.

To be sure, the impact of Hispanic-immigrant entrepreneurs extends more broadly to the U.S. macroeconomy. Contributions to tax revenues (which we return to later in this book), cannot be ignored, especially during a time of large budget deficits. But the positive impact of Hispanic-immigrant entrepreneurship on employment growth, both direct and indirect, as well as added product-market competition should also be considered.

Concluding Remarks

We highlight in this chapter that some Hispanic-immigrant entrepreneurs appear to be creating employment opportunities rather than reducing them for U.S. natives, and thus they are contributing to the economic development of the localities in which they reside. In the press there abound human-interest stories on this point, as well as on the plight of Hispanic-immigrant entrepreneurs in recent times. For example, a 2006 *Chicago Tribune* article by Sara Olkon discusses the case of Andres Macías, a Mexican immigrant who stimulated economic development in a run-down area after opening a taco stand. Also, a 2006 article in the *Sun News*, of Myrtle Beach, South Carolina, Renita Burns quotes then spokesman for the U.S. Hispanic Chamber of Commerce, Guillermo Meneses: "Whenever you see large concentrations of Hispanics moving into the area, you will see the economy grow by leaps and bounds." Our discussion of Hispanic-immigrant entrepreneurship continues under other themes in the chapters that follow.

4 Education and Hispanic Entrepreneurs

INVESTMENTS IN EDUCATION HAVE BEEN WELL DOCUMENTED as having a positive impact on individuals' labor-market outcomes. Much of the empirical evidence comes from literature exploring the relationship between education and earnings of salaried workers. Conceptually, this relationship has been attributed to the enhanced productivity that education provides workers and to the positive signal that education sends to employers about individuals' ability and motivation. The same theoretical arguments can be made for the self-employed, as education may promote the managerial know-how of entrepreneurs as well as provide a positive signal to stakeholders (e.g., customers, suppliers, bankers, others) with whom the self-employed interact. Education may also serve as a catalyst for selection into self-employment. Perhaps education enhances managerial ability, which in turn leads to a greater probability of entrepreneurship. Of course, these theoretical associations have been much scrutinized by economists and others, as they offer, in many cases, ambiguous predictions.

In this chapter we review some of the conceptual literature related to education and self-employment. We also provide empirical evidence of the relationship of education to sales of Hispanic-owned businesses, taking business owners' birthplace into account. Part of this discussion addresses whether a firm's location in the sales distribution affects how schooling relates to revenue. We further analyze how the relationship between education and earnings of Hispanic entrepreneurs changed during the Great Recession. This analysis includes comparisons across the distribution of earnings, across Hispanic subgroups, and in light of the previous chapter's focus, between the native and immigrant populations of this ethnic group. The chapter concludes with an investigation into how education is related to entry into the self-employment sector.

Conceptual Issues Regarding Education and Self-Employment Outcomes

From a conceptual perspective, we are interested in two questions pertaining to education and economic outcomes for Hispanic entrepreneurs. First, how does schooling relate to measures of business success and earnings of Hispanic entrepreneurs? Second, does education serve to promote or to deter entrepreneurship among Hispanics? Insight into the latter question involves considerations related to the push-pull framework discussed in Chapter 2, as the framework is tied to the underlying skill base of Hispanic entrepreneurs newly minted in the 2000s.

Education and Earnings of Entrepreneurs.   The model of human capital (defined as investments in people to enhance their productivity, such as education), made famous by Nobel laureate Gary Becker, builds on the notion that individuals will undertake a human capital investment as long as the present value of the returns from the investment exceeds the present value of the costs of making the investment. These returns are expressed in terms of not only net earnings gains from investing in human capital but also as nonpecuniary benefits. Investment costs include out-of-pocket and opportunity costs involved in the time required to undertake the human capital investment.

The conceptual question linking education and earnings, however, has been why earnings increase as individuals acquire education. One answer suggests that individuals become more productive and thus more valuable in the labor market. In particular, the knowledge base individuals acquire from schooling, as well as how this knowledge assists them in acquiring and dealing with new information, supposedly aids in enhancing worker productivity. Another answer, however, is that education serves as a signal to employers of a prospective employee's ability. For this latter reason, the impact of education on the magnitude of additional observed earnings has been called into question, as in Andrew Michael Spence's (also a Nobel laureate) 1973 study on job market signaling. That is, if the source of additional earnings is the inherent ability of the worker, then higher earnings do not directly result from higher levels of schooling.

With regard to self-employment, the case for education as a signal of an individual's ability appears less convincing. The self-employed would know their productivity level and would not need to rely on schooling to signal their abilities. That said, entrepreneurs could use education as a positive signal to their clients, suppliers, and creditors.

Given the disproportionate presence of immigrants among Hispanic entrepreneurs, the issue of the value of foreign education, either as a signal or as human capital, should also be considered. Economists, including Barry Chiswick in 1978 and Stephen Trejo in 2003, have contended that when education obtained abroad does not transfer easily into U.S. labor markets (or is perceived by employers to signal something negative about a worker's productivity), the returns to education should be lower for immigrants than for native workers. What remains unclear is whether a foreign education provides the same returns in the self-employment sector as education acquired in the United States, and whether a foreign education signals the same value for immigrant business owners to stakeholders.

Moreover, the quality of foreign education might have a complementary impact on other attributes of Hispanic entrepreneurs that could act multiplicatively on self-employment earnings (and other economic outcomes) of this group relative to native Hispanic entrepreneurs. For example, if the stakeholders of Hispanic entrepreneurs deem U.S. education to be of higher quality than foreign education, then native Hispanic entrepreneurs are likely to be more successful, as stakeholders might be willing to give them more business or easier access to credit. But this advantage would be magnified (in a multiplicative manner) if the quality of education were coupled with other earnings-enhancing attributes, such as motivation, ability, and drive.

The flip side is that what constitutes a low versus a high level of schooling varies across countries, given underlying differences in educational systems and access to schools. In 2010 in Mexico, for example, four out of ten (41.9 percent) adults between the ages of twenty-five and sixty-four had at most a sixth-grade education, and another quarter (26.5 percent) had the equivalent of a middle school education in the United States.[1] In El Salvador, three-quarters (76.0 percent) of adults in the same age group had completed no more than the equivalent of middle school in 2007; in fact, a full 72.0 percent had not advanced beyond the sixth grade. Only about one-third of Mexico's population, and one-quarter of El Salvador's population, had completed twelve or more years of education. As such, while someone without a high school diploma is considered "low skilled" in the United States, the same individual might be viewed as "skilled" in other countries, particularly someone who studied beyond the ninth grade.

For these reasons, and for others that might involve the relationship between schooling and access to financial capital and physical capital (e.g., computers, machines, equipment), providing empirical predictions on the impact of education on the productivity of Hispanic entrepreneurs becomes difficult. It follows that the relative role of education in the earnings of both salaried workers and the self-employed adds to this interpretive complication. That said, and as we empirically discuss below, this conceptual formulation allows us to develop hypotheses regarding Hispanic entrepreneurs, some of which we test with the data at our disposal.

Education and Choice of Self-Employment. The relationship between education and the choice of self-employment among Hispanics is also of interest. On the one hand, it can be argued that education promotes self-employment, as this investment in human capital may lower barriers to credit access, enhance managerial ability, and make an individual more aware of available entrepreneurial opportunities. If so, we would expect that Hispanics who start their own businesses have more education than the average Hispanic worker. On the other hand, schooling might increase a worker's labor-market value, thus leading to more job opportunities for the educated, which could serve to push less educated workers into the self-employment sector.

The empirical literature has borne out the conceptual ambiguity of the relationship between entrepreneurial choice and education. In two 2008 reviews of studies exploring this relationship in the United States and in other countries, Pat Dickson, George Solomon, and K. Mark Weaver in one, and Justin van der Sluis, Mirjam van Praag, and Wim Vijverberg in the other, find that education does not seem to enhance the likelihood of becoming an entrepreneur.

At the same time, these reviews did not specifically explore this relationship for Hispanics in the United States—a population with below-average education levels and high shares of immigrants. Indeed, Timothy Bates assesses this literature for minorities in the United States in his 2011 study and reports, "High educational attainment is a strong, positive predictor of entry into certain high-barrier fields (where average owner remuneration is high) for minorities generally, but not into lower barrier industries (including personal services, where average owner remuneration is low)" (p. 203). In contrast, Lofstrom and Wang suggest in their 2009 study that Hispanics lacking college degrees may be more likely to opt for self-employment than their college-graduate counterparts.

Education of Hispanic Entrepreneurs and Nonearnings Business Outcomes

Consistent with the Hispanic population in general, Hispanic entrepreneurs have less education on average than their non-Hispanic counterparts. For example, in the 2007 SBO nearly one-fifth of all Hispanic business owners had less than a high school education—more than four times the share of non-Hispanic business owners with this level of education. Just about a quarter of Hispanic entrepreneurs had at least a four-year college degree that year, compared to 45.9 percent of other firm owners. Despite their relatively low education levels, Hispanic entrepreneurs were more educated than the average Hispanic adult in general. To illustrate, in the 2007 ACS, one third of all Hispanic workers in the United States between the ages of twenty-five and sixty-four had not completed high school, and 15 percent were college graduates.

Still, part of the reason for the relatively low education levels of Hispanics pertains to the relatively high share of Hispanic immigrants. Recall from the previous chapter that in 2007, more than one-quarter of Hispanic-immigrant business owners had not completed high school, compared to one out of eleven U.S.-born Hispanic entrepreneurs. One-fifth of Hispanic foreign-born owners and 28 percent of U.S.-born Hispanic firm owners had graduated from college. While these figures point to the relative "undereducation" of Hispanic-immigrant entrepreneurs, we note in the previous chapter that they were more educated than the average foreign-born Hispanic worker in the paid-employment sector that year.

Although smaller in magnitude, when focusing only on firms with paid employees, considerable education gaps between Hispanics and non-Hispanics also existed in 2007: one out of every eight Hispanic employers did not have a high school education, versus three out of one hundred other employers. Similarly, only a third of Hispanic employers, but about half of non-Hispanic employers, had a bachelor's degree or higher. It follows that if education matters for entrepreneurial success, a disproportionate share of Hispanic-owned enterprises (including those with paid employees) will likely lag behind. Given the dramatic growth in the number of Hispanic-owned businesses, such information is important for economic development in the United States.

For insight into the role of education on business success measures of Hispanic entrepreneurs, we first analyze sales using the 2007 SBO PUMS. We then focus on other business outcomes discussed in previous chapters (namely profits and the likelihood that profits reached key benchmarks) using the 2003 SSBF. Later in this chapter, we investigate how education relates to the labor-market income of Hispanic entrepreneurs, as well as the role it plays in the likelihood of becoming self-employed.

Education and Sales of Hispanic-Owned Businesses in 2007. On the surface, having at least a bachelor's degree seems to matter with respect to sales of Hispanic-owned businesses. Those businesses owned by college graduates had average sales of $551,300 in 2007, compared to $121,100 for firms whose owners did not have a high school diploma and $173,300 for other Hispanic-owned companies. When logarithmically transforming sales, firms of Hispanic college graduates outperformed those of their less educated counterparts, with their sales being (statistically significantly) 51.8 percent higher than those of high school graduates. Of interest, those owned by the latter had lower sales (by 16.6 percent) than firms whose owners had not completed high school.

Among non-Hispanic-owned businesses, the four-year college degree also seemed to matter the most (and by a similar magnitude as for Hispanics). The sales of firms owned by non-Hispanic high school graduates were significantly lower (by 55.8 percent) than those of college graduates, and they were statistically the same as those owned by high school dropouts. These findings highlight the role of a college education in the success of businesses, at least as measured through revenue, but they say little about a high school diploma versus lower schooling levels overall.

Part of the reason for the lack of a significant difference in the sales of businesses with owners who had completed high school versus those who did not appears to be immigration. When focusing only on Hispanic-immigrant-owned firms, those owned by high school graduates had sales that were 23.7 percent lower than those of college graduates and 18.4 percent higher than those whose owners had not completed high school. An almost identical pattern emerges when focusing exclusively on firms of U.S.-born Hispanics. Those owned by high school graduates had 22.2 percent lower sales than their college-graduate peers and 21.9 percent higher sales than their less educated peers. Repeating these comparisons for the businesses of non-Hispanic immigrants (and then for non-Hispanic U.S. natives) provides similar results.

We realize that some of these differences may relate to other owner or firm characteristics. For example, education can serve to sort workers into particular industries, such that we might be observing an industry effect instead of one driven exclusively by education. However, when accounting for industry and other observable owner and firm characteristics (see Appendix B), we find that Hispanic business owners with a high school diploma had significantly higher sales (by 19.5 percent) than their less educated counterparts and significantly lower sales (by 31.3 percent) than their college-graduate peers. Similar patterns also emerged when replicating the analysis specifically for employer firms (Hispanic owned or otherwise) as well as for companies owned by (1) Hispanic immigrants, (2) Hispanic natives, and (3) non-Hispanics. Among nonemployers, however, the relationship between education and sales was weaker. A four-year college degree enhanced sales by only 8.5 percent for Hispanics and 7.5 percent for non-Hispanics when controlling for other owner and firm characteristics, while a high school diploma had virtually no effect on sales for either group compared to lower schooling levels.

Education and Sales Distribution in 2007.   Perhaps the weaker relationship between education and revenue among nonemployer firms pertains to their clustering at the lower end of the sales distribution. Firms at the higher end of the distribution include more employers, who might be more likely to depend on human capital resources than companies with low sales. To explore this issue, Figure 4.1 presents the effects of having a college education on revenue for firms at different places in the sales distribution in 2007, with other traits held constant.[2] The horizontal axis in Figure 4.1 measures the percentiles with respect to the natural logarithm of sales, and the vertical axis shows the estimated premium of having a four-year college degree (relative to a high school diploma) on sales, when controlling for other observable characteristics.

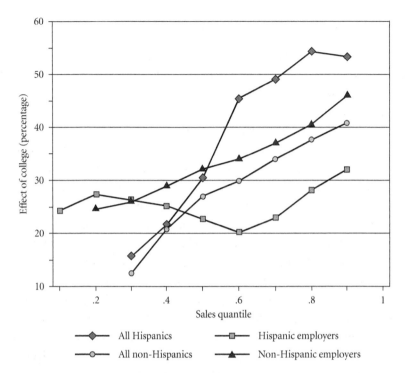

FIGURE 4.1 Effect of a college education on the sales of Hispanic-
and non-Hispanic-owned small businesses in 2007, by selected sales
quantiles

SOURCE: Authors' estimates using 2007 SBO PUMS data.
NOTES: The comparison group includes firms whose owners had at least a high
school diploma but not a four-year college degree; the results for firms with owners
who did not complete high school are not shown, to conserve space. For estimation
details, see Appendix B.

In 2007, the role of a college education on the revenue of all Hispanic-
owned firms rose with respect to each sales decile (particularly until the sixth
decile), except the ninth decile. That is, other than at the very top of the sales
distribution, the premium associated with a college diploma increased in importance as Hispanic-owned firms moved up in the distribution. To illustrate, compared to otherwise similar firms whose owners had graduated from
high school, the revenue of Hispanic businesses with college-graduate owners
was 15.8 percent higher in the third sales decile but 54.4 percent higher in the

eighth decile. The revenue "penalty" for businesses owned by those who did not graduate from high school similarly rose in magnitude as they moved up in the sales distribution; the sales of these businesses were 11.1 percent less than those owned by high school graduates at the third decile, but 37.2 percent less than those at the top of the sales distribution (to conserve space, we do not show this in Figure 4.1).

It should be noted that when we replicated this analysis by splitting Hispanic businesses according to owners' birthplace (results not shown because of space constraints), similar patterns (and magnitudes) emerge. Among Hispanic-immigrant businesses, as well as those owned by U.S. natives, having a college education became increasingly important as they moved up in the sales distribution; both groups reached their peak at the eighth decile. It follows that the relationship between schooling and revenue does not seem to be uniquely affected by the birthplace of Hispanic business owners.

Figure 4.1 also reports the effect of a college education for non-Hispanic-owned businesses. As for their Hispanic counterparts, having a college degree led to higher revenue among non-Hispanic-owned firms, and this relationship became stronger as they moved up the sales distribution. However, the magnitude of the relationship appears stronger for Hispanic companies in the same relative sales percentiles, which again suggests the importance of this human capital variable on the revenue generated by this group.

It is of interest that these patterns do not hold when focusing exclusively on Hispanic businesses with paid employees. The revenue premium associated with a college degree declined as these firms moved up the sales distribution until reaching a trough at the sixth decile, after which point the premium then rose. Similarly, the penalty for not having a high school diploma (not shown) was smallest in magnitude (at 9.0 percent) for Hispanic-owned employer firms in the seventh sales decile. It therefore appears that education played a larger role in the success of Hispanic employers at the tails of the sales distribution than for those located in the middle. This was not the case for other employers, as the link between education and revenue followed the same trend as for all non-Hispanic-owned businesses.

Part of the reason for the strong association between education and sales observed for all Hispanic-owned enterprises likely stems from a particularly strong link between education and the probability of being an employer firm among this group. Our empirical evidence supports this point.

When analyzing how observable characteristics, including education, relate to the likelihood of having paid employees, we find that a college degree had more than twice as much of an impact on the likelihood of being an employer for businesses owned by Hispanics than by non-Hispanics (5.7 percent versus 2.5 percent), all else being equal. As such, education appears to play a different role in business outcomes for Hispanic entrepreneurs than for other business owners.

Education and Other Outcomes Among Small Businesses.   We now use the SSBF data to consider how education related to other business outcomes for Hispanic-owned small firms in the mid-2000s. In these data, similar to employer firms in the SBO, slightly more than one-third of Hispanic small business owners had a four-year college degree or higher, compared to nearly half of non-Hispanics. Also, 5 percent of Hispanics did not have a high school diploma or equivalent—three times the 1.6 percent of other small firm owners with this level of schooling.

On average, in the mid-2000s, small firms owned by Hispanic college graduates had sales of $890,100 and profits of $232,600, compared to sales of $731,400 and profits of $86,100 among businesses of less educated Hispanics. When logarithmically transforming revenue, small businesses owned by Hispanic college graduates significantly outperformed those of their less educated counterparts, as their sales were 66.7 percent higher. Moreover, small firms owned by Hispanics without a high school diploma had significantly lower average sales and profits than did those of other Hispanic enterprises in 2004 and 2005. On the surface, these findings highlight the role that education plays in the success of Hispanic small businesses.

Of course, as with our analysis of sales using the SBO PUMS, some of these differences may relate to other owner or firm characteristics. To explore this possibility, we reconsider the relationship between education and small business outcomes in the SSBF while controlling for characteristics, including the owners' experience, race, and gender, as well as the industry, firm age, and other firm traits. The findings from this exercise suggest that, in the mid-2000s, small firms owned by Hispanic college graduates had approximately 70 percent higher sales than otherwise similar firms with Hispanic owners who had lower schooling levels. However, Hispanic small businesses had similar revenue between those with owners who had graduated high school and those who had not, such that the negative sales effect observed earlier appears to be driven by differences in other owner or firm traits.

Among non-Hispanic small business owners, to a lesser extent than their Hispanic counterparts, college graduates also outperformed their less educated counterparts (by about 17 percent) with respect to sales. As such, similar to the SBO results, having a college degree was positively related to the revenue generated by small businesses in 2004 and 2005, and this relationship was particularly strong for those small businesses owned by Hispanics. As with the case of Hispanics, small firms owned by non-Hispanic high school dropouts had comparable sales to those owned by high school graduates.

In terms of the profit outcomes of Hispanic-owned small enterprises, the effect of education varied according to the specific benchmark being considered. For example, when controlling for other characteristics, education did not play a significant role with respect to average profit levels or the odds of having at least $10,000 in profits. At the same time, when analyzing the likelihood of breaking even in the mid-2000s, compared to the likelihood of otherwise similar firms owned by Hispanic high school graduates doing so, this likelihood was about 33 percent lower for firms with less educated owners and 14 percent higher for firms owned by college graduates. For non-Hispanics, firms owned by college graduates had higher average profits, but they were not more likely to break even or to generate $10,000 in profits than those businesses owned by their less educated peers.

In general, these findings suggest that a college education mattered more for Hispanic entrepreneurs than for non-Hispanics with respect to measuring business success through sales and the odds of breaking even in the mid-2000s. It is of interest that this was not the case five years earlier; the education levels of Hispanic small firm owners did not play a significant role in any of the business outcomes considered here when we analyzed the 1998 version of the SSBF. Thus, the influence of schooling on the success of Hispanic entrepreneurs might be sensitive to changes in macroeconomic conditions as well as to the presence of changes in self-employment push versus pull factors.

In all, these empirical exercises illustrate that education did not exhibit the same effect on business outcomes for Hispanic entrepreneurs as it did for non-Hispanics. We next explore how education related to the earnings of Hispanic entrepreneurs in the 2000s and whether this relationship changed throughout the course of the business cycle.

Returns to Education for Hispanic Entrepreneurs in the 2000s

As discussed above, in the mid-2000s education mattered with respect to key outcomes of Hispanic-owned firms. What role did education play in the labor-market income of Hispanic entrepreneurs during this time? For insight, we specifically focus on the years explored in detail in earlier chapters (2002, 2007, and 2010) to estimate the returns to education; namely, how much did an extra year of schooling contribute to labor market earnings? In this exercise, the returns to education for self-employed Hispanics were 2.8 percent in 2002, all else being equal. On average, this means that high school graduates who did not attend college earned 33.6 percent more than their otherwise similar counterparts without any education (2.8[12]) and 5.6 percent more than those with ten years of schooling at that time (2.8[12 − 10]). By 2007, these returns had significantly increased to 4.2 percent, which means that education became a more valuable predictor of entrepreneurial earnings over the five-year period.

It should also be noted that the returns to education among Hispanics in the paid-employment sector changed as well, from 3.8 percent in 2002 to 4.3 percent in 2007 and 4.7 percent in 2010. The shift from nearly identical returns to education in 2007 to lower returns three years later in the entrepreneurial versus paid-employment sectors follows with the presence of self-employment push conditions after the Great Recession began. Hispanics having difficulties securing paid-employment jobs may have become willing to accept lower schooling returns in the self-employment sector instead of becoming unemployed or dropping out of the labor force.

It is also worth noting that Hispanics received lower returns to education than their non-Hispanic counterparts, possibly due to immigration. In 2002, self-employed non-Hispanics accrued a premium on their education, as their schooling returns of 10.3 percent were greater than both the 2.8 percent return that self-employed Hispanics earned and the 9.5 percent return that non-Hispanics received in salaried positions. By 2010, the returns to schooling for non-Hispanics fell to 9.9 percent in the self-employment sector and rose to 9.7 percent in the paid-employment sector.

Returns to Education for Self-Employed Hispanic Immigrants Versus Natives. Some of the difference between Hispanics and non-Hispanics in the returns to education likely relates to the large presence of immigrants in the Hispanic population. Recall from our conceptual discussion above that if education obtained abroad does not easily transfer into U.S. labor markets, or if it signals a relatively low schooling quality, then immigrants should earn lower returns to education than their native counterparts. Moreover, if relatively low schooling levels by U.S. standards mask considerable variability in educational outcomes in immigrants' home countries, then the returns to formal education might also be lower for immigrants than for natives in the United States.

For insight, we note that U.S.-born Hispanics had relatively low returns to education in the self-employment sector (3.5 percent) in 2002, although these returns increased significantly later in the decade, to 7.7 percent in 2007 and to 9.2 percent in 2010. In contrast, the schooling returns for foreign-born Hispanic entrepreneurs rose mildly between 2002 and 2007, from 3.1 percent to 3.5 percent, but by 2010, they had fallen below their 2002 level (to 2.3 percent). Consider, too, that the education returns in paid employment for this group rose from 2.5 percent in 2002 to 2.8 percent in 2007 and 3.3 percent in 2010. This divergence between U.S.- and foreign-born Hispanic entrepreneurs, particularly during the Great Recession, suggests that birthplace differences in the returns to education are not a stable phenomenon. One explanation is that such differences reflect birthplace-related push and pull factors into the self-employment sector along the education dimension.

Immigrants Educated in the United States Versus Abroad.   To further explore the returns to schooling for foreign-born entrepreneurs, consider that a small but nontrivial number of immigrants migrated with their parents, and thus received some (or all) of their education in the United States. While somewhat ignored in the literature, previous studies have referred to these groups in terms of "fractionalized" immigrant generations.[3] "Generation 1.75" refers to those who migrated before starting school; they appear similar in many respects to their U.S.-born counterparts, as their entire educational experience occurred in the United States. In contrast, "Generation 1.5" refers to those who migrated after completing some, but not all, of their schooling abroad. The true first generation includes immigrants who finished their education before arriving to the United States.

We estimate that in 2010, Generation 1.75 comprised 4.7 percent and Generation 1.5, another 15.1 percent, of self-employed Hispanic immigrants between the ages of twenty-five and sixty-four. These shares were statistically lower than their corresponding shares among foreign-born Hispanic workers in the paid-employment sector (7.1 percent and 17.2 percent, respectively). In addition, the self-employment rates were lower among Generations 1.75 and 1.5 (7.7 percent versus 10.0 percent, respectively) than among other Hispanic immigrants (11.8 percent), but higher than among U.S.-born Hispanics (6.6 percent). The location and timing of when foreign-born Hispanics acquired their education in their life cycles therefore appears related to their entrepreneurial propensities.

Still, we have not uncovered evidence that acquiring an education in the United States instead of abroad mattered in terms of the average schooling returns accrued by Hispanic-immigrant entrepreneurs, at least in the years we considered. When splitting education into years of U.S. schooling versus foreign schooling, the returns to both were statistically similar for foreign-born self-employed Hispanics. Also, similar to the case for all Hispanic-immigrant entrepreneurs discussed above, these returns seemed to diverge from the schooling returns for U.S.-born Hispanics after 2002. To illustrate, each year of education obtained in the United States enhanced the earnings of self-employed Hispanic immigrants by 3.7 percent in both 2002 and 2007, but by 2.2 percent in 2010.

We do not observe similar patterns for foreign-born Hispanics in the paid-employment sector. For this group, U.S.-acquired schooling generated significantly higher returns than education acquired abroad in all three years (3.3 versus 2.4 percent in 2002; 3.4 versus 2.8 percent in 2007; and 3.8 versus 3.2 percent in 2010). Moreover, the returns to both U.S. and foreign education rose over time for these immigrants, surpassing the schooling returns accrued by their self-employed counterparts by 2010. Such differences again suggest a growing presence of push factors into self-employment among foreign-born Hispanics during the Great Recession.

Education Returns and Distribution of Earnings.   The discussion thus far on the earnings effect of education for Hispanic entrepreneurs has centered on their average returns. Perhaps these differed according to where workers were located in the earnings distribution. To test this proposition, we estimate these relationships along various earnings deciles, similar to our analysis of sales above.

For visual aid, Panel A of Figure 4.2 displays the returns to schooling for nine deciles of earnings for Hispanic entrepreneurs in 2002, 2007, and 2010.

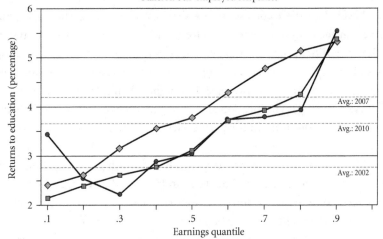

Panel A: Self-employed Hispanics

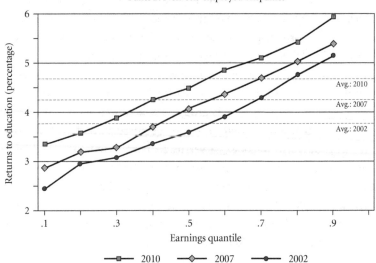

Panel B: Non-self-employed Hispanics

FIGURE 4.2 Returns to education for Hispanic workers in the self-employment and paid-employment sectors in 2002, 2007, and 2010, by selected earnings quantiles

SOURCE: Authors' estimates using ACS data in the IPUMS.

NOTES: The sample includes Hispanic workers between the ages of twenty-five and sixty-four not living in group quarters who reported labor market earnings. For estimation details, see Appendix B.

For comparative purposes, Panel B of Figure 4.2 shows the schooling payoffs for Hispanics in the paid-employment sector. The average schooling returns discussed in the previous subsection are included in this figure as well.

Several interesting features can be highlighted. First, in the three years shown, the returns to schooling were highest for Hispanics located in the top 10 percent of the earnings distribution, with little difference among entrepreneurs across the three years. This finding indicates that education mattered the most (and in a consistent manner) for the wealthiest of entrepreneurs. Second, with the exception of the self-employed in 2002, the returns to education for Hispanic workers consecutively rose with each earnings decile, which again suggests that formal schooling plays a larger role in the generation of labor-market income as workers advance in the earnings distribution.

Another point from Figure 4.2 is that in 2002, education had a greater payoff for Hispanic entrepreneurs whose earnings were in the first decile than for others whose earnings were at or below the median. In fact, self-employed Hispanics at the bottom of the earnings distribution received their highest returns to schooling in 2002 (of 3.4 percent). This observation points to the complexity of the impact of education on entrepreneurial income, and it raises the question of whether push and pull factors into self-employment depend on the location of workers in the earnings distribution.

Furthermore, the gap in the returns to education between self-employment and paid employment virtually disappeared for Hispanics in 2007 (except for those in the bottom fifth of the earnings distribution), because they rose by a greater proportion for entrepreneurs than for salaried workers. Mirroring the change in the average returns, however, the gap widened by 2010 across all wage deciles. As the schooling payoffs returned to their 2002 levels in many of the deciles shown, they continued to increase across the earnings distribution of Hispanics in the paid-employment sector. These observations again suggest the development of relatively strong self-employment push factors among Hispanics after the Great Recession began.

These push factors appear to have been particular to the foreign born. The returns to schooling among self-employed Hispanic immigrants (not shown in Figure 4.2, to conserve space) fell between 2002 and 2007 for those with earnings in all but two of the deciles, and they continued to fall across all deciles except one by 2010. In contrast, education returns increased for U.S.-born Hispanic entrepreneurs across all earnings deciles between 2002 and 2007, and they rose again in nearly all deciles by 2010, leaving self-employed native Hispanics with greater payoffs to schooling across the entire earnings distribution after the Great Recession than they had received earlier in the decade.

Returns to Education for Entrepreneurs Among Hispanic Ethnic Subgroups

Mexican Americans.   With 10.6 years of schooling on average in 2002 and 2010, self-employed Mexican Americans had the second-lowest average education levels among the four largest Hispanic entrepreneurial populations (with Salvadorans having the lowest). In 2002, Mexican American entrepreneurs also had the lowest returns to education and the second lowest (above Salvadorans) in 2007 (3.9 percent) and 2010 (3.6 percent). This population's relatively low education levels and low schooling returns probably owes to the subgroup's large number of immigrants. As discussed earlier in this chapter, education obtained outside of the country might not yield the same payoff as a U.S. education.

Following from this population's majority position among Hispanic ethnic subgroups, the increase in schooling payoffs paralleled those of Hispanic entrepreneurs in general. With few exceptions, these results are comparable to those for self-employed Hispanics overall with respect to how education affected labor-market income at different places in the earnings distribution. For example, in 2007 and 2010, self-employed Mexican Americans in the top earnings decile had the highest returns to education among all earnings deciles. Also, these payoffs increased between 2002 and 2007 in the same manner as for Hispanic entrepreneurs in general, and they fell by 2010, although they were not restored to their 2002 levels. One difference is that in 2002, Mexican American entrepreneurs in the tenth earnings percentile had higher schooling returns (3.7 percent) than the other subgroups.

Puerto Ricans.   The average education levels of self-employed Puerto Ricans were the second highest of the four groups in 2002 (12.6 years) and 2007 (13.1 years), behind Cubans, and tied with Cubans for the highest (13.2 years) in 2010. Paralleling the general changes for Hispanic entrepreneurs, the schooling returns accrued by self-employed Puerto Ricans rose from 3.6 percent in 2002 to 8.9 percent in 2007, and they fell to 4.8 percent in 2010. In both 2007 and 2010, these returns were the highest returns among the major Hispanic ethnic subgroups. This observation likely relates to the fact that nearly all Puerto Ricans are born U.S. citizens and attend American schools, either in Puerto Rico or on the U.S. mainland. At the same time, Puerto Ricans had the third lowest returns in 2002 of the four groups shown (falling behind both Salvadorans and Cubans, who have relatively high shares of immigrants), such that a U.S. education might not be the only explanation.

In all earnings deciles in 2007, and in all but the second and third deciles in 2010, Puerto Ricans also had higher education premiums across the earnings distribution than the other Hispanic ethnic subgroups. Moreover, their returns increased between 2002 and 2007, and then by 2010 fell in all earnings deciles. As for Mexican Americans, however, the decline by the end of the decade did not completely reduce the gains that Puerto Rican entrepreneurs had made before the Great Recession started, except for those in the second wage decile. Unlike self-employed Hispanics in general and Mexican Americans, in 2002, those in the bottom tenth of the earnings distribution had lower schooling returns than did their counterparts in other parts of the earnings distribution. Another difference is that these returns did not always progressively increase with respect to the earnings deciles. For example, in 2002, Puerto Rican entrepreneurs who earned the median income had lower schooling returns (virtually zero) than their peers with other income levels, except for those at the very bottom of the distribution. Even in 2007, the payoffs for schooling were lower for those with median income than for those between the twentieth and fortieth earnings percentiles.

Cubans.   Self-employed Cubans had the highest average education levels of the four subgroups in 2002 and 2007 (more than thirteen years of schooling), and they tied with Puerto Ricans for the highest level in 2010. Moreover, they had the second-highest schooling returns in all three years, being below the average returns of Salvadorans in 2002 and below Puerto Ricans in the other two years. Note that the rise in their returns between 2002 and 2007 was more than offset by a decline in 2010, which indicates that the Great Recession left Cuban entrepreneurs with lower returns to education than they received earlier in the decade. This was not the case for self-employed Hispanics in general or for Mexican Americans and Puerto Ricans.

How education rewards varied across the distribution of earnings also differed for self-employed Cubans compared to other groups. For example, in 2002, the returns steadily declined from 6.0 percent to a trough of 1.4 percent between the twentieth and sixtieth earnings percentiles; after the sixtieth percentile, their returns rose with each decile, reaching a peak (15.9 percent) in the top decile—the highest we estimated for any of the groups examined here. By 2007, schooling payoffs for self-employed Cubans increased, except for those in the top one-fifth of the distribution; they remained steady at about 8.0 percent in the eightieth percentile and fell to 5.4 percent for those at the top of the distribution. At the end of the decade, the payoffs to education had fallen for Cuban entrepreneurs in all but three of the wage deciles, and they remained steady in two of them. These rewards increased to 7.3 percent for the top earners between 2007 and 2010, but remained only half of what they were in 2002.

Salvadorans.   Among the four largest Hispanic subgroups, on average Salvadoran entrepreneurs had the lowest levels of schooling during this time period, falling from 9.7 years in 2002 to 9.4 years in 2010. A clear reason for Salvadorans' relatively low educational attainment is the fact that immigrants represented more than 95 percent of these entrepreneurs; recall that nearly three-quarters of adults between the ages of twenty-five and sixty-four in El Salvador had six or fewer years of education in 2007. It is of interest that self-employed Salvadorans had the highest schooling returns (6.5 percent) in 2002 but the lowest of the four Hispanic ethnic subgroups in both 2007 and 2010. Their relatively high schooling payoff in 2002 is puzzling because it runs counter to the notion that education obtained abroad has lower returns than a U.S. education.[4] Their relatively low schooling premiums in the other years, however, were consistent with expectations.

Unlike the other three Hispanic ethnic subgroups, Salvadoran entrepreneurs lost ground with respect to their returns to education between 2002 and 2007. This loss tracks the distribution of earnings, as their schooling returns were lower in 2007 than in 2002 for all earnings deciles, and they continued to decline in 2010. In fact, the returns became negative in the second through seventh earnings deciles in 2010, reaching a trough of −2.8 percent for entrepreneurs with median labor-market income. These negative returns indicate that education served to dampen, not enhance, earnings of Salvadoran entrepreneurs in the middle of the earnings distribution that year. Education had virtually no payoff for those in the top and bottom fifths of the earnings distribution.

Education and the Likelihood of Becoming
Self-Employed

One of the striking features of Hispanic entrepreneurship in the first decade of the 2000s was the rising self-employment rates in the Hispanic workforce. What role, if any, did education play in this growth in Hispanic entrepreneurship? As discussed earlier in this chapter, the literature has found a weak link between formal schooling and entrepreneurship. Yet to our knowledge, a test of this link for newly self-employed Hispanics (a population with relatively low education levels) has not been conducted.

We now address this question using data from the CPS. These data contain information on individuals' primary labor-market activities both in the previous calendar year and at the time of the survey. We can therefore observe individuals who had recently joined the self-employment sector by identifying those who were not self-employed in the previous year but were self-employed at the time of the survey.

Education and the Newly Self-Employed in 2002, 2007, and 2010.   In 2002, 13.8 percent of Hispanic entrepreneurs had recently joined the self-employment sector, meaning that they had not been self-employed in the previous year. These newly self-employed Hispanics had an average of 12.9 years of education, or 0.8 years more than the 12.1 years attained by more tenured Hispanic entrepreneurs and 1.6 years more than the 11.3 years of Hispanics in the paid-employment sector.[5] Mirroring this difference, among these new entrepreneurs, 29.5 percent were college graduates, and 18.7 percent did not have a high school diploma or equivalent, compared to 22.1 percent and 29.1 percent of the tenured entrepreneurs with these schooling levels, respectively.

Despite a decline in average schooling levels among Hispanic workers in general, higher schooling levels among new entrepreneurs remained in 2007, as they had an average of 12.4 years of education compared to 11.5 years among longer-term entrepreneurs. College graduates that year represented 23.2 percent of new Hispanic entrepreneurs and 16.8 percent of other self-employed Hispanics, while those without a high school degree accounted for a quarter of the former and a third of the latter. Similar to 2002, the newly self-employed represented about 13.3 percent of Hispanic entrepreneurs.

We do not observe differences in average education levels between new and established non-Hispanic entrepreneurs in either year, as both groups had the same schooling (14.1 years in 2002 and 14.2 years in 2007). This information suggests that education exerted a positive influence on the entrepreneurial tendencies of Hispanics before the recession began, but this influence does not seem to be part of a larger trend in terms of what was happening among new entrants into the self-employment sector in general. Recall from Chapter 2 that the period from 2002 to 2007 appears to have been a time when Hispanics were attracted into the entrepreneurial sector. The seeming education advantage for "newly minted" Hispanic entrepreneurs fits with this possibility.

Turning to 2010, Hispanics who had recently joined the self-employment sector represented about 11.9 percent of all Hispanic entrepreneurs. Unlike their previous counterparts, however, these new entrepreneurs did not possess an apparent schooling advantage, as their average of 11.7 years of education was comparable to the 11.4 years of other self-employed Hispanics that year. Both groups also had similar shares of college graduates (18.6 percent for the newly self-employed versus 16.7 percent for others) and high school dropouts (31.4 percent versus 34.2 percent, respectively). Education levels among non-Hispanics, too, did not differ between the newly versus longer-term self-employed, and they were virtually the same in 2002 and 2007.

We interpret the merging of the relative education levels of new versus longer-term Hispanic entrepreneurs as evidence that the Great Recession served to disproportionately push less educated Hispanics into the self-employment sector. It therefore seems that a loss in paid-employment opportunities for lower-skilled workers is part of the reason for the rising self-employment rates among Hispanics at the end of the decade.

A Closer Look at the Characteristics of Newly Self-Employed Hispanics.   Of course, other socioeconomic and demographic factors besides education affect the decision to become self-employed. In light of these possibilities, we next consider the role of education in the likelihood of Hispanics becoming self-employed when holding constant other observable characteristics. In this exercise, we compare Hispanic entrepreneurs who were not self-employed in the previous year with those who were (i.e., the longer-term entrepreneurs).

We find that education enhanced the probability of Hispanics joining the self-employment sector in both 2002 and 2007 (albeit by a small magnitude), even when accounting for other observable characteristics that affect self-employment tendencies. In both years, an additional year of schooling enhanced the likelihood of becoming self-employed by 0.06 percent.[6] However, by 2010, education no longer played a significant role in explaining new entrepreneurship among Hispanics.

Our findings further indicate that birthplace was not a good predictor of newly minted Hispanic entrepreneurs in 2002. However, in both 2007 and 2010, foreign-born Hispanics were 0.4 percent more likely than otherwise similar U.S.-born Hispanics to be newly self-employed. This observation is consistent with the growing presence of immigrants among Hispanic entrepreneurs, discussed in the previous chapter. That is, immigrants disproportionately drove the growth in Hispanic entrepreneurship as the 2000s progressed. As immigrants have less education on average than U.S.-born Hispanics, their rising presence in the self-employment sector might also explain the weakening role of education over time.

Concluding Remarks

Throughout the first decade of the 2000s, the average education levels of self-employed Hispanics between the ages of twenty-five and sixty-four rose from 10.8 years in 2000 to 11.2 years in 2010. Despite this improvement, these schooling levels were considerably lower than those of non-Hispanics in the self-employment sector, whose education fluctuated between 13.9 years and 14.1 years between 2000 and 2010. Nevertheless, they reflect the relatively low average schooling levels of Hispanic workers in general. As discussed earlier in this chapter, part of the reason for this relatively low educational attainment is the large share of immigrants.

Our findings point to the importance of a college education for the entrepreneur's success, as measured by sales and labor-market earnings. Given their relatively low educational attainment, and given the recent increase in the number of Hispanic-owned businesses, the extent to which education matters for the business and earnings outcomes of Hispanic entrepreneurs has increasingly important implications for the future development of the United States, and not just for the Hispanic community.

5   Hispanic Female Entrepreneurs

FEW STUDIES HAVE ANALYZED HISPANIC ENTREPRENEURSHIP specifically through the prism of gender. Aside from the academic and public policy relevance of such analysis, this endeavor matters to the study of Hispanic entrepreneurship in the first decade of the 2000s for several reasons. First, Hispanic women represent a nontrivial share of Hispanic entrepreneurs, and their businesses differed in some important respects from those owned by Hispanic men. According to the 2007 SBO, of the more than two million Hispanic firms, 34.9 percent were owned by women and 54.3 percent were owned by Hispanic men; the remainder were equally owned by men and women. This survey shows, however, that a disproportionate number of female Hispanic-owned firms had no paid employees compared to those owned by their male counterparts (93.3 percent versus 87.2 percent). The average sales of the female-owned firms of this ethnic group were also about one-third of those of their male counterparts.

Second, as shown in Figure 5.1, the self-employment patterns differed between female and male Hispanics during this time, and they did not follow patterns similar to those of non-Hispanics in the first decade of the 2000s.[1] The top panel in this figure shows that the self-employment rates of Hispanic men increased almost every year during the decade, such that they reached their highest rate (10 percent) in 2010. Hispanic women also had growing entrepreneurial tendencies in the first part of the decade, but their rates stopped increasing mid-decade, reaching a peak of 8.4 percent. Despite a decline after

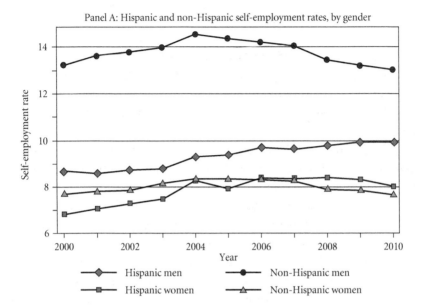

Panel A: Hispanic and non-Hispanic self-employment rates, by gender

Hispanic men ◆ Non-Hispanic men ●

Hispanic women ■ Non-Hispanic women ▲

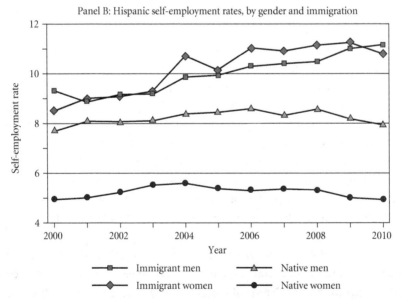

Panel B: Hispanic self-employment rates, by gender and immigration

Immigrant men ■ Native men ▲

Immigrant women ◆ Native women ●

FIGURE 5.1 Hispanic self-employment rates, by gender and immigration, and non-Hispanic self-employment rates, by gender, 2000–10

SOURCE: Authors' estimates using IPUMS and ACS data in the IPUMS.

NOTE: The sample includes workers between the ages of twenty-five and sixty-four not living in group quarters.

the Great Recession, Hispanic women ended the decade with a higher self-employment rate (8.0 percent) than when the decade began. In contrast, the self-employment rates of non-Hispanics tended to move with changes in economic growth, peaking in 2004, which corresponded to the height of the business cycle. Moreover, until the Great Recession, Hispanic women were less likely to be self-employed than their non-Hispanic counterparts, but this reversed after 2007.

Third, gender-related differences exist with respect to entrepreneurial tendencies between U.S.- and foreign-born Hispanics, as shown in the bottom panel of Figure 5.1. For example, in 2010 the self-employment rate of foreign-born Hispanic women more than twice exceeded that of U.S.-born Hispanic women (10.8 percent versus 4.9 percent), while among Hispanic men, this rate was about one-third higher for immigrants than for natives (11.2 percent versus 8.0 percent). We note, too, that although the self-employment rates of U.S.-born Hispanics were relatively flat during the first decade of the 2000s, the entrepreneurial tendencies of foreign-born Hispanics increased throughout the decade, especially among Hispanic-immigrant women. In fact, between 2005 and 2009, the self-employment rates of Hispanic-immigrant women surpassed those of their male counterparts, leading the growth in the Hispanic entrepreneurial population in the 2000s.

Finally, gender differences existed in the labor-force dynamics of Hispanics in the first decade of the 2000s. We noted in previous chapters that the Great Recession had a disproportionate negative impact on the employment opportunities of Hispanics, and that this potentially pushed them into self-employment. However, the labor-force participation rates (LFPRs) of Hispanic men were considerably higher (with an average LFPR of 80.1 percent) than were those of Hispanic women (averaging LFPRs of 56.5 percent) over the 2000s. As such, self-employment push versus pull conditions might have varied along gender lines.

In general, the foregoing observations (as well as others that we mention below) point to the importance of studying female versus male Hispanic entrepreneurs in the first decade of the 2000s. In this chapter, we parallel some of the previous topics discussed in this book by focusing on gender-related differences in business outcomes and self-employment earnings. For these outcomes, Hispanic female entrepreneurs appear to be at a relative disadvantage compared to their male counterparts. However, additional comparisons between foreign-born and U.S.-born entrepreneurs point to the presence of stronger pull versus push conditions for female Hispanic natives than for immigrants.

Gender-Related Differences in Hispanic Business Outcomes

In this section, we explore the business outcomes of female and male Hispanic entrepreneurs in the first decade of the 2000s. In addition to providing an overview, we also discuss explanations for why Hispanic female entrepreneurs lag behind their male counterparts with respect to many, but not all, of these outcomes.

Sales and Employer Representation Among Female Hispanic-Owned Firms in 2007. Our discussion of sales and employer representation among female Hispanic-owned firms in 2007 starts with a simple observation: businesses owned by Hispanic men had an overall earnings advantage (as well as a per-firm sales advantage) over firms owned by their female counterparts in 2007. In particular, the SBO indicates that despite representing a third of all Hispanic-owned businesses, the $55.7 billion in sales ($71,000 per firm) generated by female Hispanic-owned firms accounted for only 15.9 percent of total sales of Hispanic-owned businesses. Businesses owned by Hispanic men, in turn, had sales of $256.4 billion ($209,000 per firm), representing nearly three-quarters of total sales generated by Hispanic-owned businesses. (The remainder of sales were generated by Hispanic businesses equally owned by men and women.)

These sales advantages of male Hispanic entrepreneurs over their female counterparts also exist in firms with paid employees. Businesses owned by Hispanic women represented slightly more than one-fifth of all Hispanic employer firms in 2007. This is a smaller share than their presence among firms in general, which indicates the underrepresentation of Hispanic women who owned businesses with a payroll. Moreover, their $39.6 billion in sales ($746,000 per firm) amounted to about one-seventh of sales of all Hispanic-owned businesses with employees. In contrast, employer firms owned by Hispanic men accounted for nearly two-thirds of all Hispanic employers, but their sales of $210.6 billion ($1.3 million per firm) represented three-quarters of the total.

We also observe a male sales advantage in firms without paid employees. In particular, nonemployer firms owned by Hispanic women represented more than one-third of all Hispanic-owned firms in this category, but their sales of $16.1 billion ($21,800 per firm) accounted for only slightly more than one-fifth of the total. Men owned more than half of nonemployer Hispanic firms; they generated nearly $45.9 billion in sales ($42,900 per firm), or nearly two-thirds of the total.

The underrepresentation of Hispanic female entrepreneurs among employers warrants further attention. As such, we turn to the SBO PUMS to test whether female Hispanic entrepreneurs had different propensities than their male counterparts to be employers when controlling for other characteristics of the owners (e.g., education) and firms (e.g., industry). As with our other major empirical analyses throughout this book, the details of this test are discussed in Appendix B. This investigation indicates that Hispanic women were 5.5 percent less likely than men to own employer firms, all else being equal, such that the underrepresentation of Hispanic women among employers does not appear to be fully explained by their observable traits. Nevertheless, female Hispanic entrepreneurs do not seem to be at a unique disadvantage relative to men with respect to the likelihood of having paid employees. Indeed, our findings suggest that this underrepresentation is more pronounced among non-Hispanic business owners; non-Hispanic women were 6.9 percent less likely to have paid employees than otherwise similar men that year.

We also find with these data that gender-related sales differentials were not exclusive to Hispanic entrepreneurs when accounting for other observable characteristics. Among firms with identifiable characteristics in the SBO PUMS, those owned by Hispanic women had 79.7 percent lower sales than those owned by men in 2007, but slightly less than half (38.7 percentage points) of this revenue differential can be explained by differences in owner- and firm-level traits. This leaves an unexplained gender-related sales differential of 41.0 percentage points, which was slightly smaller in magnitude than the comparable gap for non-Hispanic-owned firms (43.8 percentage points).

Moreover, when separating employer and nonemployer firms, those owned by Hispanic women fared better in both groups with respect to the unexplained gender-related sales differentials than when combining the two. When controlling for other characteristics, female Hispanic-owned firms generated 29.6 percent less in revenue among employers and 24.8 percent less among nonemployers than did comparable firms owned by Hispanic men.

These gender-related penalties were smaller than those accrued by non-Hispanics, particularly for employers. The sales of businesses owned by non-Hispanic women were 40.7 percent lower than those owned by non-Hispanic men among those with paid employees and 27.0 percent less than those of other firms.

Sales and Profits of Female Hispanic-Owned Small Businesses in the Mid-2000s.   We can see in the SBO that businesses owned by Hispanic women lagged behind those owned by their male counterparts with respect to sales and the likelihood of having paid employees in 2007. But as we noted in earlier chapters, sales represent only part of the profit equation. Even if female Hispanic entrepreneurs have low sales, their relative profits are unknown—we need information on their business costs. We therefore turn to the SSBF to analyze the profits of small businesses owned by Hispanic women in 2004 and 2005. In addition to profit levels, we also consider the likelihood that profits reached the two benchmarks discussed in previous chapters—namely, whether the profits were positive (in which case the firm was at least breaking even) or greater than $10,000. We also revisit the gender differential in the sales reported in these data.

Women owned 37.2 percent of all Hispanic-owned small businesses in 2004–5; note the closeness of this share to that reported in the 2007 SBO.[2] Also, as with the SBO, female Hispanic-owned small firms had significantly lower average sales than those owned by their male counterparts ($443,000 versus $1 million). Small firms owned by Hispanic women were also less likely to break even than male Hispanic-owned small firms in the mid-2000s, as two-thirds reported positive profits, compared to four-fifths of those owned by men. While the average profits of $78,000 seem to be short of those accrued by Hispanic men ($178,000), given the large variance in profits, the difference is not statistically significant. Also, half of female Hispanic-owned small firms had at least $10,000 in profits, a smaller share (but not significantly so) than the two-thirds of male Hispanic-owned firms that achieved this benchmark. These figures continue to suggest that male Hispanic entrepreneurs outperform their female counterparts with respect to certain financial outcomes, but not all, in the small business sector.

Because some of these gender-related differences may be influenced by other owner or firm characteristics, we test whether the sales and profits of small businesses owned by Hispanic women differed from those of male

Hispanic-owned firms when taking such traits into account. As with the SBO PUMS, holding these characteristics constant does not eliminate the gender-related sales differences observed in the SSBF, as small enterprises owned by Hispanic women had significantly lower sales (about half) than those accrued by otherwise similar firms owned by Hispanic men in the mid-2000s. Also, we observe a statistically significant difference in profits, in which, similar to the case of sales, small enterprises owned by Hispanic women generated about half of the profits of those owned by Hispanic men, all else being equal.

Female Hispanic small business owners did not, however, fare worse than their male counterparts in all regards. When accounting for differences in observable features, the likelihood both of breaking even and of reaching at least $10,000 in profits is similar between male- and female Hispanic-owned small businesses. It follows that a characterization of male Hispanic entrepreneurs as having some type of advantage over their female counterparts does not accurately describe the case for all measures of business success.

Relative Earnings of Self-Employed Hispanic Women: 2002–7 and 2007–10

How do the relatively high sales and profits of male Hispanic business owners relate to their entrepreneurial earnings, and how can we attempt to explain them? Recall from Chapter 2 that the average decline in entrepreneurial quality resulting from entry into self-employment depends, at least conceptually, on whether the entry stemmed from pull or push reasons. Moreover, the magnitude of this decline in quality would also be related to the reason the individual became self-employed. If differences exist between Hispanic men and women regarding the relative strength of push versus pull conditions into the entrepreneurial sector, this could explain why female Hispanic business owners tend to underperform their male counterparts in terms of their sales and profit levels.

We explore potential gender-related push and pull differences using the time periods of 2002–7 and 2007–10, to compare the pre- and post–Great Recession impacts on relative self-employment earnings between Hispanic women and men. In particular, we first consider adjusted versus unadjusted relative self-employment earnings, and then we implement the JMP technique discussed in Chapter 2.

In 2002, echoing the case of sales and profits discussed above, self-employed Hispanic women faced a larger self-employment earnings penalty (39.7 percent) than that of Hispanic men (9.4 percent). This gender-related penalty difference narrows (but does not vanish) when accounting for observable characteristics that affect earnings, as doing so reduces the penalty to 28.6 percent for women and expands it to 19.3 percent for men.

Five years later, the relative earnings situation deteriorated on average for female Hispanic entrepreneurs for two basic reasons. First, their raw self-employment penalty increased to 53.9 percent by 2007, and their adjusted penalty (29.0 percent) changed little. Second, relative earnings of self-employed Hispanic men improved between 2002 and 2007, as both their total and adjusted penalties shrank. Recall from Chapter 2 that this time period seemed to kindle pull conditions that attracted more Hispanics into the self-employment sector. Since the relative earnings of Hispanic women in this sector fell, while those of Hispanic men improved, it appears that the development of pull conditions tended to be a male phenomenon.

During the Great Recession, the relative earnings of female Hispanic entrepreneurs continued to fall, such that their self-employment penalty reached 67.3 percent (unadjusted) and 31.2 percent (adjusted) in 2010. The unadjusted and adjusted penalties also declined for self-employed Hispanic men to 29.0 percent and 24.4 percent, respectively, but Hispanic men retained their relative earnings advantage over their female counterparts at the end of the decade.

Further deconstructing these earnings differences using the JMP approach, consider that the increase in the magnitude of the self-employment penalty (14.2 percentage points) among Hispanic women between 2002 and 2007 was mostly led by a relative decline in this group's observable characteristics (which contributed 13.7 percentage points). This pattern continued in 2007–10, as a relative decline in observable skills explained 11.6 of the total 13.4-percentage-point decline in their relative earnings.

In contrast, for Hispanic men the earnings differential between self-employed and salaried workers narrowed by 3.6 percentage points between 2002 and 2007. While the self-employed of this group experienced a comparative decline in observable characteristics (which should have increased their earnings disparity by almost 2.3 percentage points), the relative unobservable-skill differential between the two groups changed more than enough to offset the effect of the observable characteristics. This change in their unobservable characteristics added a 6.1-percentage-point gain to their relative self-employment earnings, which suggests a relative increase in the unobservable quality of Hispanic entrepreneurs during the period. During the Great Recession, this pattern reversed. The self-employment penalty rose by 23.3 percentage points, mainly a result of relative declines in both observable and unobservable skills, as each contributed 11.7 and 11.3 percentage points, respectively, to the total change.

So what do these results mean? First, as for Hispanics in general, the results are consistent with a relative decline in entrepreneurial quality during the Great Recession. Among Hispanic women, the decline continued that which occurred between 2002 and 2007. As we have discussed in previous chapters, this type of impact on entrepreneurial quality conceptually emanates from displaced workers being pushed into self-employment.

In the case of self-employed Hispanic men, this explanation can be supported by the increase in their self-employment rate from 9.6 percent in 2007 to 10.0 percent in 2010. The self-employment rate of Hispanic women, however, declined from 8.4 percent to 8.0 percent during this time, yet their average entrepreneurial quality also declined. A potential explanation is that the economic downturn disproportionately affected the higher-skilled entrepreneurs of the group over this short time frame. Moreover, the relative earnings gain among male Hispanic entrepreneurs between 2002 and 2007 occurred at the same time that their self-employment rate increased as well, from 8.8 percent to 9.6 percent. This change may be related to pull effects, as we have discussed before. Regardless of the cause, the relative earnings experience of Hispanic entrepreneurs has not been the same between men and women, which suggests gender-related variations in self-employment push versus pull conditions, with men seeming to have experienced more favorable pull factors before the Great Recession than women.

Education, Gender, and Hispanic Entrepreneurship

In terms of average schooling levels in 2010, self-employed Hispanic women had a slight educational advantage over their male counterparts (11.5 years versus 11.1 years of schooling) for those between the ages of twenty-five and sixty-four. Their small advantage flip-flopped between both groups over the decade, but this schooling differential remained small. Also, female Hispanic entrepreneurs had less education on average than Hispanic women working for someone else (who had 12.1 years of schooling in 2010). In contrast, self-employed Hispanic men had higher schooling levels than men in the paid-employment sector in every year but the last two; in 2009 and 2010, both groups had similar schooling levels.

These gender education gaps in self-employment versus paid employment seem to be driven by changes in the shares of immigrants in the self- versus paid-employment sectors. Throughout the decade, immigrants represented between approximately 65 percent and 72 percent of self-employed Hispanic women but only about half of salaried women. For Hispanic men, immigrants similarly represented a higher share of the self-employed (between about 63 and 69 percent) than other workers (ranging from 61 percent to 64 percent), but the gap between the two sectors was considerably narrower than for women.

Such differences suggest that Hispanic men and women experienced dissimilar push and pull factors into entrepreneurship during the decade along the lines of skills and immigration. Indeed, self-employment push factors might have been more prevalent among Hispanic women than men, perhaps owing to differences in their returns to education in the self-employment and salaried sectors. In what follows, we explore this possibility by continuing the earnings analysis from the previous section and by delving into the link between education and the entrepreneurial earnings of foreign-born versus U.S.-born Hispanics.

Gender-Related Education Returns Among Self-Employed Hispanics.   Using the same methodology as in Chapter 4, we estimate the returns to education separately for Hispanic men and women in the three years that we have been exploring: 2002, 2007, and 2010. The first two rows in Table 5.1 contain these returns. In 2002, a year of schooling generated 1.2 percent higher earnings for female Hispanic entrepreneurs; this payment was statistically indistinguishable from zero. That same year, the returns to education were 4.1 percent for Hispanic women in the paid-employment sector. Because education did not significantly enhance their entrepreneurial earnings, it appears that Hispanic women may have faced greater push than pull conditions into the self-employment sector that year. For Hispanic men, the education rewards for the self-employed (2.7 percent) were also smaller than those in the paid-employment sector (3.6 percent), but in a less dramatic manner.

TABLE 5.1 Returns to education for Hispanics by gender, self-employment, and immigrant status

Characteristic	Hispanic women			Hispanic men		
	2002 (%)	2007 (%)	2010 (%)	2002 (%)	2007 (%)	2010 (%)
ALL WORKERS						
Self-employed	1.18[a]	3.92	3.31	2.71	3.66	3.33
Not self-employed	4.06	4.93	5.02	3.55	3.76	4.37
IMMIGRANTS						
Self-employed	4.25	5.39	4.50	3.57	4.29	3.38
Not self-employed	4.64	5.30	5.31	5.03	5.15	5.64
U.S. NATIVES						
Self-employed	11.09	11.04	10.47	9.27	9.32	9.99
Not self-employed	9.96	10.52	9.82	9.68	10.66	10.25

SOURCE: Authors' estimates using ACS data in the IPUMS.
NOTES: The sample includes Hispanic workers between the ages of twenty-five and sixty-four not living in group quarters who reported labor-market earnings. For estimation details, see Appendix B.
[a]Not statistically different from zero at conventional levels.

Five years later, as for Hispanics in general, the schooling payoffs received by female and male Hispanic entrepreneurs had risen, to 3.9 percent among women and 3.7 percent among men, thus erasing the gender gap in these payoffs in the self-employment sector. While salaried Hispanic women also received higher returns to schooling (4.9 percent) in 2007 than in 2002, the smaller magnitude of their increase with respect to the self-employed served to narrow the gap between self-employment and paid employment in these returns. The small rise (one-tenth of a percentage point) in the schooling pay-offs of male Hispanic employees meant that education had virtually the same effect on their earnings as for self-employed Hispanic men shortly before the recession started.

The relatively large increase in the education returns of self-employed Hispanic women is consistent with the development of a relative education shortage in the self-employment sector between 2002 and 2007. Recall that the JMP results presented earlier suggested the incidence of relatively strong push factors among self-employed Hispanic women, as their average earnings fell relative to Hispanic women in the paid-employment sector during this time, driven mostly by a relative decline in observable characteristics. This finding, based on changes in average characteristics, masks the possibility that within this population, a group of female Hispanic entrepreneurs (e.g., the more educated) fared better in 2007 than they had five years earlier. It follows that a relatively small but highly educated group of Hispanic women could have been pulled into self-employment because of more lucrative returns to their skills, but their relative earnings gains were not enough to offset the average earnings losses experienced during this time by self-employed Hispanic women in general.

As we found in our other analyses, the Great Recession brought with it lower education returns for the self-employment sector for both female and male Hispanics (3.3 percent for both groups in 2010). In contrast, the schooling payoffs for salaried Hispanic women in 2010 had changed little from 2007, and they had risen (to 4.4 percent) for salaried Hispanic men, thus leaving both gender groups outside of the entrepreneurial sector with higher schooling rewards than what they had earned several years before.

These results are of interest given recent literature, mostly advanced by sociologists, that focuses on the systematic explanations of intersectionality. For example, in her 2011 book sociologist Zulema Valdez discusses this issue across multiple social locations while focusing on a diverse group of restaurateurs in Houston. She sets forth a theory of intersectionality that explains structural oppression and privilege depending on the intersection of race, ethnicity, class, and gender, and she relates this to the self-employment outcomes of Hispanics. In her view, female Hispanic self-employment should be studied with narrower populations in mind and should consider education and class levels. The general findings presented in this chapter support these propositions with regard to female Hispanic entrepreneurs.

Gender and the Education Returns of Self-Employed Immigrants.   In the previous chapter, we discussed why immigrants might receive lower education returns than their native counterparts. Perhaps some of the gender-related differences in the education payoffs between the self- and paid-employment sectors stems from the relatively large presence of immigrants among female Hispanic entrepreneurs.

As we saw in Table 5.1, when focusing exclusively on female Hispanic immigrants or U.S. natives, the returns to education are higher in the three years considered than those estimated when combining the two groups. In 2002, without separating immigrants from natives, self-employed Hispanic women received insignificant schooling payoffs on average. However, excluding the U.S. born from the analysis yields education returns of 4.3 percent for foreign-born Hispanic women in the self-employment sector; similarly, excluding immigrants generates returns of 11.1 percent for female Hispanic native entrepreneurs. For immigrants, these returns rose (to 5.4 percent) in 2007 and fell again in 2010, close to their 2002 level. Self-employed U.S.-born Hispanic women had virtually the same schooling payoff in 2007 as in 2002, but this payoff fell half a percentage point in 2010.

In all cases, though, these schooling returns were higher than those estimated for Hispanic women in general. These findings illustrate the complex nature of the role of education on entrepreneurial earnings. While education acquired abroad pays less on average than education obtained in the United States, within foreign-born Hispanic populations, it enhances their earnings more, especially in the self-employment sector, than the amount measured when combining them with U.S. natives. Moreover, self-employed U.S.-born Hispanic women reaped higher schooling returns than their counterparts in the salaried sector in all three years. Education also contributed more to their earnings than it did for self-employed Hispanic male natives, which was not the case in 2007 and 2010 in the paid-employment sector. These findings point to potentially profitable skill returns in the self-employment sector for some U.S.-born Hispanic women.

As a related point, recall that we previously raised the possibility that some educated Hispanic women faced pull conditions into self-employment between 2002 and 2007 even if, on average, push conditions were more prevalent for the population as a whole. When comparing changes in the relative earnings between U.S.- and foreign-born female Hispanic entrepreneurs, the results are consistent with this case. Female Hispanic natives (who tend to be more educated than female Hispanic immigrants) experienced an improvement in their characteristics-adjusted self-employment earnings penalty (from 45.6 in 2002 to 37.9 percent in 2007), which fits with the strengthening of self-employment pull conditions. In contrast, the corresponding penalty worsened for female Hispanic immigrants (from 20.8 percent to 25.0 percent) during this time, which would be consistent with more amplified self-employment push conditions.[3]

Among Hispanic men, except for the self-employed in 2010, Table 5.1 also shows that immigrants had higher returns to education than those estimated when grouping them with U.S. natives. However, unlike their female counterparts, the differences in the estimates were narrower among entrepreneurs than among immigrants working for someone else. Note, too, that the difference in schooling rewards between entrepreneurs and salaried workers was wider among immigrant men in 2010 (3.4 percent versus 5.6 percent, respectively) than in 2007 (4.3 percent versus 5.2 percent, respectively), as they had fallen for the former group but risen for the latter.

The same shift did not occur among U.S.-born Hispanic men, as the gap in their self-employment and paid-employment schooling rewards narrowed considerably between 2007 and 2010, from 1.4 percentage points (9.3 percent versus 10.7 percent) in 2007 to 0.3 percentage points (10.0 percent versus 10.3 percent) in 2010. U.S.-born Hispanic self-employed men thus received a greater payoff to their education after the recession than before it started. Complementing the discussion in Chapter 3, these changes indicate the presence of birthplace-related differences in self-employment push and pull factors, with immigrants having been particularly affected by the recession. These immigration and gender divisions thus suggest that within each gender group, U.S.-born Hispanic entrepreneurs fared better through the recession than did their foreign-born counterparts.

Education and Gender-Related Differences in Hispanic Self-Employment Decisions

In the previous chapter, we noted that Hispanic women were significantly less likely than their otherwise similar male counterparts to be newly minted entrepreneurs when controlling for education and other characteristics, at least in 2002, 2007, and 2010.[4] What we did not consider is whether these characteristics mattered differently for Hispanic men and women in their decisions to join the self-employment sector. Indeed, in a 2009 study economists Robert Fairlie and Alicia Robb provide evidence that male and female business owners tend to differ in this regard. For example, they found that female entrepreneurs were more likely than men to report meeting family responsibilities as the reason they owned a business.

We therefore return to the CPS data to analyze the odds of becoming self-employed for women versus men. During the decade, the share of women among newly self-employed Hispanics ranged from a low of 32.1 percent (in 2008) to a high of 48.6 percent (in 2000). This was a wider range than the one for non-Hispanic new entrepreneurs, among whom women represented between 39.7 percent (in 2010) and 44.0 percent (in 2006). These findings indicate that the share of women, especially Hispanic women, entering the self-employment sector did not remain constant in the 2000s. In terms of the 2002–7 and 2007–10 periods we have been exploring, the share of women among new Hispanic entrepreneurs fell from 42.1 percent in 2002 to 36.3 percent in 2007, and then rose modestly to end the decade at 37.3 percent. For these three years, the corresponding shares did not significantly differ from those of their non-Hispanic counterparts.

When accounting for other socioeconomic and demographic traits related to the odds of being newly self-employed, in 2002 education did not affect these odds among Hispanic women who had recently joined the self-employment sector; however, the odds were slightly negatively affected in the case of female immigrants. That year, female immigrants were 0.05 percent less likely to be newly self-employed, and this reduced likelihood grew with time of residence in the United States, after controlling for other observable characteristics. For Hispanic men, however, education mattered (each year of schooling increased the likelihood of new self-employment by 0.12 percent) but birthplace did not. Similar to the case for Hispanics overall reported in the previous chapter, family structure (i.e., marital status and the number of children at home) did not relate to being newly self-employed when the group was separated by gender.

Five years later, one year of education enhanced the likelihood of being newly self-employed (by 0.05 percent) among Hispanic women, but it no longer played a role in this outcome for men. Immigration continued to influence the odds of recent self-employment for Hispanic women (and remained insignificant for men). One difference from 2002 was that foreign-born women were more likely (0.6 percent more likely), not less likely, to have recently become self-employed, although this propensity marginally declined (by 0.01 percentage points) with each year that the immigrant had lived in the United States. The greater likelihood of female Hispanic immigrants versus natives to be newly minted entrepreneurs is consistent with their rising self-employment rates that we highlighted earlier in this chapter.

Another difference between 2002 and 2007 is that family structure played a role in explaining new entrepreneurship among Hispanic women and men in 2007. Being single reduced the odds of having recently joined the self-employment sector by one-quarter of a percent among women, and two-thirds of a percent among men. For Hispanic men, being divorced or having children residing in the household also diminished the odds of new self-employment that year. However, by 2010 family composition (as education) no longer mattered with respect to the likelihood of new self-employment among Hispanics, regardless of gender.

Birthplace continued to enhance the new self-employment propensities of Hispanic women in 2010, as it did shortly before the Great Recession started. It also became a significant predictor (by a slight magnitude) of these propensities among Hispanic men, as immigrants were 0.02 percent more likely than their U.S.-born counterparts to be newly self-employed, and these odds increased the longer that immigrants had been in the country.

The lack of a consistent influence of family composition on business formation for either Hispanic men or Hispanic women is interesting. It might relate to the relatively low education levels of the Hispanic population. Sociologists Jimy Sanders and Victor Nee in a 1996 study note that entrepreneurs can draw on labor and financial resources when establishing or operating a small business, but these resources depend on human capital. We therefore replicate this analysis for non-Hispanic women and men. For non-Hispanic women, in all three years, wives were significantly more likely to be newly self-employed than their unmarried counterparts, and the presence of children in the household further increased these odds. For non-Hispanic men, as was the case for Hispanics, only in 2007 did marital status matter, which suggests that the effect of the family on small business formation goes beyond average human capital levels.

The Representation of Microentrepreneurs Among Hispanic Business Owners

Earlier in this chapter, we noted that rising self-employment rates among Hispanic men and women in the first decade of the 2000s did not seem to coincide closely with the business cycle. When considering the role of birthplace, this seemingly counterintuitive finding related to the growing entrepreneurial tendencies of Hispanic immigrants, particularly women. Regardless of self-employment push or pull conditions, these rising numbers indicate the employment creation potential of Hispanic women (at least for themselves) even during weak economic conditions. A natural question to explore is how these groups have fared in terms of creating jobs for other workers.

We indicated above that female Hispanic entrepreneurs were less likely to have paid employees than their male counterparts, at least in 2007. Nevertheless, when considering the raw numbers, the impact of female Hispanic employers in the U.S. labor market is not trivial. According to the SBO, for example, these women generated employment for more than 363,000 workers and had an aggregate payroll of more than $9.3 billion in 2007.

Another way to investigate this point is to consider the share of microentrepreneurs (i.e., businesses hiring fewer than ten employees) among self-employed Hispanic men and women. Recall from Chapter 1 that this share increased, particularly among Hispanics, during the Great Recession. Figure 5.2, which separates Hispanic women from men in the self-employment sector, shows that female Hispanic entrepreneurs had larger shares of microentrepreneurs in all years in the decade but one (2007), especially since the Great Recession ended. Indeed, their microentrepreneurship rate jumped from 91.5 percent to 96.6 percent between 2007 and 2010, such that fewer than

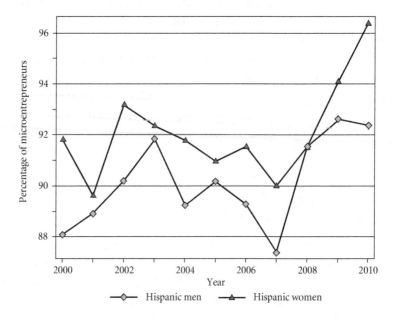

FIGURE 5.2 Representation of microentrepreneurs among self-employed Hispanics, by gender, 2000–10

SOURCE: Authors' estimates using CPS data in the IPUMS-CPS.

NOTES: The samples include self-employed workers between the ages of twenty-five and sixty-four. The year refers to the year in which the individual was a microentrepreneur (the year prior to the CPS survey).

4.0 percent of self-employed Hispanic women had ten or more workers on their payrolls that year. While this rate also increased for men during this time (from 87.4 percent to 92.4 percent), it did so in a less dramatic fashion, partly because this share was slightly lower in 2010 than in 2009. This information again fits with other evidence presented in this chapter that Hispanic male entrepreneurs outperform their female counterparts with respect to many business outcomes.

When considering differences between immigrants and natives (not shown in Figure 5.2), the changes in microentrepreneurship rates were the most dramatic among immigrants, especially women, whose rates rose from 91.5 percent in 2007 to 99.3 percent in 2010. These figures indicate that basically all self-employed Hispanic-immigrant women were microentrepreneurs after the Great Recession had ended. Female Hispanic immigrants represent one of the fastest-growing groups of entrepreneurs, and their growth has occurred mainly at the microenterprise level. This does not mean, however, that they have not affected the labor market. Consider that even if the only jobs they created were for themselves, their participation in the self-employment sector likely kept a large number from becoming unemployed or dropping out of the labor force altogether.

The shares of microenterprises among Hispanic-immigrant men tended to be lower than those of Hispanic-immigrant women for most of the decade, and the Great Recession did not change this pattern. Foreign-born Hispanic men experienced an increase in this share from 85.7 percent in 2007 to 93.8 percent three years later. As such, Hispanic-immigrant entrepreneurial growth may have had a positive impact on job creation, but mostly at the scale of smaller firms, especially near the end of the decade.

Microentrepreneurs among self-employed U.S.-born Hispanic women also increased their presence during the recession, but by a smaller magnitude, as their share rose from 87.8 percent in 2007 to 91.6 percent in 2010. However, their 2010 rate was not their highest in the decade, as it had peaked at 94.0 percent in 2002. Interestingly, U.S.-born Hispanic men had lower microentrepreneurship rates in 2010 (88.6 percent) than in 2007 (91.1 percent). This suggests that the seeming advantage that male Hispanic entrepreneurs had over their female counterparts with respect to hiring at least ten employees widened among U.S. natives during the recession.

We also considered the shares of incorporated businesses among male and female Hispanic entrepreneurs. Consistent with their relatively low share of employer firms and high rates of microentrepreneurship in the first decade of the 2000s, self-employed Hispanic women were less likely to own an incorporated firm than were their male counterparts. In 2010, for example, less than one-fifth of female Hispanic entrepreneurs had incorporated businesses, compared to more than one-quarter of self-employed Hispanic men. While both groups experienced a decline in these rates between 2007 and 2009, they started to rebound by 2010, particularly among women. Even though the Great Recession had increased the probability of Hispanics owning microenterprises, it appears that its effect on their rates of incorporation was less dramatic.

A Closer Examination of Male and Female Hispanic Microentrepreneurs. These numbers provide evidence of variations related to gender and birthplace in the shares of microentrepreneurs among self-employed Hispanics, which correspond to some of the other business and earnings outcomes reported in this chapter. A related issue is whether differences in other observable characteristics, such as education, explain these variations. We therefore explore the likelihood of being a microentrepreneur in 2007 and 2010 while controlling for a host of socioeconomic and demographic traits (listed in Appendix B).

Among self-employed Hispanic women, when accounting for differences in other characteristics, the foreign born were significantly more likely to be microentrepreneurs than their U.S.-born counterparts in 2010 but not in 2007. In contrast, Hispanic-immigrant men had lower microentrepreneurship propensities than U.S. natives in 2007, but by 2010, these propensities were about the same for both groups, all else being equal.

In terms of other characteristics related to microentrepreneurship tendencies, this exercise revealed other interesting points. First, education reduced these tendencies among self-employed Hispanic women in 2007, as would be expected. However, the role of education in the odds of being a microentrepreneur lost its statistical significance among women by 2010 and was not significant in either year for Hispanic men. Second, among female Hispanic entrepreneurs, having children residing in the household raised these odds in both years, as it did for Hispanic men in 2007. This might reflect the willingness of some Hispanic parents to own a small business for the flexibility it affords them with respect to their child-rearing responsibilities. It may also reflect the contributions of children, without being on the payroll, to the family business, which would serve to reduce the number of paid employees. Third, marital status also mattered. Being married raised the likelihood of owning a microbusiness among female Hispanic entrepreneurs, but it reduced these odds among their male counterparts. In summary, perhaps these gender-related microentrepreneurship differences reflect Fairlie and Robb's findings that female entrepreneurs have a different set of preferences than men regarding their business outcomes.

Concluding Remarks

Women represent about one-third of all Hispanic business owners. Moreover, in the first decade of the new millennium, foreign-born Hispanic women represented one of the fastest-growing entrepreneurial populations in the United States. These demographic changes indicate that understanding factors related to their business outcomes, including their earnings and employment, has become an increasingly important issue for the nation as a whole.

Many policy implications stem from these changes. For one, state and local initiatives to promote minority and female entrepreneurship could have larger effects on employment and tax revenues than they have had in previous time periods. Regarding the latter, consider that our estimates indicate that businesses owned by Hispanic women generated more than $3.16 billion in state sales taxes alone in 2007. Another is that policies designed to improve educational outcomes and English-language proficiency of Hispanic immigrants might also affect the subsequent success of Hispanic female entrepreneurs (given how these skills enhance strategic planning and access to credit, a topic we explore in the next chapter). An additional issue is whether existing policies and programs aimed at helping small businesses grow can be improved to assist newly formed Hispanic-owned microbusinesses. Finally, immigration policies should consider the importance of foreign-born Hispanic entrepreneurs to U.S. job creation (and the generation of income and tax revenue) nationally and also at the local level. We provide a more detailed discussion of such initiatives and policies in Chapter 8.

6 Strategic Issues for Hispanic Entrepreneurs—Credit Access

CREDIT ACCESS REPRESENTS AN IMPORTANT ELEMENT IN THE success of entrepreneurial enterprises. The decision to allocate resources to new investment ventures or the ability to meet payment deadlines to suppliers and employees in a timely manner often depends strongly on the entrepreneurs' ability and willingness to tap into credit markets. The purpose of this chapter is to address how Hispanic entrepreneurs fared with regard to accessing credit in the first decade of the 2000s; we also consider their primary sources of credit.

For conceptual backing, we elaborate on neoclassical discrimination theories as they apply particularly to credit markets. We also offer an alternative conceptualization: Hispanic entrepreneurs might be more reluctant than non-Hispanics to use formal credit markets either because they tend to be relatively more focused on decisions that affect them in the present or less trusting that banks will be able to assist them with their credit needs. With regard to applying for credit, we explore the characteristics of Hispanic-owned small businesses that did not apply for credit despite needing it, because they expected to be rejected. Our discussion further acknowledges the importance of studying regional differences in the credit access of Hispanics entrepreneurs. We end this chapter by anticipating some of the information in Chapter 8 on the potential importance of private and public lending programs to Hispanic entrepreneurs with respect to accessing adequate financial capital.

Conceptual Issues

Explanations for credit-access barriers faced by minorities usually focus on taste-based (that which involves a bias against a demographic group) discrimination and statistical (or information-based) discrimination. In particular, following the work of Nobel laureate Gary Becker, lenders with a "taste" for discrimination might set lower credit standards or offer lower interest rates to applicants from a preferred group than to other applicants. The more visible the less-preferred group is, the more likely taste-based discrimination is to arise.

Statistical discrimination—often discussed in the context of credit-rationing models—may also exist in the presence of imperfect information. In this case, lenders rely on screening devices, such as the applicants' demographic group, to distinguish low-risk borrowers from those with a high risk of default. Entrepreneurs from populations with traditionally weaker credit histories therefore tend to be at a relative disadvantage in accessing credit.

In a related 2011 study with coauthor Erika Mendez Garza, we discuss some of the implications of the presence of statistical discrimination in credit markets. According to our conceptualization, small business owners belong to two hypothetical ethnic groups, M and N, who have participated in past credit markets. M faced an initial amount of discrimination (stemming from some past xenophobic event) from banks, but both groups have identical distributions of creditworthy business owners. Both groups have an equal share of optimistic borrowers who are likely to misjudge the intensity of the loan search process with respect to either search time, which turns out to be longer than expected, or loan amount, which ends up being lower than expected.[1] Realistic business owners, however, correctly judge these parameters.

Finally, the probability of an approved credit application depends on being realistic about this probability, as well as on the positive correlation between pragmatic expectations and innate (or acquired) ability. It follows that both M and N will have a negative self-selection bias in the search process because each group will have a disproportionate share of optimistic loan applicants for a given search time. Following this construct, however, M will have a higher probability of loan rejection than N, all else being equal, for two reasons. First, M encounters either a longer search process than N does (more rejections than group N) or lower-than-expected loan amounts because of statistical discrimination. Second, and following from the first reason, a higher proportion of M's realistic borrowers will not participate in the current loan search process, as this group correctly identifies a greater likelihood of being rejected more often than N. This implies that a disproportionate share of M optimistic (less realistic) borrowers apply for loans, which further lowers the average quality of M's applicant pool.

An important outcome from this model is that current M applicants could reinforce the statistical discrimination. Studies on racial and ethnic differences in credit access should therefore consider the characteristics of individuals who remain outside of the applicant pool as well as the applicants themselves. Still, we should note that in some of our previous work, we have found little empirical evidence of adverse selection in the loan-applicant pool among minority-owned (and other) small firms.

An alternative conceptualization for the relatively low usage of credit markets by Hispanic entrepreneurs relates to perceptions and cultural differences with respect to preferences for financial services. To illustrate, in a 1998 study economists Ken and Linda Cavalluzzo noted that, in addition to statistical discrimination, racial and ethnic differences in credit access might result from differences in borrowers' preferences for credit. The utilization of financial institutions' services by Hispanics in general appears to be lower than for other populations. For example, as noted by Thomas Stevenson and D. Anthony Plath in 2006, relative to other populations, many Hispanics seem to distrust banks and instead prefer holding and paying with cash. They also appear less likely than the overall population to hold debt in terms of installation loans and credit cards, as shown in a 2009 Pew Hispanic Center report by Mark López, Gretchen Livingston, and Rakesh Kochhar. Fitting into this literature, later in this chapter we show that Hispanic-owned enterprises were less likely than other businesses to borrow from banks and other financial institutions to finance their start-up or expansionary costs.

A cultural reluctance to participate in formal credit markets may put Hispanic entrepreneurs at a disadvantage relative to other small business owners. Arguably, entrepreneurs most likely to be successful in acquiring credit have a high level of resources and high strategic-planning skills, followed by those with either high strategic-planning skills or a high level of resources. The entrepreneurs least likely to succeed have the lowest levels of resources and poor strategic planning. According to this conceptualization, Hispanic entrepreneurs, in a relative sense, might fall in the last of these scenarios for several reasons.

First, the seeming disinclination to use the services of financial institutions reduces the potential funding resources of Hispanic entrepreneurs. Moreover, as illustrated throughout this book, these entrepreneurs have relatively low levels of financial capital (including earnings) and human capital (education). In terms of characteristics related to strategic planning, some literature suggests that Hispanics tend to be more focused on the present than the future. For example, José Medina and his coauthors reported in 1996 that, relative to other groups, Mexican Americans seem to score higher on scales that measure the immediate benefits of consumption over long-term planning. The topic of present versus future orientation among Hispanics also comes up in relation to insurance decisions. As Jongho Lee and his colleagues report in a 2005 Tomás Rivera Policy Institute study, Hispanics tend to be less likely than non-Hispanics to purchase a variety of insurance policies. Because strategic planning, by definition, involves envisioning the future direction of the firm, the extent to which Hispanic entrepreneurs are disproportionately present oriented might hinder their business performance in comparison with other small firm owners.

Credit Access Conditions of Hispanic Entrepreneurs

How did Hispanic entrepreneurs fare with respect to accessing financial capital in the first decade of the 2000s? To address this question, we first consider the 2007 SBO PUMS, which includes information on the sources of start-up capital and capital for expanding or making improvements to physical capital. As seen in Table 6.1, Hispanic- and non-Hispanic-owned companies differed with respect to their start-up capital requirements, as a greater share of the former (27.2 percent) than the latter (24.0 percent) reported that they did not need any start-up capital. This difference may relate to differences in the scale of newly established businesses between those owned by Hispanics versus non-Hispanics; recall from earlier discussions in this book that Hispanic-owned businesses tend to be smaller than other firms.

Among those that used financial capital when establishing their businesses, Hispanics were less likely than other entrepreneurs (1) to have borrowed from their family or friends, (2) to have received a loan from the government itself or one backed by the government, and (3) to have received a loan from a bank or other financial institution. For the latter, the share reporting this source of credit among Hispanic entrepreneurs was slightly more

TABLE 6.1 Sources of start-up and expansion capital among Hispanic- and non-Hispanic-owned U.S. businesses, 2007

Sources of financial capital	Start-up capital		Expansion capital	
	Hispanic (%)	Non-Hispanic (%)	Hispanic (%)	Non-Hispanic (%)
No capital needed	27.2[a]	24.0[a]	46.2[a]	48.1[a]
Capital source among those using capital				
Personal or family savings	75.2	76.6	54.0	55.6
Home equity	7.3[a]	6.6[a]	8.4	8.3
Other personal or family assets	7.2[a]	9.5[a]	6.6[a]	7.7[a]
Loans from family or friends	2.7[a]	3.1[a]	1.9	1.8
Personal or business credit cards	15.0	13.4	22.4	23.1
Loan from bank or other financial institution	6.9[a]	12.7[a]	9.1[a]	15.6[a]
Loan from (or backed by) the government	1.1[a]	1.4[a]	1.2	1.3
Profits	—	—	12.3[a]	18.7[a]
Could not access capital despite needing it	—	—	5.3[a]	3.3[a]

SOURCE: Authors' estimates using the 2007 SBO PUMS.

NOTES: Only firms reporting whether they needed or used these sources of capital are included. More than one source could be reported. Acquiring capital for expansion purposes (which include physical-capital improvements) pertains to such activities in 2007 only. Other sources not shown include venture capitalists (which represented the source of start-up and expansion capital for 0.3 percent of both Hispanic and non-Hispanic entrepreneurs) and grants (which represented the source of start-up capital for 0.3 percent, and the source of expansion capital for 0.4 percent, of both Hispanic and non-Hispanic entrepreneurs).

[a]Difference between Hispanics and non-Hispanics is statistically significant at the .01 level; the remaining differences are not significant at the .10 level.

than half of the size of that of non-Hispanics (6.9 percent versus 12.7 percent). Table 6.1 also shows that Hispanics were more likely than non-Hispanics to have used their home equity, other nonsavings personal and/or family assets, and personal or business credit cards to finance their start-up costs. For Hispanics and non-Hispanics, personal and/or family savings represented the main source of start-up financial capital, as three-quarters of both groups reported using their savings when they started their businesses.

With respect to acquiring credit to expand or make physical capital improvements during 2007, 46.2 percent of Hispanic business owners reported that they had not needed to do so; this was a statistically smaller share than the 48.1 percent of non-Hispanics reporting the lack of requirements for expansion capital. Among firms that had acquired credit to finance the growth of their operations, a smaller share of those owned by Hispanics than non-Hispanics reported using personal and/or family assets besides savings or home equity (6.6 percent versus 7.7 percent), borrowing from banks and other financial institutions (9.1 percent versus 15.6 percent), or using their profits (12.3 percent versus 18.7 percent). The distribution of other sources of expansion capital shown in Table 6.1 did not differ between Hispanic- and non-Hispanic-owned firms.

It is of interest that while only a small share (5.3 percent) of Hispanic-owned businesses reported being unable to access credit for expansion or improvement purposes when they needed it during 2007, this share exceeds the corresponding 3.3 percent share of other firms. Coupled with their lower tendencies to borrow from banks and other financial institutions, on the surface, Hispanic entrepreneurs seem to have had a harder time than their non-Hispanic peers in acquiring the capital needed for business growth.

At the same time, these differences may reflect differences related to the underlying characteristics of the firms owned by Hispanics versus non-Hispanics. As we have discussed in other parts of this book, employer firms represent a smaller share of Hispanic-owned enterprises than other firms. When focusing exclusively on employers, the Hispanic and non-Hispanic differential in credit access for expansion objectives narrows, as the share reporting being unable to access such credit falls for both groups (to 1.7 percent among Hispanics and to 1.2 percent among non-Hispanics). However, this gap between Hispanics and non-Hispanics remains statistically significant. For nonemployers, a significant gap exists as well, as 6.2 percent of firms owned by Hispanics were unable to access financial capital to expand or improve, compared to 4.1 percent of those owned by non-Hispanics.

When accounting for differences in owner (e.g., gender, education, age) and firm (e.g., industry, age, geographic location) characteristics, the odds of being unable to access capital for expansion or improvements remain relatively high for Hispanic-owned businesses in general, as well as for non-employers. (See Appendix B for empirical details.) Indeed, we find that on average, firms owned by Hispanics were 0.8 percent less likely than otherwise similar non-Hispanic-owned firms to have acquired credit to expand or to make physical capital improvements in 2007.[2] We also observe a similar pattern when focusing only on nonemployer firms. However, among employers, Hispanics had statistically similar tendencies to access credit as other entrepreneurs when taking into account other owner- and firm-level traits.

Perhaps the Hispanic and non-Hispanic differential among firms in general relates to differences in how financial institutions perceive Hispanic versus non-Hispanic creditworthiness based on other characteristics not identified in the SBO PUMS. We therefore turn to the SSBF data, which include data on credit scores as well as detailed components of the firms' balance sheets in the small business sector. In the mid-2000s, 19.4 percent of Hispanic-owned small businesses had applied for new credit, and another 13.8 percent had sought an extension of existing credit sometime in the previous three years (see Table 6.2). These capital-seeking tendencies were similar to those of other small firms. Of these, 80.9 percent of Hispanic-owned small enterprises were successful in securing their loans, similar to other small firms. While this share is smaller than the one we discussed above using the SBO PUMS, this result may stem from the difference in the question itself. In the SBO PUMS, firms considered successful in accessing capital include those whose loan applications might have been rejected as long as others were approved (or they found other capital sources) in 2007 only. In the SSBF,

TABLE 6.2 Loan application characteristics of Hispanic- and non-Hispanic-owned U.S. small businesses, 2004–5

Characteristic	Hispanic	Non-Hispanic
Applied for new credit in past 3 years	19.4%	21.4%
Applied only for an extension of existing credit in past 3 years	13.8%	12.7%
All loan applications were approved (among loan applicants only)	80.9%	85.4%
Fear of rejection deterred firm from applying for a loan despite needing credit sometime in past 3 years	27.6%[a]	17.4%[a]
CHARACTERISTICS OF THE MOST RECENT LOAN RECEIVED		
Loan amount requested	$108,797[b]	$316,740[b]
Loan amount received	$107,159[b]	$313,440[b]
Interest rate on the loan	8.37%[b]	6.46%[b]

SOURCE: Authors' estimates using the 2003 SSBF.
[a]Difference between Hispanics and non-Hispanics is statistically significant at the .01 level.
[b]Difference between Hispanics and non-Hispanics is statistically significant at the .05 level.

we identify firms that were successful in acquiring credit as those whose loan applications had all been approved in the previous three years (the time frame covered in the SSBF for credit-access issues).

For Hispanic entrepreneurs, this loan-approval rate in the mid-2000s represented an apparent improvement in their ability to access credit from five years earlier. At that time, half of Hispanic entrepreneurs who applied for new credit were successful in securing it, compared to nearly three-quarters of other small firm owners.[3] On the surface, these figures suggest that Hispanic small business owners experienced a more favorable credit environment as the 2000s progressed, at least until the middle of the decade.

Nevertheless, Hispanic small business owners were more likely than other entrepreneurs to report they did not apply for loans because of fear of being turned down. Table 6.2 shows that a significantly greater share of Hispanics than non-Hispanics had not sought credit because of rejection expectations sometime within the previous three years (27.6 percent versus 17.4 percent). When excluding blacks from the non-Hispanic group (recall note 2), this difference widens, as only 15.9 percent of non-Hispanics and nonblacks reported that loan-denial concerns had kept them out of the credit application pool.

Among the borrowers, a closer examination of the terms of the loans reveals racial and ethnic differences with respect to key loan characteristics. In particular, the average loan amounts that Hispanic entrepreneurs sought and subsequently received were considerably smaller than those of other small firm owners. The most recent loans received by Hispanic-owned small businesses averaged $107,000 ($2,000 less than their $109,000 requested amounts) in the mid-2000s. These figures were only one-third of the average $313,000 loan secured (and the $317,000 loan requested) by non-Hispanic small firm owners. Given their smaller loan requests and credit approved, Hispanic entrepreneurs might have been unintentionally putting themselves at a competitive disadvantage against other small business owners, as the reduced funding limited their ability to expand or meet existing payment demands.

Moreover, despite their smaller loan amounts, Hispanic entrepreneurs tended to pay relatively high interest rates, which might have further reduced their competitive potential. In the mid-2000s, the average interest payments of 8.4 percent that these Hispanic borrowers reported significantly exceeded the 6.5 percent interest paid by their non-Hispanic counterparts (see Table 6.2).

Some of these differences may pertain to underlying characteristics of Hispanic entrepreneurs, including their credit ratings, as suggested above. Among loan recipients, fewer Hispanic firms than non-Hispanic firms had the safest credit ratings.[4] While this observation likely explains some of the higher interest rates they paid, we note that fewer Hispanic borrowers had the riskiest credit scores (5.5 percent versus 9.2 percent). It follows that credit ratings alone are not the only factor behind the relatively high interest rates paid by Hispanic small business owners.

When considering other loan conditions, compared to their non-Hispanic counterparts, a slightly smaller share of Hispanic loan recipients were required to have collateral or to have personal guarantees, cosigners, or other guarantors (henceforth, "guarantees"). Of Hispanic borrowers, 43 percent used collateral versus 50 percent of non-Hispanics, and 51 percent versus 54 percent had guarantees. The lower tendency to use collateral among Hispanic borrowers parallels their relatively high interest rates.

As with our previous discussion, other firm-level characteristics that might explain observed variations in the loan terms relate to the size of the enterprise and the education and age (or experience) of the owners. Hispanic loan recipients tended to have smaller businesses than non-Hispanic borrowers based on a variety of measures, including average number of employees, sales, assets, and profits. Because of their relatively small size, Hispanic-owned companies might not have needed as much credit as other firms to expand.

Hispanic small business owners who received credit were also younger on average than non-Hispanic borrowers, and they had fewer years of experience managing or owning a business. In terms of education, Hispanic loan recipients had similar shares of college graduates (approximately 44 percent) but a higher share of high school dropouts than other small business owners. These lower levels of human capital may further explain why Hispanic entrepreneurs borrowed less at higher interest rates, as they might have lacked experience (or the reputation) in previous credit markets, thus leading financial institutions to perceive them as "riskier." We discussed in Chapter 4 how education is related to sales and earnings outcomes of Hispanic entrepreneurs; on the surface, it appears this human capital variable also plays a role in Hispanic entrepreneurs' access to credit.

Last, the degree of competition in local banking markets might have been a factor in the differences in loan terms between Hispanics and non-

Hispanics in the mid-2000s. Since at least the late 1980s, studies have discussed this possibility.[5] In our sample of loan recipients, in the mid-2000s, only a quarter of the small businesses owned by Hispanics operated in areas with concentrated banking markets, compared to almost half of those with non-Hispanic owners. For Hispanic-owned small firms in general, one-third existed in areas with less competitive banking markets. These observations provide supporting evidence that banking market structures continued to affect Hispanic entrepreneurs' access to credit in the mid-2000s.

An Analysis of the Loan Conditions of Hispanic Entrepreneurs

The findings thus far indicate Hispanic small business owners received lower average loan amounts and paid higher interest rates than non-Hispanic entrepreneurs during the mid-2000s. To analyze whether these gaps can be explained through differences in observable owner and firm characteristics between the groups, we employ a more rigorous analysis by decomposing differences in the loan amounts (and interest rates) into two components: one explained by differences in average characteristics between small firms owned by Hispanics versus those owned by non-Hispanics and nonblacks, and the other by differences in the underlying structure of approved loans. The latter component is analogous to the characteristics-adjusted self-employment earning penalties discussed in earlier chapters.

Hispanic borrowers received 61.6 percent less in credit than did non-Hispanics and nonblacks. Differences in observable characteristics (including other loan conditions such as whether collateral or a guarantor was required, the local banking market concentration, firm-level characteristics such as credit rating, and the owners' characteristics) accounted for slightly more than a quarter of this differential. It follows that the vast majority (44.0 out of 61.6 percentage points) of the difference in loan amounts secured by Hispanic-owned small businesses versus their non-Hispanic and nonblack counterparts in the mid-2000s do not seem to be explained by observable differences in key underlying firm and owner characteristics, including credit ratings.

We repeat this exercise for interest-rate differentials. Small firms owned by Hispanics paid on average two percentage points more in interest than did non-Hispanic-owned and nonblack-owned businesses on their most recent loans (8.2 percent versus 6.2 percent) in the mid-2000s. The conditions of the loans, firm and owner characteristics, and banking market concentration explain only a small portion of this gap, leaving a significant adjusted interest-rate differential of 1.8 percentage points. Because the higher interest rates paid by Hispanic entrepreneurs with respect to their non-Hispanic and nonblack counterparts in the mid-2000s do not appear to solely reflect differences in observable characteristics, equal access to credit remains an important consideration for Hispanic small business owners, even if their loan approval rates are similar.[6]

Geographic and Industry Differences. Are these differences in loan amounts and interest rates between Hispanics and non-Hispanics the same across geographic regions and industries? Some of the discrimination theories mentioned in this book, particularly Gary Becker's discrimination theory, predict that bias against a particular group is strongly related to this group's visibility. To the extent that the presence of Hispanics varies across geographic regions, as discussed in Chapter 1, the general results might under- or overstate barriers to credit access faced by Hispanic entrepreneurs in particular geographic areas. Credit access might also differ because of geographic-specific credit market structures. For example, state laws differ with respect to business owners' allowable exemptions when filing for bankruptcy. As discussed in a 2004 study by Jeremy Berkowitz and Michelle White, variations in these exemptions might lead to regional differentials in credit access, as lenders take account of the amount they will be able to recover after a firm declares bankruptcy. With respect to differences in credit access across industries, venture capital firms serving minority-owned businesses could target specific industries over others, as discussed by Timothy Bates and William Bradford in a 2008 study. For example, non-electronics manufacturing firms appeared to be a popular investment choice for venture capitalists.

Because of the relatively small sample size of the SSBF, we cannot analyze all the specific regions and industries discussed in earlier chapters. We thus consider differences across broad categories. When replicating the analysis described above while partitioning the sample into three regions (South—South Central, Middle Atlantic, and South Atlantic; North—North Central and New England; West—Mountain and Pacific), our findings indicate that Hispanic entrepreneurs who received credit had significantly smaller loan amounts in the South (about 66.2 percent less) and West (39.3 percent less) in the mid-2000s than did non-Hispanic and nonblack small business owners, when controlling for other observable characteristics. Moreover, average interest rates paid by Hispanic borrowers were significantly higher in the South and West (by 2.2 percentage points in the South and 1.8 percentage points in the West) than for otherwise similar non-Hispanic and nonblack loan recipients. (Despite the smaller loan amounts in the West than the South, neither loan amounts nor interest rates significantly differed between the two regions.)

In the North, however, Hispanic and non-Hispanic and nonblack entrepreneurs had similar average loan amounts and interest rates at that time, which suggests that Hispanic small business owners fared better with respect to accessing credit in that region versus the other two when accounting for other owner and firm traits that can affect conditions placed on loans. Consider from Chapter 1 that the concentration of Hispanics in the South and West geographic areas exceeds their concentration in the North, such that these observations relate to the visibility hypothesis regarding discrimination.

We also find some surface support for this hypothesis in the SBO PUMS when testing whether the geographic concentration of Hispanics (measured by the share of Hispanics among the population in a state) related to the ability of Hispanic entrepreneurs to acquire credit to expand or make physical capital improvements in 2007. This analysis indicates that as the concentration of Hispanics increased, so did the likelihood of Hispanic entrepreneurs being unable to access financial capital for this purpose. A further test indicates that non-Hispanic entrepreneurs in states with large shares of Hispanics also tended to lack credit access versus those in other areas, though to a lesser extent.

With respect to industry, we first divide the loan recipients in the SSBF into two broad groups: one in manufacturing and construction and the second for all other industries. In this case, the lower average loan amounts and higher interest rates of Hispanic small business owners versus non-Hispanics and nonblacks discussed above did not significantly differ between the two industry categories. This finding suggests that broad industry classifications did not have a major impact on the characteristics of the loans received by Hispanic entrepreneurs.

We use the SBO PUMS to further consider how studying a more detailed set of industries was related to the likelihood of Hispanic entrepreneurs having access to financial capital to grow or improve their businesses in 2007. With respect to acquiring this type of credit, we find that, compared to their otherwise similar counterparts in professional services, Hispanic entrepreneurs (1) in construction (as well as those in the finance, insurance, and real estate, or FIRE, industries) fared just as well; (2) in manufacturing, wholesale and retail trade, and transportation, as well as arts, recreation, entertainment, and food services, fared better; and (3) in education and health-care services fared worse.

Hispanic Entrepreneurs Outside of Formal Credit Markets

Earlier in this chapter, we provided information on the importance of studying individuals who remain outside of credit-application pools. One fundamental point from that section is that Hispanic entrepreneurs might be relatively reluctant to seek credit from financial institutions. Indeed, our estimates presented earlier are consistent with this possibility; recall, for example, that fewer than one out of ten (9.1 percent) Hispanic business owners, but nearly 16 percent of non-Hispanic business owners, borrowed from banks or other financial institutions to expand or make improvements to physical capital in 2007.

Anecdotal evidence throughout the country further bears out this prospect: "Almost 90 percent of the (Latino) businesses I've seen started with a little savings and borrowing from friends and relatives." This quote is from an October 15, 2004, report in the *Business Portland Journal*, and is from the liaison between economic development organizations and Hispanic businesses of that city. A featured article in the October–November 2010 issue of *Poder: Hispanic Enterprise* magazine contains more anecdotal evidence; two Hispanic graduates from Stanford's business school wanted to open a bakery in Los Angeles but felt that "bank financing wasn't an option," such that they sought out "angel" (venture capital) investors, mostly friends and family.

To gain insight into Hispanic entrepreneurs who opt to stay outside of formal credit markets, we turn to a closer inspection of Hispanic small business owners in the SSBF who needed credit at some point in the previous three years but did not apply for it using conventional means because they expected to be denied.[7] These entrepreneurs appear to have been relatively realistic (instead of overly optimistic) in terms of their chances of securing loans in the mid-2000s, as they tended to have lower credit ratings than other Hispanic small business owners. To illustrate, among Hispanics fearing rejection, 3.7 percent had the safest credit scores and 12.4 percent had the riskiest scores; among other Hispanic entrepreneurs, 8.5 percent had the safest credit ratings, and 8.0 percent had the riskiest ones.

Hispanics deterred from seeking credit also owned smaller firms than other Hispanics in terms of their sales ($554,000 versus $861,000), assets ($215,000 versus $382,000), and profits ($46,000 versus $171,000) in the mid-2000s. Moreover, Hispanic entrepreneurs expecting to be denied loans had, on average, less human capital than other Hispanic small business owners, which further reveals a level of realism in their expectations of receiving credit. With respect to education, 5.2 percent of those who feared rejection had not completed high school and 28.3 percent had graduated from college, compared to 4.8 percent and 39.1 percent of other Hispanic small business owners who had those schooling levels. Measures of experience also reveal that Hispanic owners of small firms who feared loan rejection had 1.5 fewer years of experience in owning or managing a business than did other Hispanic entrepreneurs, and they were on average 4.4 years younger. In terms of industry, 18.0 percent of Hispanic business owners who feared rejection worked in construction and manufacturing, compared to 14.8 percent of other Hispanics in the mid-2000s.

When asked why they expected their loan applications to be turned down, only 4 percent of Hispanic small business owners at that time stated they had anticipated ethnic and/or racial discrimination as the primary reason. As such, the expectation of "taste-based" discrimination does not seem to have been a major deterrent for Hispanic entrepreneurs to participate in formal credit markets in the mid-2000s. The most frequently reported reasons for expecting a loan application to be rejected pertained to perceived creditworthiness: 26 percent did not apply because of concerns over their balance sheet, another 21 percent felt they were already overextended on existing loans, and 18 percent were uneasy with their credit history. These creditworthiness issues accounted for two-thirds of Hispanic entrepreneurs who did not apply for loans despite the need for funding, a greater share than the 56 percent of their non-Hispanic and nonblack counterparts who reported one of these three explanations for not applying for credit they needed. In summary, on the basis of their characteristics, it appears that Hispanic entrepreneurs form realistic expectations over their odds of being approved for credit before applying.

At the same time, regional distributions significantly differed between Hispanic entrepreneurs who remained out of credit pools because of loan-rejection expectations and other Hispanic owners of small firms. Among those who anticipated being denied, only 4.2 percent were located in the North, whereas 71.9 percent were in the South and South Central regions. Other Hispanic entrepreneurs had a more dispersed geographic distribution, with 18.4 percent in the North, 42.0 percent in the South and South Central regions, and 39.6 percent in the West. Moreover, the banking market concentration differed between those expecting to be turned down and other Hispanic entrepreneurs; more than half of those expecting to be turned down operated their business in concentrated banking markets, whereas one-quarter of the latter did. These observations suggest that banking market structures could affect Hispanic entrepreneurs' credit access, in terms of not only the likelihood of approval but also the likelihood of applying for needed loans.

The existence of regional differences suggests that something specific to geography could be affecting business owners' formation of loan-approval expectations. Beyond the degree of banking competition, perhaps regional banking legislation (e.g., states' bankruptcy exemption laws) affects credit-applicant pools. If specific Hispanic populations have different cultural foundations related to cautiousness and willingness to borrow from financial institutions, then the regional effects observed here could reflect the locations of Hispanic subgroups discussed in Chapter 1 (e.g., the greater presence of Mexican Americans in the West and South Central regions versus Cubans in the South Atlantic), as well as various areas of immigrants versus U.S.-born Hispanics considered in Chapter 3. Unfortunately neither the SSBF nor the 2007 SBO PUMS provides information on specific Hispanic ethnic subgroups to determine the extent to which each population participates in credit markets. When exploring whether Hispanic-immigrant entrepreneurs have had a different experience from that of their U.S.-born counterparts in accessing financial capital for expansion or improvements to physical capital, it is of interest that we do not find a statistically significant difference, at least among firms that reported owner birthplaces in the 2007 SBO PUMS.

Concluding Remarks

In this chapter, we find that Hispanic entrepreneurs were more likely than their non-Hispanic counterparts to report being unable to access the financial capital they needed to expand or improve their operations in 2007. Furthermore, among small businesses in the mid-2000s, Hispanic entrepreneurs appeared to face other barriers to credit access that manifested in the form of smaller loan amounts and higher interest rates relative to non-Hispanic small business owners, even when accounting for differences in owner and firm characteristics. Some extensions to the latter findings suggest that the results seem to be more magnified in the West and South (regions with a higher concentration of Hispanics) than in the North. In Chapter 8, we return to these points in our discussion of programs and policies that aim to lower potential barriers to credit access that Hispanic entrepreneurs face.

The conceptual framework presented here raises the issue of potential discrimination by creditors. However, a closer inspection of the reasons for anticipating loan rejections (at least from the perspective of the survey respondents) suggests that expected racial and/or ethnic discrimination did not deter the vast majority of Hispanic entrepreneurs from participating in formal credit markets. Instead, they appeared more concerned about their creditworthiness. An alternative explanation of our findings relates to cultural forces: Hispanics seem to be relatively conservative in their credit demands and less likely to trust traditional methods of financing, such as loans from banks and other financial institutions.

7   Strategic Issues for Hispanic Entrepreneurs—Technology Usage

A S THE PREVIOUS CHAPTER HIGHLIGHTED, ACCESS TO financial capital arguably matters to the success of entrepreneurs. By the same token, access to physical capital is also positively related to business outcomes. We argue in this chapter that Hispanic entrepreneurs should consider digital technology, in light of recent reports, such as those by Pew Hispanic Center researchers Mark Hugo López and Gretchen Livingston, suggesting that Hispanics as a population tend to lag behind the nation as a whole with respect to using information technology. With the rapidly advancing nature of the global technological world, this area of research clearly informs policies that aim to bridge information divides that exist across populations. This type of research is also of interest to entrepreneurs given that businesses have increasingly adopted new technology as part of their daily operations. Aside from the obvious efficiency benefits of employing digitally led information systems, other technological advances include the utilization of online resources for the recruiting of employees, advertising to prospective customers, and increasing the network of suppliers in the production and service processes.

The understanding of Hispanic entrepreneurs' technological engagement and its effect on business outcomes becomes more relevant given the rapid growth in the Hispanic population. To the extent that Hispanics have a comparative advantage in offering goods and services to their fellow Hispanics, the expansion of business opportunities for Hispanic entrepreneurs requires state-of-the-art business technology.

While studies have considered technology access and usage among Hispanic populations, we are unaware of any that have analyzed these tendencies specifically among Hispanic business owners in detail. Melvin Delgado in his 2011 book discusses the importance of technology for the Hispanic entrepreneur, but he does not empirically investigate the issue. Delgado identifies three domains at the core of the development of Hispanic entrepreneurship: (1) operational and economic success, which includes duration, profitability, number of employees, core customer base, and "owner-customer Latino-origin congruence"; (2) cultural capital success, which deals with engagement in community cultural events and beautification or "Latinization" of neighborhoods; and (3) social capital success, which requires participation on agency or advisory boards and committees as well as task forces and coalitions, mentorship, and support for community economic development. In this discussion, he calls for technological progress in the Hispanic small business sector, which includes computer usage and website development. To support his discussion, he cites a 2002 report by the Community Development Technologies Center of Los Angeles that concludes that businesses using the latest computer technology have greater revenues and employment growth.

With the newly available SBO data as well as the SSBF, in this chapter we explore whether Hispanic entrepreneurs use digital technology differently than their non-Hispanic counterparts. We also analyze whether the usage of such technology relates to business outcomes between Hispanic- and non-Hispanic-owned small firms. It should be noted that these data were five to eight years old when we were completing this chapter. In light of the dramatic technological advancements that have occurred in the past few years, our analysis might not reflect the usage of information technology by today's Hispanic entrepreneur.

Website Usage and E-Commerce Among Hispanic-Owned Firms in 2007

To motivate our subsequent analysis on the technological business gaps between Hispanics and other groups, we start off with some evidence that is "low-hanging fruit." In particular, according to the 2007 SBO, of the firms reporting their technology usage, more than 125,300 Hispanic firms (16.0 percent) and some 3.1 million non-Hispanic firms (24.4 percent) had a website for advertising their business operations.

While few businesses in general received a significant portion of their commercial sales and other operating receipts through e-commerce (i.e., transactions occurred via the Internet), Hispanics continued to be underrepresented. For example, only 4.3 percent of Hispanic-owned firms reporting this form of technological usage had any e-commerce sales, and 1.7 percent had e-commerce generating a tenth or more of their total sales. These numbers are smaller than those for comparable non-Hispanic-owned businesses, 6.7 percent of which had some type of e-commerce and 3.2 percent (twice the share of Hispanics) of which received at least a tenth of their sales through the Internet. This technological gap between Hispanics and non-Hispanics also occurred among those making online purchases, as more than a quarter of Hispanics (26.1 percent) versus 38.2 percent of non-Hispanics did so.

We further note that this ethnic digital divide in the business sector was fairly stable across gender. The advantage that non-Hispanic female entrepreneurs had over their Hispanic counterparts with respect to having a website was close to eight percentage points (23.0 percent versus 15.2 percent) among firms reporting their technological usage. This was about the same advantage that non-Hispanic male business owners had over Hispanic male entrepreneurs (24.7 percent versus 16.5 percent). In terms of e-commerce, similar percentages of firms owned by Hispanic women and men (4.5 versus 4.2 percent) generated some of their sales through the Internet, which was a smaller gap than the difference between female- and male-owned non-Hispanic businesses (7.0 percent versus 5.9 percent). The gender of the owner also did not appear to be a factor with respect to firms making online purchases.

Still, an ethnic divide was more pronounced for male owners than female owners when considering only firms with paid employees. The website usage gap was close to ten percentage points in the case of male employers, whereas the female gap was narrower, at 7 percent. This smaller ethnic divide among female owners' website usage reflects the fact that Hispanic female entrepreneurs with paid employees were more likely than their male counterparts to have a website (33.1 percent versus 30.2 percent). In contrast, in these types of businesses, 40 percent of those owned by non-Hispanic men and women had websites.

To the extent that business website usage and online sales and purchasing reflect general trends in digitally led information systems to aid entrepreneurs, the digital divide reported between Hispanic and non-Hispanic populations seems to have permeated into the business sector (at least five years prior to the writing of this chapter). Of course, the decision to use such technology is not a random one, and it likely has greater consequences in some industries over others. We already know that Hispanic-owned enterprises tend to be smaller on average than other businesses. Perhaps the seeming relatively low technology usage by Hispanic entrepreneurs merely relates to their underlying business characteristics rather than a lack of access to information technology.

To analyze this possibility, we turn to the SBO PUMS. We define digitally connected (or technologically engaged, or other variations thereof) firms to be those with a website, that had e-sales, or that made online purchases. Table 7.1 shows the representation of digitally connected firms among businesses owned by Hispanics and non-Hispanics (among other demographic

TABLE 7.1 Representation of the digitally connected among all U.S. businesses owned by Hispanics and non-Hispanics in 2007

Characteristic	Hispanic (%)	Non-Hispanic (%)
All firms	31.8	44.5
Female owned	31.3	43.6
Male owned	32.0	44.9
Employers	51.5	63.6
Nonemployers	27.7	38.6
Immigrant owned	26.6	38.1
U.S. native owned	42.0	47.7
Construction industry	20.6	31.1
College graduate owner	54.5	56.6
Owner younger than 35 years old	35.1	46.6

SOURCE: Authors' estimates using the 2007 SBO PUMS.
NOTES: "Digitally connected" includes firms that had a website, had online sales, or made online purchases. Only firms reporting their technological utilization are included here. Difference between Hispanics and non-Hispanics for each category is statistically significant at the .01 level.

dimensions) that reported their technological usage. In light of the discussion above, it is not surprising that the digitally connected represent a significantly smaller share of Hispanic than non-Hispanic entrepreneurs (31.8 percent versus 44.5 percent), with a similar pattern reported for firms when separating them by owner gender. Moreover, this gap between Hispanic and non-Hispanic businesses existed among both employer firms (in which the technologically engaged comprised more than half of those owned by the former but almost two-thirds of the latter) and, to a greater extent (in relative terms), nonemployers.

The use of information technology also varies with respect to birthplace. As Table 7.1 indicates, slightly more than a quarter (26.6 percent) of businesses owned by Hispanic immigrants were digitally connected, compared to four out of ten (42.0 percent) of those owned by Hispanic U.S. natives. This finding is consistent with a 2010 Pew Hispanic Center report by López and Livingston that foreign-born Hispanics are less likely to use information technology than their U.S.-born counterparts. The immigrant-native digital divide in the overall population therefore spills into the business sector. Recall that immigrants account for a relatively large share of Hispanic business owners; as such, part of the overall technological differential between Hispanics and non-Hispanics can be explained by differences in the representation of the foreign born between the two groups. Even so, such a gap exists among firms with foreign-born owners as well as U.S. natives, although for the latter, it is considerably smaller (42.0 percent versus 47.7 percent).

Other demographic features related to information technology usage pertain to the human capital of the owners. Table 7.1 shows that more than half of firms owned by Hispanic college graduates (54.5 percent) were technologically engaged (a share just slightly less than that among their non-Hispanic counterparts); this was about five times the representation of the digitally connected among businesses owned by Hispanics without a high school diploma. Age played a role as well, as firms with younger owners were more likely to be connected than were those with older owners. It appears that a generational digital divide exists among entrepreneurial populations, Hispanic or otherwise.

The strong presence of the technologically engaged among the more educated entrepreneurs is consistent with other studies documenting the complementarity between physical capital (which embodies technology) and human capital (education). In Chapter 4 we discussed the importance of education in business and earnings outcomes among Hispanic entrepreneurs; it also appears that education plays a role in information technology usage. At the same time, the results for the owners' age suggest that technology and age (experience) are substitutes.

Given that the technological gap between Hispanics and non-Hispanics in the business sector relates to demographic characteristics, does a gap still exist when comparing Hispanic-owned and non-Hispanic-owned firms with similar traits? To address this question, we test whether Hispanic-owned businesses had different propensities to be digitally connected while accounting for a variety of owner and firm characteristics, including owner education and birthplace as well as industry. Our results indicate that Hispanic-owned firms were 6.5 percent less likely than their non-Hispanic-owned counterparts to be connected, all else being equal. While statistically significant, this difference is relatively small, indicating that a considerable segment of the underutilization of digital technology by Hispanic entrepreneurs can be explained by their demographic and socioeconomic characteristics.

When conducting this analysis separately for employer and nonemployer firms, the digital gap between Hispanics and non-Hispanics narrows to 4.9 percent among employers and remains about the same (at 6.3 percent) for nonemployers. Separately analyzing female-owned businesses from those owned by men also shows a digital differential between Hispanics and non-Hispanics (7.0 percent and 6.7 percent, respectively) that hovers around the gap observed when combining the groups. Finally, this differential is more pronounced for businesses owned by immigrants than those owned by U.S. natives. Compared to their non-Hispanic counterparts, the likelihood of being digitally connected was 8.2 percent lower for Hispanic immigrant entrepreneurs but 5.2 percent lower for U.S.-born Hispanics.

In terms of other characteristics related to the usage of digital technology, this exercise supports some of the patterns observed in Table 7.1. Technological usage tended to be higher among firms with owners who were more educated, younger, U.S. natives, and men than among other businesses. In terms of industry effects, compared to businesses in professional services, the propensity to be digitally connected was lower in construction; agriculture; mining; transportation; finance, insurance, and real estate (FIRE); and education and health-care services—but it was higher in manufacturing, trade, and information, as well as the arts, recreation, and food services industries.

Digital Technology and the Sales of Hispanic-Owned Firms in 2007

Another issue worth exploring pertains to the underutilization of information technology among Hispanic entrepreneurs, their business outcomes, and their sales more broadly. Recall from previous chapters that Hispanic-owned firms have considerably lower sales than other businesses, but differences in observable characteristics between Hispanic- and non-Hispanic-owned enterprises explained much of this sales gap. Perhaps digital technology is another contributing factor.

In the SBO, the sales of technologically engaged firms are higher than those of other firms. While the decision to use information technology is not random, we are interested in determining whether this relationship, causal or otherwise, differs between Hispanic and non-Hispanic entrepreneurs. Compared to the unconnected, the sales of businesses employing digital technology were 68.6 percent higher among Hispanics and 90.6 percent higher among non-Hispanics. It follows that the sales differential between Hispanics and non-Hispanics is wider among the digitally engaged than among the unengaged; compared to their non-Hispanic counterparts, Hispanic-owned firms had 30.5 percent lower sales among the connected but 8.5 percent lower sales among the unconnected.

Other characteristics of owners (e.g., gender, education, age) and businesses (including industry) explain much of this ethnic sales differential, as it shrinks to 10.9 percent for technologically engaged firms and to 2.2 percent for unconnected businesses when controlling for such factors. (Appendix B contains the empirical details.) Therefore, the seeming underutilization of digital technology does not fully explain the relatively low sales of Hispanic entrepreneurs. What we cannot observe with these data are potential differences in the quality of technology (e.g., website navigability) between Hispanic- and non-Hispanic-owned firms.

Additional analyses reveal that the larger Hispanic/non-Hispanic revenue gap in connected versus unconnected firms exists when restricting the sample to firms along several demographic dimensions, including the owner's gender, birthplace (United States versus abroad), and education (college graduate, less than high school, and other). For the latter, it should be noted that the largest gap in the sales differential between Hispanic and non-Hispanic connected and unconnected firms occurred for those with owners who had not completed high school. Among these less educated entrepreneurs, technologically engaged Hispanics had 22.1 percent lower sales than their non-Hispanic counterparts, but revenue of the unconnected did not differ between Hispanics and non-Hispanics.

In all, the results indicate that technologically engaged Hispanic entrepreneurs did not fare better on average than their non-Hispanic counterparts in 2007, at least with respect to their revenue; in some cases, they appeared to fare worse. Nevertheless, later in this chapter, we provide evidence using alternative data collected a few years before the SBO that suggests otherwise.

Information Technology Characteristics of Hispanic-Owned Small Businesses

With the foregoing SBO findings in mind, we use the two most recent versions of the SSBF to consider whether the adoption of information technology by Hispanic-owned small businesses differed from that of other firms when taking other characteristics into account. These data cover the periods 1999–2000 and 2004–5. Consider Table 7.2, which provides the shares of Hispanic and non-Hispanic entrepreneurs who used information technology in different capacities in their businesses. As with the SBO PUMS, in the late 1990s, a statistically significant digital divide existed between Hispanics and non-Hispanics with respect to the digitally connected (defined in this analysis as using e-mail, purchasing or selling goods and services online, applying for credit online, or using other online banking services for business purposes). Connected firms represented slightly more than half (52 percent) of Hispanic-owned small businesses, compared to 62 percent of non-Hispanic-owned small firms.

This divide was also apparent in the late 1990s in the usage of e-mail (in which about half of Hispanic-owned small firms, but 58 percent of those owned by non-Hispanics, used e-mail), and in the basic utilization of computers in the workplace (71 percent versus 77 percent). It is of interest that, among firms that employed computers as part of their business practices at the time, the intensity of the technology usage was the same between Hispanic- and non-Hispanic firms, as each used computers for an average of 3.5 tasks (e.g., word processing, accounting).[1] This information indicates that Hispanic entrepreneurs did not lag behind other firms in all technical aspects

TABLE 7.2 Technology usage by small businesses

	Surveyed 1999–2000		Surveyed 2004–5	
Technology usage	Hispanic	Non-Hispanic	Hispanic	Non-Hispanic
Digitally connected	51.7%[a]	60.4%[a]	75.4%	79.8%
Uses e-mail for work	49.8%[a]	57.8%[a]	74.4%	78.2%
Uses Internet for purchases or sales	28.9%	27.3%	62.0%	64.6%
Uses computer for business purposes	70.9%[b]	76.5%[b]	85.2%	85.9%
Among firms using computers, number of different uses (ranges between 1 and 8)	3.5	3.5	4.5	4.4

SOURCE: Authors' estimates using the 1998 and 2003 SSBF.
NOTE: "Digitally connected" includes firms that had a website, had online sales, made online purchases, or used the Internet for online banking.
[a]Difference between Hispanics and non-Hispanics is statistically significant at the .05 level.
[b]Difference between Hispanics and non-Hispanics is statistically significant at the .10 level.

at that time. Similarly, approximately the same share of both groups (more than a quarter) purchased or sold goods and services online.

By the mid-2000s, evidence pointing to a potential digital divide between Hispanic and non-Hispanic small business owners vanished, as the adoption of technology increased more among Hispanics than among other entrepreneurs. Three-quarters of Hispanic-owned small firms were digitally connected—a statistically similar share to that among firms owned by non-Hispanics. Three-quarters of both groups used e-mail, and slightly less than two-thirds purchased or sold goods online. Also, during that time, 85 percent of all small businesses (Hispanic-owned or otherwise) used computers in some capacity, averaging about 4.5 different functions.

It would appear that the technology differential between Hispanics and non-Hispanics in the business sector overall observed in the 2007 SBO cannot be generalized to the small businesses represented in the SSBF. Perhaps the discrepancy exists because of the types of firms included in each data set (see Appendix A). Some support for this suggestion can be garnered when considering that the percentages of small firms using digital technology in the mid-2000s SSBF were closer to those among employer firms in the 2007 SBO.

Furthermore, we include firms using e-mail in identifying the digitally connected in the SSBF but not in the SBO PUMS, which does not provide such information. As such, the digitally connected in the SSBF should include a larger share of businesses than the SBO. When redefining the connected in the SSBF to exclude e-mail users who did not have other digital activities, the shares of the connected fall (to 68.2 percent among Hispanics and to 68.8 percent among non-Hispanics). However, while these shares are closer to those among employer firms in the SBO PUMS, they continue to suggest the lack of a digital divide between Hispanics and non-Hispanics in the small business sector. In addition, the latest numbers reported in Table 7.2 relate to 2004–5, a couple of years before the SBO. Because technological advancements continued to surge in the second part of the decade, we cannot say whether the disappearance of the digital divide between Hispanics and non-Hispanics among small business owners between the late 1990s and mid-2000s did not resurface later in the decade.

What implications did these changes have on racial and ethnic differentials in the potential success of small businesses? For insight into this question, we return to some of the business outcomes of interest discussed in previous chapters: sales, profits, and whether the profits were positive or reached $10,000 or higher.[2] Table 7.3 reports the average outcomes while splitting the samples by digital connection status. Panel A includes Hispanic-owned small businesses, and Panel B reports characteristics for non-Hispanic firms.

As with the SBO PUMS, it is not surprising that being connected relates to most of the business-success measures in both time periods: connected small businesses (Hispanic-owned or otherwise) had higher sales; higher profits; greater shares of firms earning profits of $10,000 or more; and, with the exception of non-Hispanic-owned firms, positive profits. These observations indicate that connected firms tended to be larger and more successful, consistent with conventional wisdom. As we noted above, these results should not be interpreted to mean that adopting new technology will automatically increase the pecuniary success of a business.

Comparing Hispanics with non-Hispanics, in the late 1990s, the digital-divide differences in annual sales and profits were narrower, similar to the SBO PUMS findings for sales. For example, the sales of connected Hispanic firms were 85 percent higher than those of their unconnected counterparts. For non-Hispanic firms, the sales of connected firms doubled the sales of their unconnected counterparts. Nevertheless, the gap between digitally engaged and not engaged regarding the presence of firms with profits of at least $10,000 was wider among Hispanic-owned businesses (ten percentage points) than for other firms (four percentage points). Connected Hispanic-owned

TABLE 7.3 Average success outcomes measures of small businesses, by digital connection status and Hispanic ethnicity

Characteristic	Surveyed 1999–2000		Surveyed 2004–5	
	Digitally connected	Not connected	Digitally connected	Not connected
PANEL A: HISPANIC-OWNED FIRMS				
Annual sales	$603,886	$248,782	$954,918	$229,637
ln(sales)	$11.95	$11.10	$12.21	$10.67
Profits	$50,495	$32,092	$172,637	$24,415
Profits $10,000+ (1998 $)	67.4%	57.3%	62.1%	32.3%
Positive profits	83.1%	76.2%	77.2%	60.6%
College graduate owner	57.2%	19.2%	43.8%	12.4%
Managerial experience (in years)	14.95	16.58	14.82	19.68
Age of owner (in years)	46.27	49.69	45.58	50.55
Age of firm (in years)	10.30	11.69	9.46	16.40
PANEL B: NON-HISPANIC-OWNED FIRMS				
Annual sales	$1,475,000	$320,555	$1,248,000	$294,215
ln(sales)	$12.36	$11.36	$12.31	$11.44
Profits	$184,487	$62,956	$201,557	$59,903
Profits $10,000+ (1998 $)	65.5%	61.5%	60.3%	54.0%
Positive profits	77.9%	81.8%	75.3%	75.0%
College graduate owner	59.9%	32.4%	52.2%	27.5%
Managerial experience (in years)	17.60	19.43	19.11	20.90
Age of owner (in years)	49.22	51.81	51.31	53.47
Age of firm (in years)	12.51	14.96	13.89	16.66

SOURCE: Authors' estimates using the 1998 and 2003 SSBF.

businesses also had a greater share of firms breaking even than the unconnected (83.1 percent versus 76.2 percent), a difference not observed among other enterprises.

By the mid-2000s, technologically engaged small firms continued to be more successful than other enterprises. Of specific interest to this book, unlike the sales results discussed above using the SBO PUMS, many of the connected-unconnected differentials in the small business outcomes were particularly pronounced among Hispanics during this time. To illustrate, these differentials were as follows (with the first figure in each item referring to Hispanics, and the second referring to non-Hispanics): (1) 154 percent versus 92 percent higher sales, (2) 6.1 times versus 3.4 times more in profits, (3) 29.8 percentage points versus 6.3 percentage points in the share of firms earning $10,000 or more in profits, and (4) 16.6 percentage points versus 0 percentage points with respect to the share breaking even. On the surface, it appears that small business outcomes not only related to digital technology; this relationship also was stronger for Hispanic entrepreneurs than for non-Hispanics in the mid-2000s. This was not the case in the 2007 SBO PUMS.

Why might these differences between Hispanic- and non-Hispanic-owned firms exist? To address this question, we consider differences in the observable characteristics of the small business owners and of the businesses themselves, given that information technology usage depends on individual choice. Table 7.3 reports selected average characteristics of owners and firms.

With respect to human capital, we observe many of the same differences among small business owners in the SSBF as for the businesses in the SBO. Compared to the unconnected, in both time periods, those employing online resources had higher shares of college graduates, fewer years of managerial experience (defined as experience in owning or managing a business), younger owners, and younger firms. In terms of differences between Hispanic- and non-Hispanic-owned firms, the shares of college graduates fell for both groups over the five years, but the ratio of connected to unconnected college graduate business owners rose for Hispanic entrepreneurs. The share of college graduates among digitally engaged Hispanics was triple that of unconnected Hispanics in the late 1990s. Five years later, the representation of college graduates among Hispanics in this category exceeded that of others by 3.5 times but changed little from 1.8 times for other small businesses. The disproportionate presence of the highly educated among technologically engaged Hispanics with respect to those Hispanics who were not has potential implications for their connected-unconnected differentials in the average business outcomes of small businesses during this time frame, particularly in light of our findings on education in Chapter 4.

The experience and age of owners and the age of the firm are inversely related to whether a Hispanic-owned small business is digitally engaged, but these gaps exceeded those among non-Hispanics, particularly in the later time period. To illustrate, in the mid-2000s the average experience levels and age of connected Hispanic business owners were about five years less than other Hispanic business owners at that time, compared to about two years' difference among other firms in general. Unconnected Hispanic-owned firms had also existed an average of seven more years than the connected, compared to three years for small businesses owned by non-Hispanics. The increase in the relative age of business owners (and therefore a likely greater propensity to adopt new technology) of technologically engaged Hispanic-owned businesses could have played a role in explaining their relative improvement in business outcomes among the unconnected between the late 1990s and mid-2000s.

Although not shown in Table 7.3, relatively few Hispanic-owned small businesses operated outside of metropolitan statistical areas (MSAs), although they increased their presence among the connected during this time period (from 5 percent to nearly 10 percent). A similar change did not occur among other Hispanic business firms, as the non-MSA group represented 10 percent in both time periods. Perhaps the improvement in the relative success of technologically engaged Hispanics related to their increased usage of information technology by businesses opening in rural areas as a means to reach new customers, suppliers, and potential employees.

Isolating Information Technology Effects for Hispanic-Owned Small Businesses

What do these numbers mean in terms of the importance of being digitally connected for Hispanic entrepreneurs? It might be that the seeming development of an advantage that technologically engaged Hispanic small business owners had over their non-Hispanic counterparts in the earlier part of the decade could relate to changes in some of their observable characteristics. We control for these characteristics to isolate potential technology effects on business success. In this exercise, being connected positively related to three of the four outcomes for small businesses in general: annual sales, profits, and the probability of having profits of $10,000 or more (in 1998 terms) in both time periods. For example, in the late 1990s, connected small firms had sales that were about 72 percent higher than otherwise similar unconnected firms. They were also 5.7 percent more likely to have $10,000 or more in profits. A further test indicates that the relationship between online technology and these success measures did not significantly change between the late 1990s and mid-2000s.

These findings parallel those of other studies reporting the importance of information technology in the small business, but they suggest that there was not an early-adopter advantage between the two time periods, given the lack of an additional boost in the earlier period. We realize that these results might simply reflect the correlation between the utilization of Internet resources and the underlying ability of the owners (or managers). However, this finding can be capturing more than an unobserved ability bias, as it does not seem to have an across-the-board effect on various success measures of small businesses. The use of online resources did not significantly correspond to the likelihood that firms broke even.

Considering Hispanic-owned small businesses, in the late 1990s, those using online technology fared the same as non-Hispanic small businesses with respect to the four success measures. It follows that the differences in the outcomes observed in Table 7.3 for technologically engaged Hispanics versus non-Hispanics at that time can be explained by differences in observable owner and firm-level characteristics.

However, five years later, connected Hispanic-owned small firms outperformed otherwise similar non-Hispanic-owned small businesses in terms of their sales, breaking even, and having real profits of at least $10,000. Unconnected Hispanic entrepreneurs fared significantly worse with respect to three outcomes than other unconnected firms at that time, ceteris paribus. Using sales to illustrate this, connected non-Hispanic firms sold approximately 62 percent more than their otherwise similar unconnected counterparts in the mid-2000s. Technologically engaged Hispanic-owned businesses, however, sold approximately 150 percent more than other Hispanic-owned firms and 80 percent more than non-Hispanic unconnected small firms.

These findings indicate that Hispanic-owned small firms utilizing digital technology in the mid-2000s had a significant advantage over other small businesses with respect to their sales and achieving profits above certain benchmarks—an advantage that did not exist five years earlier. With these data, however, we cannot definitively explain why this is the case. One possibility is that Hispanic entrepreneurs who adopted this technology in the 2000s were more innovative than other small business owners in terms of tapping into potential customer, supplier, and employee bases. The results might also reflect differences in these outcomes related to birthplace (which is not reported in the SSBF). Recall from our SBO results that a digital divide existed between U.S.-born and foreign-born entrepreneurs.

With respect to customers, we noted earlier that the growth in the overall Hispanic population arguably led to an increase in the demand for Hispanic products. Perhaps some Hispanic-owned businesses realized this rising demand and subsequently made their goods and services more accessible through the Internet. We continue to explore the relative improvement in the sales of connected Hispanic-owned firms in the following section.

In terms of the business owners' human capital levels, education did not have a consistent effect on small business success. Firms owned by college graduates outperformed those owned by less educated entrepreneurs only with respect to their profit levels as well as having at least $10,000 in real profits in the mid-2000s. This finding does not necessarily mean that owners with college diplomas did not play a role in the success of small businesses. Recall from earlier that connected firms had relatively high shares of college-graduate owners, which suggests the complementarity between formal education and the use of information technology. Finally, the experience of the owners enhanced the odds of success of the enterprises, albeit at a diminishing rate. Unlike education, experience appears to be a substitute with technological engagement. In a similar fashion, the age of the firm also related to more successful outcomes among small businesses (except for the probability of being an employer firm in the late 1990s).

Other Considerations.   Our findings indicate that technologically engaged Hispanic-owned small businesses outperformed not only unconnected Hispanics but also their connected non-Hispanic counterparts in the mid-2000s. Five years earlier, Hispanic- and non-Hispanic-owned small firms employing online resources had similar advantages over their unconnected peers. Perhaps the seeming development of a Hispanic technological advantage in the small business sector between the late 1990s and early 2000s simply reflects greater general physical capital investments (and an increased utilization of this capital) rather than specifically the use of online resources by Hispanic versus non-Hispanic small business owners. To address this issue, we first reanalyzed the four outcomes when considering the small firms that employed computers in general (not just for online purposes). The results from this exercise indicate that firms utilizing computers were more successful than uncomputerized small businesses in both time periods with respect to sales, profit levels, and reaching the profit benchmark of at least $10,000. However, unlike our findings for online technology, Hispanic-owned small businesses with computers had similar advantages to those of their non-Hispanic counterparts.

As a related exercise, we considered the total number of functions that computers served in the small business. These alternative estimates show that the variety of tasks computers performed significantly related to successful outcomes among small businesses, with the exception of breaking even. Similar to the findings reported above for sales, this relationship mattered more for Hispanic-owned small firms than other enterprises in the mid-2000s. Unlike our previous results, Hispanics entrepreneurs fared the same as their non-Hispanic counterparts in terms of how the number of computer functions related to other business outcomes. Combined, these exercises suggest that the seeming Hispanic-technological advantage in the small business sector in the mid-2000s was particularly acute with respect to the utilization of online resources and not simply related to the usage of computers in general.

JMP Analysis of Sales.   Did the relative improvement in connected Hispanic small business outcomes between the late 1990s and mid-2000s occur because of shifts in their underlying characteristics or because the relationship between these characteristics and business success measures itself changed? To elaborate on this point, we employ the JMP technique discussed in previous chapters to analyze the change in the sales differential (rather than earnings) between Hispanic- and non-Hispanic-owned small businesses between the two time periods.

Because race mattered in terms of the sales of non-Hispanic-owned small firms (where those owned by blacks had significantly lower sales, and those owned by Asians had higher sales), in this analysis, we exclude firms owned by these groups. As such, our comparison is between Hispanic versus non-Hispanic, nonblack, and non-Asian (non-HBA) firms. The sales gap between Hispanic-owned and non-HBA-owned businesses among the technologically engaged shrank from a 44.7-percentage-point differential to 13.4 points—a relative improvement of 31.3 percentage points for Hispanic entrepreneurs during this time. In contrast, among unconnected firms, Hispanics lost ground relative to non-HBA small businesses between the late 1990s and early 2000s, as the sales differential between Hispanic-owned and non-HBA-owned businesses widened by 47.1 percentage points.

The four JMP effects provide insight into factors behind these changes. Among connected firms, Hispanic-owned firms should have experienced a deterioration in their relative sales of 10.7 percentage points with respect to their non-HBA peers, given a widening of the gaps in observable characteristics between the two groups from the late 1990s to the mid-2000s. The returns to these characteristics on sales during this time should have further widened the sales differential between Hispanic-owned and non-HBA-owned businesses by (a slim) 0.6 percentage points. Changes in the returns to unobservable traits should have also slightly increased this differential by another 0.8 marginal points. Still, connected Hispanic-owned firms made significant improvements with respect to their unobservable attributes over non-HBA small businesses employing online technology, thus reducing the potential sales gap between the two groups by 43.4 percentage points. It follows that the relative improvement of the sales of technologically engaged Hispanic-owned small firms over the five-year time span seems to have been driven by a relative improvement in unobservable characteristics.

In terms of these unmeasurables, perhaps technologically engaged Hispanic-owned businesses became more innovative or were able to tap into growing demand for their products more efficiently than the unconnected. Factors associated with immigrant-native human capital differentials could have also played a role, especially if birthplace relates to innovation among entrepreneurs or the likelihood of adopting new technology. Indeed, recall from earlier that immigrant business owners in the SBO were less likely to be digitally connected than their U.S.-born counterparts, all else being equal. The SSBF data do not provide information on the birthplace of small business owners, such that the analyses we presented here could not distinguish across countries of origins.

Concluding Remarks

Data from the 2007 SBO indicate the presence of a digital divide between Hispanic and non-Hispanic entrepreneurs with respect to having a website and conducting e-commerce, although differences in observable characteristics explained a considerable portion of this gap. The use of digital technology did not appear to benefit Hispanic-owned firms more than other firms with respect to sales. However, our analysis of the SSBF data indicated that while a digital divide seemed to exist between Hispanic- and non-Hispanic-owned small businesses in the late 1990s, it had vanished by the mid-2000s. Furthermore, being technologically engaged in the mid-2000s had a significantly stronger relationship for Hispanic-owned small firms than other small businesses with respect to their sales, profits, and in the likelihood of breaking even, which was not the case five years before.

We provide further evidence that the relative improvement made by connected Hispanics between the late 1990s and mid-2000s was not explained by shifts in, or returns to, their characteristics. They were more likely explained by a set of unobserved differences in the characteristics between the immigrant and native Hispanic self-employed populations. Given the discontinuation of the SSBF, this data source cannot be used to examine whether the role of digital technology in Hispanic-owned small business outcomes continued to evolve during the course of the Great Recession. Perhaps future versions of the SBO will continue to include questions pertaining to technological utilization, thus allowing researchers to track the technological progress of Hispanic entrepreneurs.

8 Current Policy Issues for Hispanic Entrepreneurs

A S DISCUSSED IN THE PREVIOUS TWO CHAPTERS, ACCESS TO capital—both financial and physical—is a primary determinant of a firm's success in the marketplace. Seeming disparities in accessing capital between majority and minority entrepreneurs have, as expected, generated public concern and subsequent policy action to help correct these gaps. Public authorities are, of course, a focal point in this regard, but policy also usually manifests itself in grassroots community policy involvement. The reader must bear in mind as this chapter unfolds that entrepreneurs' decisions to use public or community-based programs depend on (1) the availability of and assistance offered by the programs, (2) the recognition of which programs exist (as well as the processes of how to apply), and (3) their preferences for using them.

The appendix to this chapter focuses on the first point by outlining some of the larger public programs designed to promote the development and growth of traditionally disadvantaged small businesses, such as those run by Hispanic entrepreneurs. It also provides examples of similar programs sponsored by nongovernmental agencies. When writing this chapter, it was never our intention to put together an exhaustive list of all major programs providing assistance to minority-owned enterprises in the first decade of the new millennium; instead, we aimed to provide illustrative examples of such programs.

To gain insight into the latter two reasons behind entrepreneurs' decisions to seek public or private assistance, we provide a cursory analysis of the usage of public funding between Hispanic and non-Hispanic entrepreneurs using data from the SBO, the SSBF, and the Small Business Administration (SBA). This investigation is suggestive of potential untapped opportunities for Hispanic entrepreneurs because they either lack awareness about existing opportunities or, as we mentioned earlier in this book, are reluctant to use them.

This chapter continues by discussing issues that have shaped and might continue to shape Hispanic entrepreneurship in the United States, from public policy and private-sector perspectives to changing demographic trends across the country. Many of these perspectives relate to funding opportunities emanating from the interactions between both public and private ventures and Hispanic entrepreneurs. But others, as we discuss below, relate to education programs to help would-be and existing entrepreneurs, new risk-assessment measures, and fiscal issues such as the tax revenues generated by Hispanic businesses to local state and federal entities. The changing demographic trends are likely led by varying entrepreneurial opportunities across regions and differences in regional socioeconomic dynamics.

We also provide a critical assessment of issues facing Hispanic entrepreneurs in this new millennium. We particularly highlight the importance of education, immigration, and statistical-discrimination-reducing policies as catalysts for Hispanic entrepreneurship growth, and in so doing, we provide a critique of existing discourse on how to best help the Hispanic business sector. A common thread throughout this discussion identifies policies, such as certain categories of employment based ("EB") visas, which serve as a means to attract Hispanic-immigrant entrepreneurs, and ones focusing on U.S. workers, such as ACCION Texas's attempts to identify new rubrics to find potentially successful Hispanic entrepreneurs outside of conventional methods. (More on ACCION can be found in this chapter's appendix.)

Finally, we note some of the current dialogue that has, in some measure, centered on issues of ethnic representation of agencies that serve small businesses and the definitions used by public authorities to determine whether a firm is eligible for public programs. We argue that this dialogue has come at the expense of other potentially more fruitful avenues, like EB visas, as well as other pro-business immigration policies, to help grow the Hispanic entrepreneurial sector. In addition, less attention has been paid to the effectiveness of private education programs that have been promoted by banking institutions such as Bank of America and Wells Fargo, as well as attempts by some private organizations to find new ways to identify prospective entrepreneurs.

An Analysis of Hispanic Entrepreneurs' Utilization of Government Programs

The examples in this chapter's appendix of public and private programs designed to assist small and minority-owned businesses suggest a multitude of opportunities for Hispanic entrepreneurs to access credit, receive government procurement, and obtain technical assistance. Therefore, a clear takeaway from this discussion is that, with regard to availability, public and community-based organizations exist to mitigate potential financial hardships faced by historically disadvantaged entrepreneurs. Whether Hispanics actually use these programs, and whether the programs are effectively administered (particularly during weak economic conditions—the times when they might be most needed), are additional questions worth posing.

With respect to the first question, we consider how frequently Hispanic entrepreneurs use programs from the public sector. We explore the second question later in this chapter. Our desired aim is, to the extent possible, to learn more about Hispanic entrepreneurs' knowledge of and preferences for these opportunities. But realistically, these analyses point more to the usage of these programs for those who know about and have a preference to use them. In Chapter 6, we provided evidence that the fear of loan rejection deterred a greater share of Hispanic small business owners than other entrepreneurs from applying for credit despite the fact that they needed it. Could fear of rejection also shape the preference of Hispanics for using these programs? Also, in our introductory comments in this chapter, we acknowledged that Hispanic entrepreneurs might not use some programs because they are unaware of the opportunities that they provide.

Preferences of Hispanic Entrepreneurs for Financial Services Providers. While data to systematically identify why Hispanic entrepreneurs participate (or not) in these programs are difficult to obtain, the SSBF data contain some information about the underlying preferences of entrepreneurs for using certain institutions as providers of financial services. According to the two most recent versions of these data, only about 1 percent of Hispanic-owned small businesses used a government agency as one of their top three sources of financial services—a percentage similar to that of non-Hispanic small firms. Instead, the vast majority (about nine out of ten) reported that banks represented at least one of their top three primary financial services providers.

When asked about the main reason they selected their providers, none of the Hispanic small firm owners in the sample, and less than 1 percent of non-Hispanic owners, reported that they did so because the institution offered or assisted with SBA-guaranteed loans (described in this chapter's appendix). Instead, features such as a previous or ongoing relationship with an institution and its proximity topped the list for both Hispanic and non-Hispanic entrepreneurs. This type of nonresponse could reflect either a lack of knowledge of SBA programs by the surveyed Hispanic small business owners (who are supposed to be nationally representative) or a stronger preference for other characteristics associated with institutions offering financial services.

It is also possible, however, that the socioeconomic characteristics of entrepreneurs themselves, as well as those of the firms they operate, might be explanatory factors in the usage of public programs. For example, Hispanic-owned firms tend to be smaller and newer than other firms. Perhaps these characteristics reduced the perceived success of receiving certain financial and training assistance, thus deterring such firms from attempting to use certain programs. Moreover, smaller businesses might not have the resources to invest in learning about existing programs (or about the application processes), such that their share might be reduced in the pool of firms seeking assistance from public programs.

To address this issue, we analyze the likelihood that small enterprises used a government agency as one of their top three sources of financial services while controlling for other factors, such as education of the owners, characteristics of the firm (including its size, age, and credit rating), concentration of the banking market, and other features. This exercise reveals that few of these characteristics related to small business owners' decisions to use government agencies for financial services. Firms that were not sole proprietorships, with a larger number of employees, and those in the construction and trade industries were more likely to use these agencies than were smaller firms in other industries. Hispanic-owned small firms were statistically indistinguishable from other companies in this regard.

As noted above, the citing of an institution's offering of, or assistance with, SBA loans does not mean that entrepreneurs do not have access to them.

However, the correlation between using a government agency as a financial service provider and the size of the firm could indicate either a lack of awareness of government-sponsored financial programs or the expectation among very small businesses of being denied credit access. In the case of the latter, so-called mom-and-pop shops and microentrepreneurs (which, as we indicated earlier in this book, represent the vast majority of Hispanic entrepreneurs) might view current programs as inaccessible.

This analysis further revealed that Hispanic-owned small businesses with less educated owners, as well as newer firms, tended to be more likely than other small firms to utilize government agencies as financial service providers. As such, this information provides some surface evidence that government-sponsored lending programs could help offset the potential effects of lower human capital levels and being on the initial learning curve on the credit access of Hispanic entrepreneurs.

Hispanic Representation Among SBA Loan Recipients.   Of course, many Hispanic entrepreneurs might not consider SBA programs even when they know they are available. To understand the basic utilization of SBA programs by Hispanic entrepreneurs, we turn to data reported in 2010 by the SBA regarding the demographic characteristics of its business loan recipients in recent years. In fiscal year 2010, more than three thousand SBA 7(a) loans were approved for Hispanic-owned businesses, representing 5.8 percent of the total loans awarded. Moreover, the amount of the loans for Hispanics was $570 million, or 4.5 percent of the total $12.6 billion approved. Given that Hispanics represented more than 11 percent of the self-employed U.S. population in 2010, the SBA numbers suggest that Hispanics are underrepresented among loan recipients.

Hispanic-owned small businesses represented a smaller share of the total SBA loan amounts than among the number of loans because their average loan size of $187,000 was considerably less than the $242,000 average received by non-Hispanic business owners. Similarly, the average loan received by Hispanics through the SBA's CDC/504 program that year was smaller than that for non-Hispanics, such that their representation among the number of approved loans in this category (6.2 percent) exceeded their representation in terms of the dollar value of the loans (5.6 percent). Recall from Chapter 6 that Hispanic entrepreneurs in the mid-2000s applied for (and thus received) smaller loans than their non-Hispanic counterparts. This discrepancy also appears to have existed with respect to SBA loans at the end of the decade.

How did Hispanic entrepreneurs fare with respect to these loans during the Great Recession? A key feature of the recession was the tightening of credit markets, which hit small businesses. These data indicate that Hispanic entrepreneurs experienced a disproportionate decline, both absolute and relative, in the number and dollar value of approved SBA loans during this time. To illustrate, in fiscal year 2007, 10 percent of all approved 7(a) loans went to Hispanic small business owners (ten thousand of the one hundred thousand loans), which represents 7 percent of the total loan values ($1.0 million out of $14.3 million). Just two years later, Hispanic entrepreneurs comprised only 5 percent of the total number of loans (two thousand out of forty-four thousand) and 4 percent of the total loan amounts ($400,000 out of $9.3 million). While the 2010 figures indicate an improvement in the proportion of Hispanics among SBA loan recipients over 2009, the proportion did not return to its pre-recession level.

Hispanic Entrepreneurs' Credit Access Through Public Programs.   The SBO PUMS represents another data set that can be used to measure the outcomes of public program usage among Hispanic entrepreneurs, although, unfortunately, we cannot assess the effects of the Great Recession at this time. These data indicate that in general, few Hispanic (and non-Hispanic) entrepreneurs utilize public programs to access credit for start-up or expansionary purposes. Recall from Chapter 6 that only 1.2 percent of Hispanic-owned businesses that accessed financial capital had loans from (or backed by) the federal, state, or local governments to expand or make capital improvements in 2007. This figure was similar to the 1.3 percent of non-Hispanic-owned firms with these types of loans. The SBO PUMS also indicates that similar shares of Hispanic- and non-Hispanic-owned enterprises had funding from grants for expansionary purposes (0.4 percent). When focusing only on employer firms, a greater share of those owned by Hispanics than other businesses borrowed from the government (1.2 percent versus 0.9 percent) or had government-guaranteed loans (0.9 percent versus 0.7 percent).

Even though these numbers are quite small, the data initially suggest that Hispanic entrepreneurs fared just as well as (or slightly better than) their non-Hispanic counterparts in terms of accessing credit for expansion purposes through some of the aforementioned public programs, at least in 2007. Nevertheless, we noted in Chapter 6 that a slightly greater proportion of Hispanics reported being unable to access financial capital for expansionary or capital-improving circumstances (5.3 percent versus 3.3 percent). We note that these differences exist independent of ethnic-related variations in the distribution of firms in the expansionary mode; recall that a slightly higher share of Hispanic-owned businesses versus other firms were expanding or improving their capital in 2007.

Also, with regard to accessing credit for business acquisition, Hispanic entrepreneurs were less likely than non-Hispanics to use government lending resources. In particular, 1.1 percent of Hispanic-owned businesses had accessed government (or government-backed) loans to help with start-up costs, compared to 1.4 percent of non-Hispanic-owned firms. Only 0.3 percent of Hispanic entrepreneurs had some type of grant to establish or purchase a company—about the same as non-Hispanic aspiring business owners. As such, taken together, these statistics do not indicate that Hispanic entrepreneurs utilized public programs as major sources of credit shortly before the Great Recession.

Public Procurement and the Hispanic Entrepreneur.   The appendix to this chapter discusses selected programs established to help minority entrepreneurs access government procurement. Our estimates using the 2007 SBO PUMS suggest that Hispanic entrepreneurs appear to be benefiting from these programs at the federal level more than other entrepreneurs, but not necessarily at levels below the federal one. In 2007, the federal government was a major client (i.e., it represented at least 10 percent of a firm's total sales) of 2.2 percent of all Hispanic-owned firms reporting such information and 1.7 percent of those owned by non-Hispanics. A similar gap exists when focusing exclusively on employer firms: 3.2 percent of Hispanic employers had the federal government as a major customer, compared to 2.6 percent of non-Hispanic employers.

At the same time, state and local governments were less likely to be major clients of Hispanic-owned businesses (employers or otherwise) than of other firms. To illustrate, for 4.6 percent of Hispanic entrepreneurs in general (and 6.6 percent of Hispanic employers), state and local governments accounted for at least one-tenth of total sales, compared to 5.0 percent of all non-Hispanic business owners (and 7.1 percent of non-Hispanic employers). These findings point to an unclear assessment of the relative benefits of government procurement to Hispanic entrepreneurs. Unfortunately, we do not have the data to determine the precise percentage of sales represented by federal, state, and local governments for Hispanic-owned versus non-Hispanic-owned enterprises, nor do we know the share of Hispanic entrepreneurs who actively seek opportunities for public procurement. Such information would provide more clarity into Hispanic entrepreneurs' utilization of government procurement programs.

Public Ventures and Policies and the Hispanic Firm

Public institutions and policies matter to entrepreneurs because of the importance of government procurement to the business sector and the role it plays in funding business ventures. Strategically, in order to grow, the Hispanic business sector needs to position itself in the most favorable manner to meet guidelines for these types of lucrative business opportunities. Two strategies that have recently received public attention in this regard involve the potential impact of the official definition of a small business on Hispanic entrepreneurs and the Hispanic representation among community development financial institutions (CDFIs).

Size of Hispanic-Owned Businesses.   Before discussing how Hispanic businesses fare in terms of business size, we need to generally address the controversial topic of what constitutes a small business. At the heart of this controversy exists the competitive edge that some larger businesses have over the "truly" small business. This controversy has been well noted in the popular press. For example, in a *Washington Post* article from February 22, 2012, the U.S. Small Business Administration's spokesperson Molly Brogan says, "For the majority of businesses that have about 9 to 11 employees, it's hard to compete against a company that has 500 employees." Brogan's comments were in response to research from the American Small Business League (ASBL) showing that seventy-two large companies received $16.4 billion in federal small business contracts as well as some confusion on how new small business guidelines would address these issues.

In the middle of the controversy over small business guidelines sits the SBA. Under Public Law 85-236, the SBA has the authority to establish standards on small business size for federal government programs. In establishing these standards, the SBA takes account of underlying differences across industries and its ability to assist small businesses across sectors as a means of encouraging and strengthening their competitiveness in the economy.

For example, the SBA considers $7.0 million in receipts as a benchmark for services, retail trade, and construction; five hundred employees for manufacturing and mining; and one hundred employees for the wholesale trade industry. The SBA does not consider these three levels as "anchor size standards" per se, but as benchmarks or starting points.

To the extent that small businesses should have a competitive edge in public-driven programs, there is interest in determining whether Hispanic-owned firms compete well in this regard compared to non-Hispanic firms. Statistics from the 2007 SBO on the average size and revenues of firms by ethnicity relate to this purpose. Recall from Chapter 1 that Hispanic-owned businesses had about half the sales receipts as those of non-Hispanics in this survey ($974,000 to $1.98 million)—although the sales of firms owned by Cuban Americans ($1.57 million) were closest to the non-Hispanic average. Firms owned by non-Hispanics also had a larger number of workers on average than did Hispanic-owned businesses. These statistics seemingly support the view that Hispanic entrepreneurs have a competitive edge over other business owners in public procurement and funding programs geared toward small businesses; as such, these firms might stand to benefit from smaller size standards.

But this view is overly simplistic. To explain why, consider the following example. In terms of overall eligibility, Hispanic-owned employer firms accounted for 4.4 percent of all such businesses in the United States in 2007. We select two industry classifications, wholesale trade and accommodation and food services, which have near-average and above-average rates of public procurement and eligibility for public funds to Hispanic-owned businesses. This percentage is 3.9 percent in wholesale trade and 6.2 percent in the accommodation and food services sectors, respectively. We adopt the small business definition of fewer than one hundred workers for the wholesale trade industry and less than $7 million for the accommodation and food services sector to determine the share of Hispanic businesses that qualify under SBA small business regulations. The eligibility percentages marginally increase to 4.0 percent for wholesale trade and 6.3 percent for accommodation services.

We then impose a more stringent benchmark of fewer than fifty workers for wholesale trade and less than $3.5 million for accommodation and food services as a means to determine how these Hispanic-eligibility percentages would change. The Hispanic business share increases slightly to 4.1 percent in wholesale trade and to 6.7 percent in the accommodation and food services sector. Arguably, while we find that more Hispanic businesses would qualify for the aforementioned programs, the relative impact is quite small. This stems from the fact that changes in business-size standards would affect both Hispanic and non-Hispanic firms.

What would happen if the SBA policy imposed a more favorable business-size standard for Hispanic-owned businesses than for other firms? The SBA has, for example, considered regional distinctions as a means to make adjustments to the definition of small businesses. If regional distinctions were made, could business-size definitions alternatively include underrepresented gender, race, and ethnicity parameters?

Consider the following back-of-the-envelope analysis on how this idea might work. Say that a public policy goal aims to match, as closely as possible, the share of eligible Hispanic firms for public procurement programs and other aid to the share of the adult Hispanic population in the United States (currently about 14 percent). To start, according to the SBO 2007 statistics, very few sectors would see marked improvements in the eligibility of Hispanic firms for public procurement and programs. The accommodation and food services sector, however, would come close: if the SBA defined as eligible non-Hispanic firms with no more than nine workers, the share of Hispanic businesses would rise from 6.5 percent to 13.2 percent, as there would be 31,200 Hispanic firms of the 237,000 firms in this sector.

Aside from the likely politically charged ramifications of public policy such as this one, and while the characteristics and needs of a particular SBA program may necessitate these types of distinctions, the SBA (at least for regional distinctions) has deemed them confusing and difficult to implement. The SBA recently settled on having a single table of size standards for all programs and regions. To account for inflation, monetary-based standards have gradually increased, such that small firms can have up to $35.5 million in average annual receipts. However, as a result of improved labor productivity, these adjustments have also led to other issues related to the timing of adjustments to money-based definitions of size as well as employee-based standards. These types of controversies were particularly evident in the popular press following the revised SBA size standards, effective March 12, 2012, which included thirty-seven new standards for thirty-four industries and three subindustries (among other revisions).

Hispanic-Owned Business Representation.   The second point of this public discourse relates to whether Hispanic entrepreneurs are well positioned to take advantage of public procurement and public-aid opportunities. In this light, the ability of community-based organizations, particularly CDFIs,[1] to assist Hispanic businesses has been called into question by some. For example, Javier Palomares, chief executive officer of the U.S. Hispanic Chamber of Commerce, stated at a Federal Reserve System conference on July 12, 2010, that this number is alarmingly low:

> CDFIs are very much the fabric of the communities they serve. And, perhaps, no other institution out there understands the needs of small businesses because they're part of that community, they understand the issues, the challenges. And, often times, they're not only the administrator of the loan, but become the business consultant on an ongoing basis. And, if the business makes it, often times, it's because the CDFI held their hand. And, I commend that. That said, I would say that, of about the 800 CDFIs in this country, there's [sic] only three that are Hispanic based or Hispanic backed or managed by Hispanics. And yet, when you look at the growth of small business in America, Hispanic small business outpaces all others at a rate of about four to one. And, when you look at women owned Hispanic businesses, they outpace the rate of growth and startup at a rate of about six to one. So, there's a huge gap in the Hispanic community as it relates to the needs for Hispanic owned, managed, and focused CDFIs.

To add to Palomares's point, the CDFI fund (housed in the Treasury Department) recently awarded close to 180 grants to CDFIs throughout the country. Of these, only seven CDFIs were Hispanic run or in predominantly Hispanic areas, four of which were ACCION CDFIs (in Chicago, Albuquerque, New York City, and San Antonio, Texas; for a description of ACCION, see the chapter appendix).

On the surface, this public discourse ties the issue of Hispanic accessibility to public aid for small businesses to the "Hispanicity" of the CDFIs (however measured), and it raises an important question: what role does the cultural affiliation of a CDFI to its Hispanic community play in facilitating lending to Hispanic entrepreneurs? A 2008 paper by Spencer M. Cowan, Danielle Spurlock, Janneke Ratcliffe, and Hoiou Zhu provides insight into this question. Their results indicate that CDFIs provide minorities with more services relative to their transactions, but all CDFIs, regardless of the ethnicity of the owners, provide larger loans to whites.

These authors also interviewed some of the CDFIs used in their empirical analysis; their interviews suggest that minority-owned CDFIs tend to be more likely to lend in census tracts with large minority populations, but mostly because of their propensity to lend in low-income census tracts. An interesting finding from these interviews is that a CDFI's familiarity with the cultural norms of customers seemingly matters, as Palomares's comments above would suggest, a finding that would create a level of trust between the owner and the borrower and potentially more access to credit for would-be Hispanic entrepreneurs. That said, while the results of this recent paper are mixed, the area of inquiry between ethnic representation in public programs and Hispanic business success warrants future investigation, given its potential impact in shaping the Hispanic entrepreneurship experience in the future, an experience that has increasingly important national ramifications.

Immigrant Visas for Entrepreneurs.   The foregoing two issues, while potentially important to the growth of Hispanic entrepreneurship in the United States, might be taking too much light away from others in the public domain, such as underrepresented, eligible Hispanic immigrant entrepreneurs. As we discussed in Chapter 3, Hispanic immigrants (especially women) have higher entrepreneurial tendencies than their U.S. native counterparts. As we note below, in states with the fastest-growing Hispanic entrepreneur populations between 2000 and 2010 (Arkansas and South Carolina), the ratio of foreign-born to U.S.-born Hispanic business owners has grown to close to three to one. Also, our estimates indicate that Mexican immigrants in Texas-Mexico border areas have higher self-employment rates than U.S.-born Mexican Americans as well as Mexican immigrants in the rest of Texas and in the United States overall. These observations indicate the vital role of Hispanic immigrants in local business sectors.

So where does immigration reform stand in terms of promoting (or discouraging) would-be foreign-entrepreneurs? Consider one potentially policy-driven tool to bolster the entrepreneurial rates of Hispanics, the EB-5 visa, spawned by the Immigration Act of 1990. Among other major changes, this act created five different employment-based (EB) categories under which immigrants are eligible for a U.S. visa. The fifth category, the EB-5, created the opportunity for the issuance of immigrant visas based on foreign investment in the United States. As a follow-up to this act (and the EB-5 in particular), in 1993, Congress also established the Immigrant Investor Pilot Program to encourage immigrant investment in a range of business opportunities in so-called designated regional centers.

In fact, the EB-5, referred to as the investor's visa, serves to attract foreign capital to the United States, that is, investors who can eventually settle
in this country as permanent residents. The EB-5 issues the investor permanent residency, or a green card, which allows the investor to begin the road
toward naturalization and, with it, eventual citizenship. To be eligible for
the EB-5 visa, the immigrant investor must meet specific criteria, which includes investment of $1 million, the creation of ten jobs, and immigration
qualification status. The EB-5 can also be awarded to immigrants who wish
to invest $500,000 in capital in a new commercial enterprise that employs five
workers in a "targeted employment area" (those with unemployment rates of
150 percent of the national unemployment rate, or rural areas as designated by
states). Under this program, immigrants initially receive conditional perma-
nent-resident status in the United States for a two-year period. After this time,
upon satisfying EB-5 program conditions, the immigrants become uncondi-
tional lawful permanent residents of the United States.

While a common criticism of this program is that it allows foreign busi-
nesspeople to "buy" U.S. residency (purportedly providing an unfair advantage to wealthy individuals), the EB-5 has actually not been as popular
as anticipated. The visa has become more attractive to Asian investors since
2005, but EB-5 participation rates since its inception have been remarkably
low among Latin American immigrants. Figure 8.1, which displays the visa
issuances made to EB-5 recipients who were new arrivals, illustrates these
trends. Notice the steady rise in EB-5 visas for Asian immigrants, from virtually none in 2002 to more than 400 in 2007, and then rising sharply to 2,500
in 2009. Except for Latin Americans, this pattern is paralleled by immigrants
from other regions, albeit at a much slower pace.

Arguably, it is of policy interest to determine why the participation rate of
Hispanic-immigrant entrepreneurs in the EB-5 program falls short of other
groups. Explanations range from an inadequate number of Hispanic entrepreneurs who meet the minimum requirements for this visa to less-than-
efficient marketing strategies of this program in Latin America. Anecdot-
ally, the economic development agencies of some cities near Mexico, such as
McAllen, Texas, have started to enhance their outreach efforts to attract immigrant entrepreneurs by establishing EB-5 offices as reference points for potential entrepreneurs from south of the U.S. border.

Some of the features of the EB-5 program might also be sufficiently allur-
ing if they are well disseminated to entice Hispanic immigrant entrepreneurs

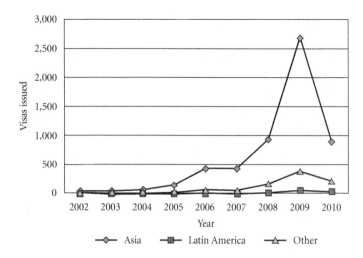

FIGURE 8.1 New issuances of EB-5 visas, 2002–10

SOURCE: Authors' estimates using the "visa statistics" from the Bureau of Consular Affairs, U.S. Department of State.

NOTE: These data exclude EB-5 recipients who adjusted their status.

to the United States. For one, the creation of EB-5 regional centers, such as the one in McAllen, offer preexisting or pooled projects that help investors participate in the program without having to start a new business from the ground up. Moreover, the possibility that potential immigrant investors can participate in this program with lower monetary and employment-creation requirements may attract Mexican and other Latin American investors to areas considered economically depressed along the along the U.S.-Mexico border.

To be sure, the future of the investor visa continues to be debated in Washington, DC. For example, Alejandro Mayorkas, director of the U.S. Citizenship and Immigration Services Division of the U.S. Department of Homeland Security, recently suggested the department's intentions to promote this program in a policy memorandum draft. In addition, the creation of an EB-6 visa has been considered. This new plan, unofficially dubbed "The Social Entrepreneur," would allow for a substantially lower investment to qualify for a visa and would be financed through capital investments as opposed to foreign cash infusions. This employment-based visa category would also allow talented foreign entrepreneurs, such as engineering students or technology-skilled immigrants with potential entrepreneurial ventures, to find domestic or international funding to start and grow businesses in the United States while simultaneously receiving immigration benefits. These nascent immigration policy efforts, along with a policy agenda to promote these opportunities in Latin America, might serve to strengthen the Hispanic entrepreneurial base in the United States.

The EB-5 might also be helpful in addressing the existing gap between Hispanic firms and non-Hispanic firms in the share of employer firms. To illustrate, consider the construction sector, in which only 11.2 percent of Hispanic-owned businesses had paid employees in 2007, only half of the presence of employer firms among corresponding non-Hispanic firms. In Arkansas, the state with the fastest-growing Hispanic entrepreneurial population, this number was 3.4 percent. Arguably, potential job creation serves as a policy issue in the development of programs to grow Hispanic entrepreneurship in an era of high unemployment; the EB-5 employment requirements for would-be entrepreneurs might be an avenue to create more of these types of businesses. Indeed, recent reports, including one from 2010 by M. Keil Hackley and Summer Robertson, have shown that the EB-5 is becoming a viable option among international construction entrepreneurs as developers learn to attract foreign investment capital.

Private Ventures, Entrepreneurship Education, and Hispanic Entrepreneurship

While it can be difficult to disentangle the public and private issues shaping Hispanic entrepreneurship, some issues of interest specific to the private sector exist. The ones we discuss here relate to efforts (or lack thereof) on the part of banking institutions to promote Hispanic entrepreneurship. We discuss these issues while keeping in mind that these institutions must balance the risk and return of their portfolios as they attempt to find creative alternatives to assist minority-owned businesses. We also outline examples of educational programs to help would-be entrepreneurs that target Spanish-speaking populations in the United States.

Hispanic Entrepreneurs and Banking Institutions. We have detected through anecdotal evidence that in the first decade of the 2000s, banks were more inclined to fund Hispanic-owned firms that had already demonstrated success (e.g., those with successful profit ratings). For example, a 2004 *Port-*

land Business Journal profiles Francisco Díaz, owner of three Portland-area *taquerías*, who borrowed money from a friend in the early stages of his business. Díaz noted, "It's very hard when you are first running a business to get access to capital. When you ask for a loan or line of credit, they want your two-year work history. You have to come up with other strategies." Also, in a 2004 *San Francisco Business Times* article, Judith Harkham Semas noted that Alan Fisher, then executive director of the California Reinvestment Coalition, mentioned that community banks do a better job of serving their local communities than do multistate banks. Fisher says, "The big banks have credit-scored, mass-production programs that aren't particularly sensitive to California's diversity."

Some of these concerns, of course, are not particular to Hispanic entrepreneurs. The banking business, as is the case for most other private firms, does business to make a profit. What distinguishes the banking industry from others pertains to its high degree of regulation. Depending on the charter of a bank, a bank might be regulated by as many as three agencies (e.g., nationally chartered banks are regulated by the Office of the Comptroller of the Currency, the Federal Deposit Insurance Corporation, and the Federal Reserve System). This regulatory framework has been justified largely by the fact that banks, as financial depository institutions, safeguard the vast majority of savings of U.S. residents. So banks, by law, must be prudent in their lending practices and are expected to vet closely their prospective loans. In so doing, banks mitigate asymmetric information such as adverse selection and moral hazard.

Put in this perspective, issues of a Phelps-type statistical discrimination in the lending process, as we discussed in Chapter 6, might arise. In sorting through loan applicants, banks might ascribe the average characteristics of a population of borrowers to an individual who belongs to that population. As such, the individual who belongs to a group with a relatively high default-risk premium might find it more difficult to obtain a business loan from a bank.

But this type of discrimination might extend beyond individuals who belong to certain racial, ethnic, or gender populations. The distinction might depend on a type of business as well. Indeed, in a recent Federal Reserve System conference, the composition of firms between so-called gazelle and mom-and-pop businesses was discussed by bankers, academics, CDFI representatives, and policy makers in light of issues related to job creation in the United States. Gazelle firms are usually technology-based start-ups with little collateral, which creates potential funding barriers for these types of businesses. The irony, mentioned at this meeting, is that when successful, gazelles tend to grow and create most of the new employment opportunities in the U.S. economy.

While it is difficult to identify an industry that would have a disproportionate number of gazelle firms, as an approximation, we consider the information sector. The 2007 SBO reports that 2.9 percent (2,100 Hispanic firms out of nearly 73,000 overall) of firms operating in the information sector were Hispanic owned, compared to the 4.3 percent we report above for all employer firms. On the one hand, it would appear that the foregoing issue of gazelles and mom-and-pop firms is of relatively less importance for Hispanic entrepreneurs. On the other hand, the low participation raises issues regarding the potential for Hispanic entrepreneurship as an engine of employment growth in the United States, especially when considering the rapid population growth of Hispanics.

There are nascent attempts by the private sector to develop assessment measures to identify low-risk entrepreneurs by using creative tools outside of the traditional ones. An example, albeit one primarily used in developing countries, is the Entrepreneurial Finance Lab (EFL). The EFL was founded in 2006 as a means to find low-cost screening tools and alternative financial contracts as methods to stimulate entrepreneurial finance in developing countries. For example, a psychometric assessment tool (which prospective entrepreneurs take over a thirty-five-minute session) purportedly identifies low-risk entrepreneurs. In 2010, the EFL became an independent private organization, with the goal of promoting economic growth across the developing world.

This idea has been received with interest by some CDFIs attempting to develop new assessment tools, beyond the traditional financial ones, to identify Hispanic microenterprises that might be successful but fall short of meeting the traditional criteria for accessing credit. At least one of these, ACCION Texas, recently issued a request for proposals for the creation of a tool to reach out to Hispanic communities by identifying better ways to reduce information barriers of the statistical discrimination type. In particular, ACCION Texas's goal is to create a standardized assessment mechanism to risk grade those entrepreneurs who might be rejected under current underwriting criteria. ACCION Texas aims to expand those small businesses' access to credit without negatively affecting their portfolio quality. Their target population of entrepreneurs includes those seeking loans of $5,000 and less for start-ups less than six months old and without a source of income outside the business, or those that lack sufficient collateral. Ultimately, the assessment matrix would incorporate repayment data to improve the accuracy of the tool and would run parallel to existing systems assessing risk.

Banking Institutions, Economic Education, and Hispanic Entrepreneurship. There have been some interesting efforts by banks that might help fuel future generations of Hispanic entrepreneurs. Consider, for example, the efforts of some major banks along the lines of education on strategic business planning, which also encompasses financial and tax education policy. For example, major bank holding companies, such as Wells Fargo and Bank of America, have undertaken significant strategic-planning programs at the K–12 level, such as Wells Fargo's Hands On Banking and Bank of America's Financial Fitness for Life, to teach children and young adults the importance of financial strategic planning.

Financial Fitness for Life is a personal finance curriculum for students with materials for four grade levels: kindergarten to second, third to fifth, sixth to eighth, and ninth to twelfth. A novel aspect of these materials is that, along with a teacher guide, both students and parents receive guides as well. That is, all lessons provided by teachers have student and parent involvement. The lessons delve into important aspects of personal finance, such as earning income, spending, saving, investing, and so forth. Of relevance to some Hispanic populations, all of the lessons are available in both English and Spanish.

Hands on Banking, also available in both Spanish and English, is offered free on the Internet, without commercial content or product placement, for adults, young adults, and school-aged children. The new Hands on Banking Entrepreneurship site is particularly relevant to educating future entrepreneurs—the site features articles, business templates, and lessons aimed at teaching students and adults about various facets of entrepreneurial activities, from developing business proposals to managing and growing a business.

These entrepreneurship education programs, of course, assume that business strategic planning programs matter in the long run. But this proposition is testable, and results from such research might be instrumental in shaping pedagogical programs in the United States that aim to promote entrepreneurship, particularly for Hispanic populations. While little is known about the impact of entrepreneurship education on entrepreneurial behavior, there has been a growing interest in identifying whether such a casual relationship exists. For example, Dev Dutta, Jun Li, and Michael Merenda provide evidence in a 2011 study suggesting that entrepreneurship education alone might not be sufficient to foster entrepreneurial activity. Rather, they argue that it should be a part of a diverse educational experience that eventually leads to an increase in the entrepreneur's personal income and net worth. In contrast, Ivana Bilic, Ante Prka, and Gaia Vidovic, also in a 2011 study, test an index that measures entrepreneurial orientation on undergraduate and graduate business students at a Croatian university. They find that graduate students have a higher entrepreneurial orientation than their undergraduate counterparts and that those who took entrepreneurship courses tested the highest on this index.

Tax Revenue and the Influence of Hispanic Entrepreneurs

The significance of Hispanic-owned small businesses on local, state, and federal tax revenues is another issue that, at least on the surface, likely weighs on the political clout of the Hispanic entrepreneur and, in so doing, shapes this sector's future. We tackle this issue by first estimating the absolute and relative contribution of Hispanic entrepreneurs to public coffers and then addressing the broader issue of tax revenues and political influence, keeping the level of geographic aggregation in mind.

Hispanic-Owned Business Tax Revenues.   While precise estimates of the total tax revenue generated by Hispanic entrepreneurs are difficult to determine, as discussed in previous chapters, the CPS IPUMS can be used to measure average income taxes paid by the self-employed based on their earnings. We estimate that in 2010, Hispanic entrepreneurs paid an average of $550 in state income taxes, another $2,270 in federal income taxes, and $3,576 in their share of FICA taxes. Aggregating these figures suggests that they contributed $793 million to state tax coffers, $3.27 billion in federal income taxes, and another $5.16 billion in their share of the payroll tax in 2010 alone, not counting the amount they paid in payroll taxes for their employees, corporate taxes, or sales taxes generated from their goods and services.

For the latter, using the SBO PUMS, our estimates indicate that Hispanic-owned businesses generated more than $20.15 billion in state sales taxes in 2007 alone, based on their sales, receipts, and the value of shipments received (henceforth, "sales"). In terms of corporate taxes, consider that the $350.7 billion dollars generated in sales by Hispanic-owned firms accounted for 1.2 percent of all sales reported in the 2007 SBO. Based on a 2008 report from the Internal Revenue Service, the U.S. government received $433.5 billion in tax revenues from corporations. This would put Hispanic-owned businesses' corporate-tax contribution at more than $5 billion (approximating state corporate tax revenues as well). While not a small amount in absolute terms, it is admittedly small with respect to total corporate taxes paid.

Hispanic-Owned Businesses' Public Policy Influence.   But what do these tax numbers mean in terms of the influence of Hispanic-owned businesses in the formation of public policy, particularly that which might promote Hispanic entrepreneurship? There is a fairly robust literature that deals with the influence of the business sector on public policy. One recent example is a 2005 study by Christopher Witko and Adam Newmark that considers the potential influence of the business sector on improving policy to create a more favorable business climate. Their findings indicate that political contributions improve the business climate. If so, the relatively low corporate tax revenue estimates for Hispanic businesses at the national level would put their political clout at a relatively low level. This is not to say, of course, that other factors should be ignored, such as the degree of unionization and state campaign-finance regulations, as the authors of the study suggest.

Timothy Bates reminded us in 2011, "Politicians allocate public resources to political strength, which inner cities rarely possess; bankers allocate loan funds seeking secure returns, and their consensus view is that inner-city lending is risky; mobile residents seeking attractive opportunities often depart" (p. 293). In this light, we should note that the representation of Hispanic-owned businesses varies greatly not only in the intracity dimension but also across U.S. regions, as suggested elsewhere in this book. Statewide, the greatest presence of Hispanic-owned firms in the business sector in 2007 was highest in New Mexico (23.7 percent), Florida (22.4 percent), and Texas (20.6 percent). Hispanic businesses in New Mexico and Florida also contributed close to 5 percent of state business receipts and, as such, the taxable base for these states. Of interest, these statistics, in rank order, are as expected for New Mexico, given that this state has the highest share of Hispanics in the United States (46 percent according to the 2010 census).[2] However, Florida's comparable Hispanic share is 22 percent (close to Texas's 21 percent), yet

Texas's Hispanic business sector contributed less than half of what those in Florida contributed to the business tax base.

The political clout of Hispanic-owned businesses in states such New Mexico and Florida might serve as clues to what the future will bring at a national level as the Hispanic population in the United States becomes more prominent. Of course, the Hispanic demographic profiles of these states, from the share of immigrants, their age and education, and the specific populations of Hispanic ethnic subgroups in these states (e.g., Cuban Americans in Florida, Spanish American versus Mexican American in New Mexico) would need to be taken into account to make more informed projections of the political clout of Hispanic businesses in the future.

Recent research in political science suggests that this type of clout is not necessarily in the best interests of the efficiency of those businesses who seek it, at least not at the regional level. For example, Raj Desai and Anders Olofsgard present an interesting argument in a 2011 study that political influence improves, but also hurts, the business environment for influential firms. Using the World Bank's Enterprise Surveys of approximately eight thousand firms in forty developing countries, they find that the potential privileges from political influence come at a political cost, namely via a reduction in the firms' ability to reduce variable costs associated with workers' employment. They go on to note that these political restrictions might adversely affect firms' productivity even if they earn higher profits than noninfluential firms.

What remains to be seen is the significance and sustainability of Hispanic-owned small businesses on local and state tax revenues, and whether it would be mutually advantageous for local agencies to partner with Hispanic entrepreneurs. This information would go beyond the traditional literature that usually focuses on the impact of small businesses at the national level (e.g., their effect on gross domestic product), and not on state and local coffers.

Regional Demographics and Hispanic Entrepreneurship

As we have highlighted throughout this book, Hispanic entrepreneurship grew at an uneven pace across the United States in the first decade of the 2000s. According to the SBO, for example, the number of Hispanic-owned businesses in both South Carolina and North Carolina nearly doubled between 1997 and 2007. Two other neighboring states, Kentucky and Tennessee,

had growth rates during this time of up to 150 percent in the Hispanic entrepreneurial sector. Arkansas, however, between 2000 and 2010 had the fastest
annual growth rate, 15.4 percent, in the number of Hispanic-owned businesses, according to the ACS, followed by South Carolina (at 13.2 percent).
These regional patterns are quite significant, given that prior to the 2000s,
relatively few Hispanics resided in these states.

So what is driving this uneven growth pattern in Hispanic entrepreneurship across states and regions? An answer to this question might further help
inform policy that aims to foster Hispanic entrepreneurship in the 2000s. To
provide insights to this question, we consider research by urban economists
Edward Glaeser, Stuart Rosenthal, and William Strange (henceforth GRS),
who conceptualized in a 2010 study why entrepreneurship differs across regional dimensions. We then outline a case study using Arkansas and South
Carolina because of their stated unusually large growth in Hispanic entrepreneurial activity over the first decade of the 2000s.

The first hypothesis that GRS posit is that regional entrepreneurial activities depend on entrepreneurial returns across regions. For example, consider
the returns on Hispanic entrepreneurship in South Carolina's construction
sector relative to those in the United States according to the SBO 2007. (We
focus on the construction sector here because of the aforementioned growing predominance of Hispanic entrepreneurs in this sector). In particular,
Hispanic entrepreneurs in this sector in firms without employees had annual
sales receipts of $74,700, compared to the national average of $50,000. For construction firms with employees in South Carolina, their average labor costs
were $21,800, compared to $34,200 for Hispanic entrepreneurs nationwide.

Interestingly, however, not all of these statistics generally favored Hispanic
entrepreneurs in Arkansas. While the average payroll for Hispanic firms with
employees was $30,800, still less than the national average, the average annual
sales receipts were about $8,000 higher for Hispanic entrepreneurs who did
not employ workers in this sector. The second and third hypotheses offered
by GRS might help explain the fast growth in Hispanic entrepreneurs: differential entrepreneurial growth over space reflects differences in the availability
of inputs to entrepreneurship (including human capital) and the supply of
ideas in a given region. In this regard, according to the ACS, Arkansas saw a
large increase in its Hispanic population between 2000 and 2010 (111 percent),
as did South Carolina (148 percent). The difference between the two states,
however, is that more immigrants became entrepreneurs in Arkansas (the

ratio of Hispanic immigrants to natives in the business sector doubled from 1.4 to 2.8 during this time interval) than in South Carolina (the comparable ratio changed from 2.3 to 3.0). As such, it could be argued that Arkansas relatively benefited from an infusion of Hispanic immigrants with strong entrepreneurial tendencies.

The final hypothesis set forth by GRS for variations in entrepreneurship growth across areas is that differences exist in the local culture, political system, or endowments. Do Arkansas and South Carolina have relatively favorable attributes in this regard? To address this point, we consider the study mentioned above by Witko and Newmark. They developed a "business policy climate" index based on policy indicators that include tax policies, probusiness legal reforms, wages, and pollution regulations, among others. According to this index, South Carolina ranked eighth among states and Arkansas nineteenth in the nation (South Carolina's score is 4.77 and Arkansas' is 1.511, where the mean score is zero and the larger the score the better the state's business climate). Both of these states have above-average business climates, which supports the view that these conditions foster entrepreneurial formation.

In all, given the role of local socioeconomic and demographic conditions (including the customer base, industrial compositions, and costs) in stimulating entrepreneurship, the foregoing case study of Arkansas and South Carolina points to the developing Hispanic self-employment patterns across geographic regions since 2000. This information is important because, as noted earlier, Hispanic populations (particularly immigrants) have been moving into nontraditional geographic areas.

Concluding Remarks

Various public and private programs have been designed to provide small businesses with opportunities to access credit and government procurement, acquire training, and receive technical assistance. In general, as we discussed in this chapter, few Hispanic entrepreneurs (as well as other small business owners) seem to use these programs. We have suggested that knowledge about government programs and the willingness to use them might be root causes for these findings. Yet the efficiency of these programs might also play a role, especially during times when the small business sector might need them the most.

Take the case of the SBA lending programs. Surface evidence points to a decline in the SBA's banking partners from effectively financing small businesses when credit markets started tightening, even before the Great Recession officially started. For example, a May 31, 2007, *New York Times* article reported that between 2001 and 2007, the SBA lost half of its budget and 31 percent of its staff. As a result, fees for many of its loan programs, such as the 7(a) program, increased, thus apparently reducing the accessibility of these loans for many entrepreneurs.[3] Local anecdotal evidence from an October 25, 2009, article in the *St. Petersburg Times* points out that in Florida in 2009: "Though a dozen new lenders arrived on the scene, about 100 lenders actively doling out loans in 2008 didn't make a single loan last fiscal year. The total volume of bank SBA loans throughout the district plummeted 43 percent."

The decline in the representation of Hispanic SBA loan recipients between 2007 and 2010 reported in this chapter is consistent with these reports. Because postrecession data are not yet available from the SBO, we cannot at this time identify how the Great Recession affected Hispanic entrepreneurs' overall usage of public lending programs or government procurement. What we can say is that the recent credit crisis put financial pressures on existing public and private programs at a time when small businesses were most likely to seek them. Hispanic entrepreneurs, who tend to have smaller companies than their non-Hispanic counterparts, appear to have been disproportionately affected by this crisis. How quickly the lingering effects of the Great Recession wear off has yet to be seen. However, new policies and initiatives, along with revisions of existing programs, have been undertaken to restore the small business sector to pre-recession levels. The extent to which Hispanic entrepreneurs will be involved in these new programs is a topic of particular policy importance.

The future will likely bring many unexpected surprises, and Hispanic entrepreneurship will probably be affected by many of these. Already, the second decade of the 2000s is hinting at two. First, there has been a slowdown in the rate of immigration to the United States from Mexico, and second, new studies are revealing the relatively high rates of Hispanic consumers becoming digitally connected.

Regarding the first point, throughout this book we have made reference of the importance of Hispanic-immigrant entrepreneurs to Hispanic entrepreneurship in general. According to a 2012 Pew Hispanic Center report by Jeffrey Passel, D'Vera Cohn, and Ana González-Barrera, net Mexican migration to the United States has virtually come to a halt since 2005. The reasons for this migration decline include voluntary and involuntary departures (deportations) of Mexican immigrants in the United States, as well as fewer crossings into the United States by Mexicans (apprehensions of individuals of Mexican origin declined to one-fifth, or about 286,000, in 2011 from their 2005 levels). What will the slowdown in the immigration rate of Mexicans to the United States have on future Hispanic entrepreneurs? The declining number of would-be Hispanic entrepreneurs, at least in theory, should drive up the earnings of domestic entrepreneurs who would have competed against these immigrant entrepreneurs. But maybe this will occur at the expense of fewer alternatives to U.S. consumers and the potential jobs those entrepreneurs would have created.

That said, regarding the second point, a recent report (*Nielsen's State of the Hispanic Consumer: The Hispanic Market Imperative,* from April 20, 2012) on digital usage by ethnic group finds that Hispanic consumers have higher propensities than non-Hispanics to watch videos on the Internet and on mobile phones. And although Hispanics have a relatively lower rate of Internet access at home compared to the U.S. average (62 percent and 76 percent, respectively), this usage increased by 14 percent between February 2011 and 2012, compared to a rate of 6 percent for the nation. Will the more technologically proficient Hispanic consumers eventually graduate tech-savvy Hispanic entrepreneurs? To be sure, there is much more to write on this topic.

Appendix: Overview of Selected Public Programs Assisting Small and Minority-Owned Businesses

At the federal level, on the surface, quite a few opportunities exist for small businesses, minority-owned or otherwise. It should be made clear at the outset, however, that agencies of the federal government do not make loans to businesses per se. Rather, these federal agencies guarantee or facilitate loans between financial institutions and small businesses; award grants to businesses; and, perhaps more important, buy goods and services from the small business sector in the form of public procurement.

Public procurement has been recognized as an important component in American society for at least several decades. Indeed, the Small Business Act of 1953 established the Office of Small and Disadvantaged Business, and the role of this agency's director involves promoting and ensuring that each federal agency and their large prime vendors include small business concerns as sources for goods and services in their prime-contracting and subcontracting operations. Federal procurement policies (which apply to direct purchases by the government and purchases by federal grant recipients) are determined by legislative action and recommendations from the Office of Federal Procurement Policy, a subdivision of the Office of Management and Budget.

Beyond procurement issues, a variety of government agencies have been designed to enhance access to capital, provide training opportunities, and deliver other forms of assistance to small businesses. Our discussion here focuses on some of the more commonly used programs, but as noted earlier, other public programs also exist.

The U.S. Small Business Administration.   Congress created the U.S. Small Business Administration under the Small Business Act of 1953. The SBA's purpose was to "aid, counsel, assist and protect, insofar as is possible, the interests of small business concerns." Other functions of the SBA included ensuring that small businesses received a "fair proportion" of government contracts and sales of surplus property. Such missions had already existed in previous agencies that essentially served as predecessors to the SBA, including the Reconstruction Finance Corporation (RFC, a federal lending program created by President Herbert Hoover in 1932 for businesses hurt by the Depression) and the Smaller War Plants Corporation (SWPC, created by Congress in 1942 most notably to help small businesses participate in production efforts during World War II and to facilitate their access to credit by providing direct loans to entrepreneurs). With the dissolution of the SWPC after World War II, the RFC took over the SWPC's lending role. In 1952, when it appeared that the RFC would be abolished, President Dwight Eisenhower proposed the creation of the SBA.

Additional legislation relevant to the SBA includes the Investment Company Act of 1958, which created the Small Business Investment Company (SBIC) program to address concerns related to small businesses' access to technological innovations, and the Equal Opportunity Loan (EOL) program of 1964 that relaxed credit and collateral requirements for impoverished applicants seeking financial support to start new firms considered to be "sound commercial initiatives."

Currently, the SBA has a variety of programs to facilitate loans to small businesses through banking partners, to enable small firms to access federal contracts, to promote entrepreneurial development through education and technical training and assistance, to serve as an advocate for small businesses regarding congressional legislation (e.g., potential regulatory burdens), and to provide counseling and management assistance to entrepreneurs, among other functions. We should note that the SBA does not identify a small business using a single definition, and what constitutes a "small business" has been a point of contention (as we discuss elsewhere in this chapter). Depending on the industry, the SBA defines a small business by using the average number of employees over the past year or the average annual receipts over the past three years, whichever represents the largest size of the business, including its affiliates and subsidiaries.

As mentioned above, in terms of its function to facilitate loans, the SBA does not directly extend credit to small business owners but instead provides them with information and resources about loan opportunities. Some of its more prevalent financial programs include the 7(a) loan program, the Microloan Program, and the Community Development Company/504 Program. The SBA 7(a) Loan Program—the most commonly used SBA program—is named after section 7(a) of the Small Business Act, which authorized the SBA to provide business loans to American small businesses. Under this program, the SBA guarantees a portion of loans made and administered by commercial lending institutions for eligible borrowers starting, acquiring, or expanding a small business. In fiscal year 2010, nearly fifty-three thousand loans worth a total of $12.6 billion were made through the 7(a) program, averaging almost $239,000 per loan.

The 7(a) program also works through several subprograms designed for specific purposes. These include special purpose loans (e.g., the Community Adjustment and Investment Program to help U.S. firms in areas negatively affected by the North American Free Trade Agreement); express and pilot programs (targeting active-duty military personnel, veterans, and borrowers from distressed communities); export loan programs (to help develop and expand small export businesses); rural business loans (to streamline lending application processes for small community and/or rural-based lenders); and loan advantage initiatives (including the Small Loan Advantage Program and the new Community Advantage Initiative, which encourages larger SBA lenders to make loans in underserved markets).

The SBA's Microloan Program facilitates small, short-term loans of up to $50,000 through designated nonprofit, community-based organizations.

These organizations also offer business training and technical assistance to entrepreneurs. Microloans can be used for items such as working capital, inventory, supplies, furniture and fixtures, and machinery and equipment, but they cannot be used to pay existing debt. The average microloan is about $13,000.

The Community Development Company/504 Program represents another major SBA financial program. The SBA works with community development companies (CDCs, private nonprofit corporations contributing to economic development within their communities) and private-sector lenders to facilitate small ventures with long-term, fixed-rate loans to acquire major fixed assets (e.g., land) for expansion, modernization, or improvements. The maximum SBA guarantees on CDC/504 loans vary according to the expected outcomes. For example, the loan's debenture runs up to $1.5 million for small firms expected to create or retain one job for every $65,000 provided by the SBA or to meet a community development goal. It rises to $2 million for small businesses projected to meet a public policy benchmark, such as the expansion of minority firm development or business district revitalization. And the SBA guarantees up to $4 million in loans to small manufacturers expected to generate or keep one job (or improve the local economy) per $100,000 in SBA-guaranteed loans.

Beyond financial programs, the SBA has other programs to assist small businesses. For example, the SBA's 8(a) Business Development Program (named after section 8(a) of the Small Business Act) was created to enhance the competitiveness of small and disadvantaged entrepreneurial entities. Administered by the SBA district offices, this nine-year program provides access to federal and private procurement markets and offers financial training, managerial development, and technical assistance to small businesses "unconditionally owned and controlled by one or more socially and economically disadvantaged individuals who are of good character and citizens of the United States, and which demonstrates potential for success."

The Minority Business Development Agency.   The Minority Business Development Agency (MBDA), part of the U.S. Department of Commerce, is "an entrepreneurially focused organization committed to wealth creation in minority communities." It has as its mission "to foster the growth and global competitiveness" of minority-owned businesses, regardless of their size. President Richard Nixon initially established the MBDA as the Office of Minority

Business Enterprise (OMBE) in 1969 through Executive Order 11458; the name was changed to the MBDA in 1979.

In 1971, President Nixon expanded the OMBE through Executive Order 11625, which authorized the awarding of grants to public and private organizations to provide technical and management assistance to minority-owned enterprises. The OMBE established a national network in 1973 consisting of business development organizations providing seed funding to numerous minority advocacy organizations, including the National Minority Purchasing Council (now the National Minority Supplier Development Council), the Hispanic Chamber of Commerce, and the National Council of La Raza. Through Executive Order 12432, President Ronald Reagan gave the U.S. Department of Commerce and the SBA the authority to administer the establishment and preservation of federal minority business programs.

As with the SBA, the MBDA does not provide loans or grants directly to businesses. Instead, it generates grants to fund its national network of public and private (both for-profit and nonprofit) organizations, including its Minority Business Enterprise Centers (MBECs, which give financial counseling, procurement matching, and managerial and technical assistance to minority-owned firms), Native American Business Enterprise Centers (NABECs, to assist Native American firms and tribal entities), and Minority Business Opportunity Centers (MBOCs, which facilitate brokerage services, and contract and financial transactions between minority-owned businesses and public and private organizations). It should also be noted that the MBDA analyzes and disseminates information about the characteristics of minority-owned businesses, along with their challenges and opportunities, to government agencies and the general public. In fiscal year 2010, the average annual funding was $260,000 for MBECs, $219,000 for NABECs, and $219,000 for MBOCs.

The Small Socially Disadvantaged Producer Grants Program.   The program Small Socially Disadvantaged Producer Grants (SSDPG, previously called the Small Minority Producer Grant) is housed in the U.S. Department of Agriculture's Rural Development Office. This program awards competitive grants of up to $200,000. To be eligible, cooperatives and associations of cooperatives must provide a variety of financial, managerial, and technical training assistance opportunities to small and socially disadvantaged agricultural producers. Associations and cooperatives potentially qualify for grants if at least 75 percent of their membership or government boards contain small, socially disadvantaged producers. The SSDPG budget in fiscal year 2010 was approximately $3.5 million.

Private Programs Assisting Small Businesses and Minority Entrepreneurs

Beyond the public sector, a variety of national, state, and local programs exist in the private sector to help small businesses and minority entrepreneurs. The following represent some of the more visible programs in this regard.

The U.S. Hispanic Chamber of Commerce.   The U.S. Hispanic Chamber of Commerce (USHCC) is the top grassroots effort to help Hispanic entrepreneurs. As a nonprofit organization, its mission is "to foster Hispanic economic development and to create sustainable prosperity for the benefit of American society."

The USHCC was incorporated in 1979 in New Mexico after several Hispanic leaders realized that a national organization should represent the Hispanic business community in the public and private sectors, and provide a cohesive voice to strengthen the Hispanic community. Currently, the USHCC membership includes more than two hundred local Hispanic chambers of commerce, in addition to professional trade associations and business networks. The USHCC connects local Hispanic chambers and associations with Fortune 500 companies and other corporate partners for networking and procurement through its certification and education programs. The USHCC also provides technical support, leadership and management, and consulting services in business development for Hispanic entrepreneurs, and it serves as their advocate in domestic politics, trade policies (particularly between the United States and Latin America), and corporate partnerships.

Numerous examples can be found regarding its advocacy role. For example, the USHCC in the 1990s was in favor of the passage of the North American Free Trade Agreement. As reported in a June 11, 1993, *Dallas Morning News* article, and as highlighted in a September 21, 1999, *Wall Street Journal* article, it has campaigned against some large-business interests that argued for the loosening of rules on the definition of minority-owned businesses. More recently, because of concerns over how labor costs affect Hispanic entrepreneurs, the USHCC has argued against more restrictive immigration reform, as a *Washington Times* article from April 5, 2006, discussed.

National Minority Supplier Development Council.   The National Minority Supplier Development Council (NMSDC) has as its mission to "provide a direct link between corporate America and minority-owned businesses." Its foundations started in 1968, when the Chicago Association of Commerce and Industry, the Chicago Economic Development Corporation, and the Chicago Urban League partnered to introduce that city's first showcase of minority business opportunity, and the following year it was incorporated into the Chicago Business Opportunity Fair, which attracted six hundred representatives of minority-owned businesses and two hundred representatives of large Chicago firms. Other cities followed Chicago's lead and began hosting events to showcase their minority entrepreneurs. Given the apparent demand to coordinate such efforts nationally, a group of Chicago-based companies organized the National Minority Purchasing Council in 1972, which was incorporated in 1973. Its name was later changed to the National Minority Supplier Development Council.

A year after its incorporation, the U.S. Department of Commerce's Office of Minority Business Enterprise (see the Minority Business Development Agency in the previous section) contracted with the NMSDC to promote minority business development in the private sector. The government contract was renewed through 1987, but soon afterward, the NMSDC felt it had enough support from the private sector to discontinue receiving government funding. The NMSDC now certifies and matches more than 16,000 minority-owned businesses with the 3,500 corporate members in its network (including most Fortune 500 companies). In 2009, these corporate members purchased more than $101.1 billion worth of goods and services from minority-owned firms.

The NMSDC also has a nonprofit financial services program—the Business Consortium Fund (BCF)—which provides access to capital exclusively to NMSDC certified minority-owned businesses that have supplier or vendor relationships with the NMSDC's corporate members and are experiencing difficulty obtaining financing through conventional means. In addition to having a loan guaranty and loan participation program, the BCF facilitates access to credit through its strategic alliances with other national financial services firms (e.g., for equipment leasing or franchise financing).

The National Urban League's Entrepreneurship and Business Development.   The National Urban League—a civil rights organization founded in 1910—has as its goal "economic empowerment in order to elevate the standard of living in historically underserved urban communities." Consistent with this goal, the Entrepreneurship and Business Development (EBD) division works to foster "social entrepreneurship" by providing minority-owned businesses with financial investment, training, and corporate networking. As reported in a November 8, 2005, article in *USA Today*, the head of the National Urban League's Orlando affiliate, Lance McCarthy, stated that advocating, providing services, and engaging in business development "is the civil rights movement of the 21st century."

The EBD's signature program is the Entrepreneurship Center Program, which provides mentorship, counseling, and management and technical assistance to enhance entrepreneurs' access to credit and contracts that support job creation and preservation, their competitiveness, and their ability to enter new markets. This program also has a goal of increasing the number (and survival rates) of minority-owned businesses. In 2010, the services provided by these centers helped entrepreneurs obtain $20.19 million in new bonding, contracts, and financing.

ACCION USA.   ACCION USA (an affiliate of ACCION International, a global microfinance organization) was established in 1991 and has as its mission the empowerment of low- to moderate-income microentrepreneurs by providing access to capital, financial education, and business training and mentoring. It specializes in working with small business owners who are unable to access credit from traditional sources because of firm type, a short time in business, or insufficient credit history. Because of its targeted audience, minorities, immigrants, and women tend to be overrepresented among its customers. In fact, at the time this chapter was written, Hispanics represented 61 percent, and African Americans, 27 percent, of ACCION USA's active clients.

ACCION USA offers entrepreneurs loans ranging from $500 to $50,000 at competitive interest rates. In 2009, it made a total of $4.3 million in loans, with the average loan size of slightly more than $5,000. Its three categories of small business loans include business loans (up to $50,000 for profitable, established businesses), start-up loans (up to $30,000 for businesses in operation for at least six months that are not yet profitable), and transition loans (up to $30,000 for the purchase or location change of businesses in operation for at least six months). In addition, it offers nonbusiness loans from $500 to $700 to help individuals build their credit scores, and it partners with government agencies (including the SBA), corporations, and small business organizations to help increase the credit access of microentrepreneurs.

Operation HOPE's Small Business Empowerment Program.   Operation HOPE, a nonprofit organization focused on expanding economic opportunity in underserved communities through economic education and empowerment, was founded by entrepreneur John Hope Bryant in reaction to the Rodney King riots in south-central Los Angeles in 1992.[4] It was the first nonprofit social investment banking organization in the United States, and it strives for so-called silver rights: "the right to financial literacy, access to capital, and equity of opportunity for the underserved."

The HOPE Financial Literacy Empowerment Centers (a network of community-based locations that provide financial resources, literacy, and counseling to people in underserved neighborhoods) represent a major component of Operation HOPE. Under these centers is the Small Business Empowerment Program, designed for aspiring entrepreneurs from low-wealth areas. In addition to offering financial education, business training, and technical assistance, this program facilitates entrepreneurs' access to credit through its network of direct lenders, loan-packaging assistance, SBA loan program commercial financing, and lines of credit.

The National Minority Business Council.   The nonprofit National Minority Business Council (NMBC), located in New York City, was founded in 1972 to provide education and training, advocacy, and business opportunities and assistance to small, minority, and female business owners. In 2008, it began hosting its Entrepreneurship Boot Camp to assist small business owners in developing their firms, as well as to help aspiring entrepreneurs move from the paid-employment sector into self-employment. Although it does receive some public and private assistance, it is largely funded by its membership dues.

California Association for Micro Enterprise Opportunity.   An example of a state program, the California Association for Micro Enterprise Opportunity (CAMEO) is a network of microbusiness assistance programs; it has as its mission "to create jobs and to promote economic opportunity and community well-being." CAMEO started in the early 1990s when four advocates for low-income women (Mimi Van Sickle, Sheilah Rogers, Debi Clifford, and Forescee Hogan-Rowles) felt that public policy was inadequate for the needs of their clients. In addition to advocacy, CAMEO seeks to facilitate micro-enterprises (mostly businesses with up to five employees, requiring less than $50,000 in start-up costs) with access to credit, technical assistance, and managerial training. In 2010, through its members, CAMEO served twenty-two thousand microenterprises in the state, which generated thirty-eight thousand jobs.

New York Business Development Corporation.   Another state program is the New York Business Development Corporation (NYBDC), which the New York State Legislature created in 1955. It works with its lending partners to provide loans to small firms in New York, many of which would not qualify for traditional financing. The NYBDC attempts "to be more creative" in its underwriting, such as using multiple participations, SBA guarantees, flexible amortization, and long-term payouts. Its loans are generally disbursed in amounts up to $2 million and are secured by borrowers' assets and, in some cases, by the SBA. In fiscal year 2010, loans approved through the NYBDC were worth a total of $233.6 million.

The NYBDC also runs the Empire State Certified Development Corporation, which is licensed to provide an SBA 504 loan program (described above) for eligible small ventures in New York. Moreover, it manages the operations of the Statewide Zone Capital Corporation, which is a privately owned loan and investment fund that promotes the expansion of new and existing businesses in participating areas of the state. The NYBDC participates in business seminars and conferences for minority-owned businesses, and it reaches out to community organizations to help identify (and work with) potential borrowers to assist these entrepreneurs in meeting their credit needs. The NYBDC also has a microloan program (which places priority on minority- and female-owned businesses), and it provides credit-scoring alternatives for smaller loan requests.

9 In Closing

W E REPORT IN THIS BOOK THAT HISPANIC POPULATION growth was the catalyst for the sharp increase in the number of Hispanic business owners in the 2000s. However, upon closer examination of the self-employed within this group, the disproportionate growth of Hispanic business owners also came from strengthening entrepreneurial tendencies within the Hispanic population. That said, the first ten years of the new millennium witnessed historically sharp variations in the business cycle that challenged Hispanic entrepreneurs. Our findings suggest that the Great Recession disproportionately and negatively affected the Hispanic workforce. An outcome of the business cycle of the 2000s was a rapidly growing population of Hispanic microenterprises and an increase in smaller-scale Hispanic-owned businesses.

In this book, we pay some attention to the case of the construction sector as a source of Hispanic entrepreneurship during the period under study. Indeed, we suggest that the housing market appears to have been a stronger predictor of Hispanic entrepreneurship than overall economic growth. We also considered geography as a predictor of Hispanic self-employment trends and found that while Hispanic entrepreneurial activities strengthened in all regions of the United States in the 2000s, the intensity appears to have been sensitive to particular geographic areas.

One result (among many) that we found of interest regarding the importance of the construction and professional services sectors was the similarity of the industries in which Mexican American, Cuban, and Salvadoran entre-preneurs worked over the period. In general, the distributions of the major industry classifications were quite similar between self-employed Mexican Americans and Cubans.

In the first decade of the 2000s, self-employment provided an increas-ingly important means for Hispanic workers to earn a living. While Hispanic entrepreneurs earned less on average than their counterparts in the paid-employment sector, we estimate that they fared relatively better than non-Hispanic workers when controlling for observable characteristics (e.g., educa-tion, experience, industry, geographic region) related to labor-market income. The apparent relative earnings advantage of self-employed Hispanics versus non-Hispanics could partly explain the intensifying entrepreneurial tenden-cies of Hispanics in the decade.

Our results, however, indicate that changes in the relative earnings of self-employed Hispanics during the 2000s appeared, not surprisingly, sensi-tive to macroeconomic conditions, which likely affected the reasons work-ers joined the entrepreneurial sector. We note that a decline in the relative observable characteristics of self-employed Hispanics should have dampened their relative earnings between 2002 and 2007. However, this potential nega-tive earnings effect was offset by improvements in the levels of unobservable characteristics among Hispanic entrepreneurs during the time, which indi-cates the presence of pull factors related to Hispanics' rising self-employment rates before the Great Recession. During the recession, however, our findings further suggest that Hispanic self-employment rates continued to rise because many sought self-employment as a means to avoid unemployment. This push into self-employment seemed to lower the average quality of Hispanic entre-preneurs in terms of both observable and unobservable characteristics, thus reducing their relative earnings in the self-employment sector.

We also find that the entrepreneurial tendencies of foreign-born Hispan-ics appeared more sensitive to ethnic enclaves than those of Hispanic U.S. natives, even when accounting for other characteristics, such as education, which can influence self-employment probabilities. However, the Great Reces-sion appeared to have reduced some of the enclave advantages that immigrant entrepreneurs encountered. We also surveyed some of the academic litera-ture that focuses on labor-market outcomes of foreign-born versus U.S.-born workers, including the hotly debated issue of immigrant "quality" in terms of how it pertains to entrepreneurship. Our analyses of Hispanic-immigrant cohorts living in the United States in 2002 provide provocative evidence of higher entrepreneurial quality among Hispanic immigrants (particularly among non-Cubans) than among native-born Hispanics.

Several interesting features surfaced regarding our results in testing the relationship between education and the earnings of Hispanic entrepreneurs. We found that the returns to schooling were highest for Hispanics located in the top 10 percent of the earnings distribution, with little difference across the decade among entrepreneurs. This finding indicates that education mattered the most (and in a consistent manner) for the wealthiest of the entrepreneurs. With the exception of the self-employed in 2002, the returns to education for Hispanic workers consecutively rose with each earnings decile, again suggesting that formal schooling played a larger role in labor-market income as workers advanced in the earnings distribution. The returns to schooling among self-employed Hispanic immigrants fell between 2002 and 2007 for those with earnings in all but two of the deciles, and they continued to fall across all deciles except for one by 2010. Finally, in terms of education as a catalyst for Hispanic entrepreneurship, we found changes in the relative education levels of new versus longer-term Hispanic entrepreneurs to be evidence that the Great Recession served to disproportionately push less educated Hispanics into self-employment.

Our gender-related earnings analyses of Hispanic business owners suggest that there was a relative decline in both groups' entrepreneurial quality as a result of the Great Recession. As we discuss in this book, this impact on entrepreneurial quality conceptually emanates from displaced workers being pushed into self-employment. In the case of self-employed men during this period, this explanation follows from their increasing self-employment rates in the 2000s. And while over this decade we found evidence of pull effects for these groups, the Great Recession seemingly restored some of the previous self-employment push conditions for both female and male Hispanics, as their returns to education fell in the entrepreneurial sector in 2010. This was not the case for Hispanic men and women in the paid-employment sector (who had higher schooling returns at the end of the decade than at the beginning). These findings illustrate the complex nature of the effect of schooling on entrepreneurial earnings.

The association between education and Hispanic-immigrant entrepreneurship points to some potential policies and strategic remedies. Policies designed to improve the educational outcomes and English-language profi-

ciency of Hispanic immigrants might affect the subsequent success of Hispanic entrepreneurs in terms of earnings and job creation, given how these
skills enhance strategic planning, access to credit, and apparently the use of
information technology. Another issue is whether existing policies and programs aimed at helping small businesses grow can be improved to assist newly
formed Hispanic-owned microbusinesses.[1] Finally, immigration policies,
such as the EB-5 program (the immigration provision that allows immigrants
who start businesses in the United States a path to U.S. citizenship), might
consider the importance of foreign-born Hispanic entrepreneurs to job creation (and generation of income and tax revenue) nationally and at the local
level.

Our conceptual framework of the credit-access barriers that Hispanic entrepreneurs face suggests potential discrimination by creditors as a possible
explanation for the results. However, closer inspection of the reasons for loan
rejections (at least from the perspective of survey respondents) shows that
expected racial or ethnic discrimination did not deter Hispanic entrepreneurs
from participating in formal credit markets. Instead, they appeared more
concerned about their creditworthiness. An alternative explanation for our
findings relates to cultural forces: Hispanics seem to be relatively conservative
in their credit needs and less likely to use traditional methods of financing,
such as borrowing from banks and other financial institutions.

In terms of how Hispanic entrepreneurs have fared with respect to access
to physical capital, we uncover mixed evidence. On the one hand, Hispanic-
owned businesses were less likely to be digitally connected than other firms
in the SBO PUMS. However, using the SSBF, we found similar rates of technology usage between Hispanic- and non-Hispanic-owned small businesses
in the mid-2000s, which was not the case five years earlier. We also estimate
from the SSBF that Hispanic-owned small firms utilizing digital technology
had a significant advantage over other small businesses with respect to sales
and profit benchmarks in the mid-2000s, but this is not supported in the SBO.
Perhaps the difference in these findings reflects that the firms constituting the
SSBF sample are relatively more mature (as argued by Timothy Bates in 2011).

That said, in light of the growing presence of Hispanics in the United
States, understanding factors that affect the success of Hispanic enterprises
has become a topic of national interest, particularly during a time such as
the Great Recession. With technological advancements likely to continue to
surge, our results suggest that the rate at which Hispanic entrepreneurs (and

other small firm owners) integrate such technology into routine business operations has real implications for their success. To be sure, programs designed to help Hispanic entrepreneurs utilize new technology abound, including the technology center established by the St. Louis Hispanic Chamber of Commerce, which offers services in both English and Spanish (as reported in a November 14, 2004, *St. Louis-Post Dispatch* article, by Shera Dalin).

Chapter 8 reports several findings and policy recommendations to improve the standing of Hispanic and minority entrepreneurs. In addition to defining a small business, a related issue is how to define a minority-owned business. Public and private organizations (some of which are described in the appendix to Chapter 8) have tended to identify minority-owned businesses as those with at least 51 percent minority ownership, a standard set by Congress in 1978. Yet in 1999, the National Minority Supplier Development Council loosened the definition to include firms with at least 30 percent minority ownership, which generated considerable controversy. This new measure allowed previously ineligible firms to become eligible for public and private contracts, as well as government procurement programs, designed for minority entrepreneurs. Large businesses had argued that the old standards discouraged minority-owned businesses from taking on more investors and raising equity in order to keep their "minority-owned" status. Government and corporations purchasing goods and services from minority businesses were also able to have a larger pool from which to choose suppliers.

However, businesses (and their advocates) that could be classified under the old standards as "minority owned" campaigned heavily against relaxing the standards. For example, the National Minority Business Council said that non-minority-owned businesses would have an easier time creating "front companies" to pose as minority firms, in order to increase their access to public and private programs designed for minority entrepreneurs. The U.S. Hispanic Chamber of Commerce also claimed that the new standard would mean that larger companies could obtain corporate contracts at the expense of small businesses. The Small Business Administration (SBA) spoke out against the 30 percent standard. The National Minority Supplier Development Council has since returned to the 51 percent threshold.

Also, in recent years the SBA has been criticized for its delay in releasing information, such as eligibility criteria, for a new lending program (which will be part of its CDC/504 loan portfolio, described in the Chapter 8 appendix), designed to help small businesses refinance mortgages on their buildings.

Congress set an expiration date for the program of two years, but with delays in releasing the program's details, few existing small businesses will be able to benefit from the program.

We close with three general observations. First, our findings support the perspective in existing scholarship that human capital (e.g., education), financial capital (e.g., credit), and physical capital (e.g., equipment, including computers) are at the heart of business success. To the extent that minority entrepreneurs are at a disadvantage in these factors, their business outcomes will suffer relative to those of their majority counterparts. This perspective, mostly from the labor economics literature, begs the question as to why these differentials, particularly in human and physical capital, exist to begin with. From a sociological point of view, context trumps individual characteristics in explaining differentials in business outcomes between minority and majority entrepreneurs. For example, some socialists, including Zulema Valdez, believe that societal "systems of oppression" are the root cause of the relatively low business outcomes of minorities. This type of modeling helps inform on issues of intersectionality and, more broadly, on the importance of refining demographic groups along the lines of gender, class, and race. It also questions the argument that market and political contexts make this assumption untenable (at least in the long run). Conceptual insights into the competing (or complementary, according to Timothy Bates) perspectives between labor economists and sociologists can be found in the new field of stratification economics and particularly in some of the recent research by William Darity Jr. (such as his 2005 study) and his colleagues.

Second, from a behavioral social-science perspective, the role of preferences for self-employment should not be ignored. Neoclassical microeconomic theory assumes that individuals maximize utility and not income. As such, much of what we find here could be explained by different preferences for self-employment across groups. The data we use in this book, however, do not allow us to test for this proposition, although we discuss the issue of preference in the chapter on credit access (Chapter 6). However, some recent studies acknowledge the importance of preferences and business outcomes among minority groups. For example, Vicki Bogan and William Darity Jr., in a 2008 paper, review (and offer a critique) of some of the earlier work on the relationship between African American "cultural values" and African Americans' entrepreneurial activity. Also, in a 2009 article, Robert Fairlie and Alicia Robb, using a confidential Bureau of Labor Statistics data set on entrepreneurs' motivation for owning a business, found some (small) differences in preferences for self-employment across gender.

Finally, many of our findings indicate that Hispanic-owned businesses tend to be smaller than other firms along several dimensions, including sales and numbers of paid employees. With that said, the economic impact of these firms should not be underestimated. As we discuss in this book, the 2.3 million businesses owned by Hispanic entrepreneurs in 2007 generated employment beyond the jobs these entrepreneurs created for themselves. Their economic activities also contribute to federal, state, and local government coffers; indeed, we estimate that in 2007, Hispanic-owned businesses generated more than $20 billion in state sales-tax revenue alone, a figure that does not include their contributions to other tax revenues, such as local sales taxes, income and payroll taxes, and corporate income taxes.

With these closing statements (and throughout this book), we hope to have captured a flavor of issues related to the business cycle, economic outcomes, sociodemographic characteristics, access to financial and physical capital, and policy and conceptual issues that Hispanic business owners faced in the first decade of this millennium. This decade witnessed dramatic growth in the Hispanic population and the intensification of entrepreneurial tendencies among Hispanics. If these demographic changes continue as the 2000s unfold, Hispanic entrepreneurship will become an increasingly vital component of American job creation and the economic direction of the nation.

TECHNICAL APPENDIXES

Appendix A: Major Data Sets Used and Construction of Key Variables

American Community Survey

The American Community Survey (ACS), a random nationally representative sample of the U.S. population, has been conducted annually by the U.S. Census Bureau since 2000. We focus on the 2001–10 surveys contained in the Integrated Public Use Microdata Series (IPUMS, as described later in this appendix). Starting with 2005, the ACS samples contain approximately 1 percent of the U.S. population. The pre-2005 ACS samples are smaller in size (containing one out of every 232 people in the United States in 2001, one of 261 people in 2002, one of 236 people in 2003, and one of 232 people in 2004).

Sample Selection Criteria. Our ACS samples include workers (identified as those reporting a specific "worker classification") between the ages of twenty-five and sixty-four who were not residing in group quarters at the time of the survey. We exclude group-quarter residents for consistency across the years; the ACS excludes them altogether in surveys before 2006. We identify the self-employed as those individuals who reported working for their own enterprises in the worker classification variable. For individuals with multiple employment sources, the worker classification refers to where the individual spent the most time during the reference day or week. To maintain the national representation of the samples, we employ the sampling weights (constructed by the U.S. Census Bureau) in all analyses.

Our sample sizes of self-employed Hispanics in 2002, 2007, and 2010 are as follows: 3,185 (representing 1.19 million), 13,388 (representing 1.61 million), and 14,457 (representing 1.72 million), respectively. Our samples of other Hispanics workers in these years include the following: 34,480 (representing 13.36 million), 125,199 (representing 15.97 million), and 135,779 (representing 16.76 million). The sample sizes used in the analyses for other years, as well as for non-Hispanics, can be obtained from the authors.

In our analyses of earnings (Chapters 2–5), we further restrict the sample to those individuals who worked at some point in the previous twelve months. In the ACS, these earnings refer to the pretax amount the individual earned through wages, salaries, commissions, tips, and business income during the twelve months before the survey. Self-employment income excludes business expenses.

Identification of Specific Hispanic Groups.   We identify immigrants as those individuals who were born outside of the United States and its territories. However, we identify the ethnic subgroups using the self-reported Hispanic classifications provided in the IPUMS. Consequently, our Hispanic-immigrant sample contains a small share of Puerto Ricans—individuals who reported Puerto Rican ethnicity but were born outside of the United States, Puerto Rico, or another U.S. territory. For example, Puerto Ricans represented 0.3 percent of self-employed Hispanic immigrants in our 2010 sample.

Industry Variables.   In our industry analyses using the ACS and PUMS, we consider fifteen categories of nonmilitary industries: agriculture (which includes fishing, forestry, and hunting); arts and entertainment (which includes recreation, accommodations, and food services); construction; education, health care, and social services (referred to here as education and health-care services); finance, insurance, real estate, and rental and leasing; information and communications; manufacturing; mining; personal services; professional and managerial services (which includes scientific, administrative, and waste management services); public administration (in which there was only one self-employed worker in the 2010 sample); religious and civic services (which includes labor unions and political organizations); transportation and warehousing; utilities (in which there were no self-employed workers); and wholesale and retail trade (referred to as trade).

Measuring Hispanic Concentration. We obtained the Hispanic concentration measure (discussed in Chapter 3) by dividing the estimated number of Hispanics (regardless of age, work status, or group-quarter residence) by all individuals in the metropolitan area. This measure equals zero for individuals who resided outside of metropolitan areas.

Fractionalized Generations of Immigrants and Education Acquired Abroad. To determine where immigrants acquired their schooling (discussed in Chapter 4), we assumed that immigrants who arrived to the United States by the age of five completed all of their schooling in the United States; this group constituted Generation 1.75. Those who migrated after the age of five but before they completed their schooling—based on comparing the estimated age when the immigrant completed his or her schooling (education plus five) with his or her estimated age at arrival in the United States (age minus years in the United States)—represent Generation 1.5. We use this information to estimate the years of schooling immigrants acquired abroad versus in the United States.

Current Population Survey

The Current Population Survey (CPS) is a monthly household survey conducted jointly by the U.S. Census Bureau and the Bureau of Labor Statistics (BLS). We focus on the March surveys in the Integrated Public Microdata Series—CPS (which currently contains monthly surveys between 1998 and 2008, as well as the March surveys between 1962 and 2011). These data can be downloaded free of charge from the University of Minnesota Population Research Center, at http://cps.ipums.org/cps/. The March surveys contain supplemental information on income and other socioeconomic and demographic items. Our CPS samples (based on the March supplements) include workers, identified as those reporting a specific "worker classification." We employ the appropriate sampling weights in all analyses.

The CPS samples are considerably smaller than the ACS and PUMS (both of which are also described in this appendix). For example, our 2010 CPS sample includes 1,143 self-employed Hispanics (representing 1.52 million) and 12,604 other Hispanic workers (representing 16.73 million). However, only the CPS provides individuals' primary labor-market activities at the time of the survey and in the previous calendar year. For current labor-market activities, workers with more than one job are classified on the basis of the job in which they work the most hours per week. Individuals not employed at the time of the survey reported information for their most recent job. Because the CPS contains the number of employees (on a categorical basis) who worked for respondents' employers in the previous calendar year, as well as the estimated income taxes paid, we identify the self-employed through the worker classification pertaining to the previous year when analyzing microentrepreneurship and income taxes (in Chapters 1, 5, and 8). For individuals with multiple employment sources, this classification refers to the longest job held in the previous year.

Identifying the Newly Self-Employed.   When analyzing the newly self-employed in Chapters 2, 4, and 5, we identify workers between the ages of twenty-five and sixty-four who were not self-employed in the previous year but were at the current time of the survey. Admittedly, this information is not perfect, because some individuals not listed as self-employed in the previous year might have been for part of the time, as the CPS classifies the previous year's activities on the basis of the position individuals held the longest if they had multiple employment sources. Nevertheless, while we cannot determine the extent to which this occurred, we suspect that such individuals did not represent the norm.

Industries in the CPS.   Given the smaller sample size of the CPS versus the PUMS and ACS, we use a smaller set of industries in our CPS analyses than with the latter. In particular, when analyzing the likelihood of becoming self-employed during the previous year, we consider seven categories of nonmilitary industries: education, health care, managerial, professional, and social services; finance, insurance, real estate, and rental and leasing; manufacturing; other services (including personal services, public administration, and religious and civic services); transportation and warehousing; wholesale and retail trade (referred to as trade); and construction and "other" (with "other" containing industries with very few observations in the sample of newly self-employed Hispanics).

Income-Tax Estimates.   The CPS-IPUMS provides estimated tax-credit-adjusted federal and state income taxes paid in the previous year, as well as FICA taxes, constructed on the basis of an individual's income. We use this information to generate the average (and aggregated) income taxes paid by

Hispanics who were self-employed in the previous year. For example, our estimates for the income and FICA taxes paid in 2007 (or 2010) came from the 2008 (or 2011) CPS. For these estimates, we do not restrict the sample by age.

Integrated Public Use Microdata Series

The Integrated Public Use Microdata Series (IPUMS), a project of the Minnesota Population Center at the University of Minnesota, collects and disseminates U.S. census data for social and economic research. The current version, provided by Steven Ruggles and his colleagues, includes microdata from the American Community Survey (described earlier in this appendix), the Public Use Microdata Samples (PUMS) from the 1980–2000 decennial censuses (described later in this appendix), and other decennial census data going back to 1850. These data can be downloaded free of charge from the IPUMS website at http://www.ipums.org.

Integrated Public Use Microdata Series, International

The Integrated Public Use Microdata Series, International (IPUMS International) is a project of the Minnesota Population Center at the University of Minnesota. It was designed to collect and disseminate census microdata from around the world for social and economic research. As of June 2012, this data set included 211 censuses from sixty-eight countries. The data can be downloaded free of charge from the IPUMS website at http://www.ipums.org. We use the most recent data for Mexico (2010), Cuba (2002), and El Salvador (2007) to estimate the shares of the population between the ages of twenty-five and sixty-four in each country who had different levels of education. We exclude individuals who had missing information on their educational attainment.

Public Use Microdata Sample from the 2000 Decennial Census

The Public Use Microdata Sample (PUMS) from the 2000 decennial census is a nationally representative sample based on the long-form census questionnaire given to one of every six households. We focus on the 1 percent sample available in the IPUMS (mentioned earlier in this appendix), which contains approximately 1 percent of the U.S. population in 2000, and we employ the sampling weights (constructed by the Census Bureau) to maintain the national representation of the sample. We use the same sample restrictions and variable definitions as for the ACS.

Survey of Business Owners

The U.S. Census Bureau conducts the Survey of Business Owners (SBO) as part of its required economic census every five years. The Census Bureau combines data from the SBO with data from other surveys, censuses, and administrative records. The publicly available data (published on the Census Bureau's website at http://www.census.gov/econ/sbo/index.html) include summary statistics on the composition of businesses in the United States by demographic and economic characteristics, including ethnicity, race, gender, and veteran status, among other traits. The SBO identifies Hispanic-owned firms as those in which more than 50 percent of the owners are Hispanic.

The 2002 and 2007 SBO questionnaires were mailed to a random sample of businesses selected from a list of all firms in operation in 2002 or 2007 with receipts of $1,000 or more. The firms on this list were identified using a combination of business tax returns for all companies reporting business activities on certain Internal Revenue Service tax forms—including the 1040 Schedule C (Profit or Loss from Business), 1065 (U.S. Return of Partnership Income), any of the 1120 corporation tax forms, 941 (Employer's Quarterly Federal Tax Return), and 944 (Employer's Annual Federal Tax Return—as well as from data collected from other economic census reports. The list excluded the industries of crop and animal production; scheduled passenger air transportation; rail transportation; the postal service; funds, trusts, and other financial vehicles; religious, grant-making, civic, professional, and similar organizations; private households; and public administration.

Survey of Business Owners Public Use Microdata Sample

The Public Use Microdata Sample of the Survey of Business Owners (SBO PUMS) was created by the U.S. Census Bureau using responses from the 2007 SBO (described earlier in this appendix), which provides access to survey microdata. The full version of the SBO PUMS contains 155,968

Hispanic-owned firms, which we define using the SBO's measure (firms with Hispanics owning more than 50 percent of the company, and more than 2 million non-Hispanic owned firms; these represented 2.26 million and 24.13 million companies, respectively. Of these, 84,543 Hispanic-owned firms (representing 1.1 million) and almost 1.46 million non-Hispanic-owned firms (representing nearly 17 million) have detailed information on owner- and firm-level characteristics besides basic demographic features. These data can be downloaded free of charge from the U.S. Census Bureau at http://www .census.gov/econ/sbo/pums.html. All of our analyses employ the sampling weights provided by the SBO. Moreover, because of the SBO PUMS's sampling design, we employ random groups variance estimation throughout our empirical exercises when testing for statistical significance. For more information on random groups variance estimators, see the studies by Stanislav Kolenikov (2010), K. Wolter (2007), and Jun Shao (1996).

Sales—Natural Logarithmic Issue. The SBO PUMS provides sales information in $10,000 increments, such that firms with less than $5,000 in sales (which represented one-fifth of all the firms in the SBO), are coded as having $0 in revenue. To avoid dropping these firms from the sample when analyzing the natural logarithm of sales, we use the natural logarithm of $1,400—a figure that approximated the average sales of firms with less than $5,000 in revenue based on the 2003 Survey of Small Business Finances (described later in this appendix). When setting this group's revenue equal to $1 (instead of $1,400), however, many of the results discussed in this book remain unchanged.

Immigrant Versus U.S. Native Owners. The SBO PUMS reports information on the birthplace of the owners for only a subset of firms, which include 35,388 firms owned by Hispanic immigrants and 30,103 owned by Hispanic U.S. natives. When directly comparing businesses with U.S.- versus foreign-born owners, we focus only on this subset.

Industry Variables. In our analyses considering industries in the SBO PUMS, we identify twelve categories: agriculture (which includes fishing, forestry, and hunting); arts, recreation, and entertainment (which includes accommodations and food services); construction; education, health care, and social services (referred to as education and health-care services); finance, insurance, and real estate (FIRE, which includes rental and leasing);

information and communications; manufacturing; mining and utilities; professional and managerial services (which includes scientific, administrative, and waste management services); transportation and warehousing; wholesale and retail trade (referred to as trade); and "other services" (a composite group of industries not belonging to the ones already mentioned).

State Sales-Tax Estimates.   In various chapters, we discuss estimates of the state sales-tax revenue generated by Hispanic-owned businesses using the SBO PUMS. In most cases, we multiplied the 2007 state sales tax to our estimates of the total sales and receipts generated by Hispanic-owned businesses in a given state. However, the SBO PUMS does not uniquely identify seven states plus the District of Columbia (DC) because of small population sizes; instead, these are clustered into four groups: (1) Alaska and Wyoming; (2) Delaware and DC; (3) North Dakota and South Dakota; and (4) Rhode Island and Vermont. For these states, we first estimated the total sales and receipts of Hispanic-owned businesses for each of these groups. We then prorated these sales according to the distribution of self-employed Hispanics living in each state using our sample from the 2007 ACS (described earlier in this appendix) and multiplied them to the respective state sales tax. For example, for group 2, 43.53 percent of the self-employed Hispanics in our ACS sample resided in Delaware, and 56.47 percent were in DC in 2007. We therefore multiplied the Delaware sales tax to 43.53 percent of the total sales of Hispanic-owned businesses in group 2 and multiplied the DC sales tax to the remainder of group 2's sales of Hispanic-owned firms. Because we cannot identify the cities or counties in which the businesses were located, we cannot estimate the additional sales-tax revenue generated in areas with sales taxes above the state-tax rate.

Access to Financial Capital.   When discussing the shares of businesses reporting different sources of financial capital for start-up and expansion purposes (as in Chapters 6 and 8), we focus only on those firms that reported this information. The sample size of Hispanic-owned firms reporting their start-up capital sources (including those that did not need it) is 78,962; those reporting their expansionary capital sources (including those that did not need it) numbered 77,350.

Digital Technology Utilization.   In Chapter 7, when discussing digital technology, we focus only on those firms that reported whether they used this technology. The sample of Hispanic-owned firms in this discussion included 78,962 businesses.

Survey of Small Business Finances

Conducted by the Board of Governors of the Federal Reserve System between 1999 and 2000 (mostly in the second half of 1999) and 2004 and 2005 (mostly in the second half of 2004), the 1998 and 2003 versions of the Survey of Small Business Finances (SSBF) include nationally representative data on for-profit, nonfinancial, nonfarm, and nonsubsidiary business enterprises in the United States that had fewer than five hundred employees at the end of 1998 or 2003. These data can be downloaded free of charge from the Board of Governors' website at http://www.federalreserve.gov/Pubs/Oss/Oss3/nssbftoc.htm. Unfortunately, the SSBF has been discontinued, such that small business outcomes after the mid-2000s cannot be analyzed with later versions of this data set.

The SSBF data have been used in a variety of studies analyzing access to credit among small businesses (for recent overviews, see Timothy Bates' 2011 study and David Blanchflower's 2009 study). One of the drawbacks of these data, particularly when analyzing specific racial or ethnic groups, is the relatively small sample size. Of the 4,240 small firms included in the 2003 SSBF, 4,181 (representing 6.29 million small firms) had information on the racial or ethnic characteristics of the owners. The 1998 SSBF includes such information for the majority owners of all 3,561 firms in the sample (which represented more than 5.29 million small firms). To obtain a larger sample size of Hispanic-owned firms, we define them as firms in which at least half of the primary owners belonged to this ethnic group. This yields samples of 264 (representing 302,000 Hispanic-owned small firms) in the 1998 version and 170 (representing 300,000 of such firms) in the 2003 version. However, when re-estimating the empirical analyses on the basis of the SBO-definition of more than 50 percent Hispanic ownership, the results for the SSBF analyses change little from those reported in this book. In all of our analyses, we employ the appropriate sampling weights to preserve the national representation of the samples.

Readers should be cautioned that, despite the data being nationally representative, the small sample sizes of Hispanic-owned small firms are less than ideal. To illustrate, Bates notes in his 2011 study that the lack of consistent evidence on loan-rejection rates among Hispanic-owned small businesses could be due to the "smaller Hispanic SSBF sample sizes" (p. 218). Bates further mentions that because the firms in the sample "represent an older, more established, larger-scale subset of the nation's small business community," the SSBF is "not an appropriate database for investigating the credit access constraints facing young minority-owned businesses" (p. 219). These issues might explain why some of our results obtained using the SSBF do not always parallel our findings from the SBO.

At the same time, many researchers (including us) continue to use the SSBF because it contains richer information on small firms' balance sheets than other data sets. For our analysis in Chapter 7, moreover, we depend heavily on the SSBF because it includes more detailed information on technology utilization than the SBO PUMS. Another advantage with using the SSBF over other data sets is that changes in the access to financial and physical capital in the small business sector can be tracked over time.

Appendix B: Details Behind
the Empirical Analyses

Chapter 2—Earnings

Analyses of Sales Based on the SBO PUMS. To analyze whether the sales of Hispanic-owned businesses in 2007 differed from those of other firms when controlling for observable characteristics, we focus on the 84,543 Hispanic-owned businesses and 1.46 million other firms in the SBO PUMS that reported detailed demographic information. We first estimate the following using the method of ordinary least squares (OLS) for firms owned by non-Hispanics:

$$(1) \qquad ln(Sales) = f(Owner, Firm, Industry, Region),$$

where *ln(Sales)* represents the natural logarithm of annual sales. The *Owner* vector contains sets of binary variables identifying demographic and socio-economic characteristics of the majority of the owners, including race (black; Asian; Native American; and "other," the comparison group); birthplace (U.S. born [base], foreign born, and unknown), gender (female versus male), education (less than high school, high school diploma or equivalent but less than a four-year college degree [base], and four-year college degree or higher), and age [younger than thirty-five, thirty-five to fifty-four [base], and older than fifty-four). The *Firm* vector includes firm-level characteristics identified in the literature as predictors of business outcomes, such as the age of the firm measured by its time of establishment (before 1980, 1980s, 1990s, 2000–2, 2003–5, and 2006–7 [base]), and whether it was a home-based business. The vectors of *Industry* and *Region* include sets of binary variables identifying twelve different groups of industries (see the industries outlined in Appendix A under the SBO PUMS heading) and seven geographic regions (New England, North Central, Middle Atlantic, South Atlantic, South Central, Mountain, and Pacific [base]).

We then use these regression estimates to impute (predict) the sales of Hispanic-owned businesses, given their characteristics. The difference between their actual sales (in natural logarithms) and the predicted sales measures the revenue gap between Hispanic- and non-Hispanic-owned firms unexplained by their differences in observable characteristics.

Sales and Profits in the Mid-2000s Based on the SSBF. When analyzing whether Hispanic-owned small businesses differed from other firms with respect to their sales and profits in the mid-2000s while controlling for observable characteristics, we estimate the following using SSBF data.

(2) $$Outcome = f(Race/Ethnicity, X).$$

Race/Ethnicity is a vector containing binary variables indicating Hispanic, black, and Asian ownership of the firm (defined in terms of businesses with at least half of the owners from these groups), such that non-Hispanic-, non-black-, and non-Asian-owned (non-HBA-owned) firms represent the base comparison group. The vector X contains other characteristics identified in the literature as predictors of small firms' successes, including owner characteristics (gender, binary variables for education [less than high school, high school diploma or equivalent but less than a four-year college degree (base), and four-year college degree or higher], years of managerial experience, and experience squared), firm characteristics (age, age squared, industry [construction and manufacturing, transportation and trade, and other (base)], whether the firm was a sole proprietorship, binary variables for geographic region [North, West (base), and South], and whether the firm's headquarters were outside of a metropolitan statistical area), and a constant term.

We estimate Equation (2) utilizing the regression method of ordinary least squares for annual sales (in natural logarithms) and profits, and probit analysis for the likelihood that the firm had positive profits or had profits of $10,000 or more. Moreover, we reestimated Equation (2) while using the owner's age and age squared as regressors instead of managerial experience. The empirical results (available from the authors) change little from those reported in the chapter. Because of the correlation between the owner's age and experience, we do not include both variables together.

Self-Employment Earnings Penalties. For insight into self-employment earnings penalties, consider the following:

(3) $$ln(Earnings)_{Self} - ln(Earnings)_{Employed} = \text{Explained SE Penalty} \\ + \text{Unexplained SE Penalty,}$$

where *ln(Earnings)* denotes the natural logarithm of annual wages, salaries, and business income. The *Explained SE Penalty* consists of the portion of the self-employment earnings penalty that is attributable to differences in observable characteristics between entrepreneurs and other workers, and the *Unexplained SE Penalty* represents the portion of the total penalty that remains when accounting for skills and other features. The explained and unexplained components can be estimated using the "Oaxaca-type" wage decomposition method, based on the work of economist Ronald Oaxaca, such as in his 1973 study.

Specifically, we first estimate the following earnings function solely for paid employees between the ages of twenty-five and sixty-four in the PUMS and ACS to obtain the structure of wages that existed outside of the entrepreneurial sector:

(4) $$Ln(Earnings) = (Human\ Capital)\beta_1 + Other\ \beta_2 + Industry\ \beta_3 \\ + Region\ \beta_4 + e.$$

The vector *Human Capital* includes education, experience (estimated using the convention of age minus education minus five), experience squared, and limited English proficiency (LEP)—a binary variable equal to one for individuals who do not speak English language well (and zero otherwise). The *Other* vector includes other characteristics of the worker—namely, the number of annual hours worked, race (white [base], black, Native American, Asian, and other and/or mixed), gender, birthplace (a binary variable equal to one for individuals born outside of the United States or its territories, and zero otherwise), and a continuous variable for immigrants' U.S. tenure. The *Industry* and *Region* vectors include a set of binary variables for different groups of industries (see the fifteen industries outlined in Appendix A under the ACS heading) and geographic regions (New England, North Central, South Central, Middle Atlantic, South Atlantic, Mountain, and Pacific [base]).

The β_i terms represent vectors of coefficients to be estimated, and e denotes the normally distributed error tem.

Using the estimated coefficients from the β_i vectors, the wages of the self-employed can be imputed to estimate how much they should have earned in the paid-employment sector given their characteristics. The difference between their predicted earnings ($Predicted\ ln(Earnings)_{Self}$) and the earnings of paid-employment workers measures how much of the self-employment earnings penalty stems from differences in observable facets. That is:

(5) $Explained\ SE\ Penalty = Predicted\ ln(Earnings)_{Self} - ln(Earnings)_{Employed}.$

Moreover, the gap between the actual earnings and predicted earnings in natural logarithms of entrepreneurs indicates how self-employment affects average wages unexplainable by differences in observable characteristics:

(6) $Unexplained\ SE\ Penalty = ln(Earnings)_{Self} - Predicted\ ln(Earnings)_{Self}.$

That is, the *Unexplained SE Penalty* (also referred to as the adjusted penalty) reflects the self-employment earnings penalty that is not accounted for differences in observed skills and other characteristics between entrepreneurs and workers in the paid-employment sector.

JMP Estimates. We use the Juhn-Murphy-Pierce decomposition technique to analyze the components contributing to changes in the relative self-employment earnings of Hispanic entrepreneurs over time using the ACS. Consider the following earnings function for members of a particular group (G) in year t:

(7) $$Ln(Earnings)_t^G = X_t^G \beta_t^G + \sigma_t^G \theta_t^G,$$

where X_t^G represents a vector of observable characteristics (including the variables in the *Human Capital, Other, Industry,* and *Region* vectors described for Equation (4)), and β_t^G includes the returns to those characteristics. In Equation (7) θ_t^G denotes a normal standardized residual (which captures unobservable characteristics), and σ_t^G is the standard deviation of G's residual earnings in year t. It follows that the earnings differential between self-employed Hispanics and the non-self-employed (denoted by N) in year t can be expressed as:

(8) $$\Delta Earnings_t + ln(Earnings)_t^{Self} - ln(Earnings)_t^N = \Delta X_t \beta_t^N + \sigma_t^N \Delta \theta,$$

where ΔX and $\Delta \theta$ denote the differences in X and θ between the two groups.

Extending Equation (8) to explore changes in the earnings differential between Hispanic entrepreneurs and those in the paid-employment sector between two time periods ($t-1$ and t) yields the following:

$$(9) \qquad \Delta Earnings_t - \Delta Earnings_{t-1} =$$

$$(\Delta X_t - \Delta X_{t-1})\beta_t^N + \Delta X_{t-1}(\beta_t^N - \beta_{t-1}^N)$$
$$+ (\Delta \theta_t - \Delta \theta_{t-1})\sigma_t^N + \Delta \theta_{t-1}(\sigma_t^N - \sigma_{t-1}^N).$$

The four right-hand-side terms measure the four JMP components of the changes in the relative earnings of Hispanic entrepreneurs. The first term reflects how changes in average observable characteristics between two time periods contributed to the change in the earnings differential between self-employed Hispanics and those in the paid-employment sector, and the second component accounts for changes in the influences of (i.e., returns to) these characteristics on earnings. The third term estimates shifts in average unobservable traits over time, and the final component captures changes in the impacts of these unobservables on the wage differential between Hispanic entrepreneurs and salaried Hispanic workers.

Chapter 3—Immigration

Analyses of Sales of Immigrant- Versus Native-Owned Firms.   When analyzing whether the sales of Hispanic-owned firms differed between immigrants and U.S. natives when controlling for other observable characteristics in the 2007 SBO PUMS, we estimate Equation (1) first for businesses owned by U.S.-born Hispanics. We then use these estimates to predict the sales for firms owned by foreign-born Hispanics. A t-test on the difference between actual sales and predicted sales reveals the level of statistical significance.

Hispanic Enclaves and Immigrant Entrepreneurship.   To test whether Hispanic enclaves relate to the self-employment likelihood of Hispanic immigrants when controlling for other characteristics, we estimate the following using the methodology of probit regression:

$$(10) \qquad Self\text{-}Employed = f(Enclave, Human\ Capital, Industry, Region,$$
$$Demographic),$$

where *Self-Employed* equals one for the self-employed and zero for other workers. The variable *Enclave* refers to the share of Hispanics in the population in metropolitan areas. We construct this measure by dividing the estimated number of Hispanics (regardless of age, work status, or group-quarter residence) by all individuals in the metropolitan area in the ACS. This measure equals zero for individuals who resided outside of metropolitan areas.

The *Human Capital, Industry,* and *Region* vectors contain the same variables described for Equation (4). The *Demographic* vector includes other characteristics of the worker—namely, race (white [base], black, Native American, Asian, and other and/or mixed), gender, immigrants' U.S. tenure, and family structure (married with spouse present in the household [base]; married with absent spouse; single; divorced, widowed, or separated; and number of own children residing in the household). The full set of probit regression results can be obtained from the authors; the effects mentioned in the text refer to marginal effects.

Empirical Tests on Hispanic Immigrant Talent.   We obtain the adjusted self-employment earnings penalties as well as the JMP estimates through the same methodology as in Chapter 2. For the changes in relative self-employment earnings of the foreign born in the Hispanic-immigrant cohort, we estimate Equation (4) only for the U.S.-born in the self-employment sector; we then use those estimates to predict what the earnings of self-employed immigrants should have been, given their characteristics, if they had the same structure of wages as U.S. natives. The difference between their actual labor-market income and the predicted earnings measures the unexplained or adjusted immigrant penalty (if negative) or premium (if positive)—that is, the relative earnings of immigrant entrepreneurs. We then replicate this exercise for workers in the paid-employment sector.

Chapter 4—Education

Analyses of Education and Sales Using the SBO PUMS.   When analyzing whether education mattered in terms of sales when controlling for other observable characteristics in the 2007 SBO PUMS, we estimate Equation (1). We focus on the statistical significance level of the coefficients on the education variables to determine whether firms with owners with less than a high school education or those with a four-year college degree or higher differed from those owned by high school graduates.

Quantile Regression Analysis of Education and Sales.   Using the 2007 SBO PUMS, we utilize conditional quantile regression analysis to explore whether education related differently to revenue depending on the firm's position in the sales distribution. To accomplish this, we estimate a series of sales functions—based on Equation (1)—for nine sales deciles (using the "qreg" command in the software package Stata) separately for Hispanic-owned firms, Hispanic-owned employer firms, non-Hispanic owned firms, and non-Hispanic-owned employer firms. Figure 4.1 provides the coefficients on the college-graduate-owner variable for each of the regressions. For a concise discussion of quantile regression analysis, interested readers should refer to the 2001 study by Roger Koenker and Kevin Hallock.

Analyses of Education and Other Outcomes Using the SSBF.   Similar to the sales analysis conducted using the SBO PUMS, to test whether education mattered in terms of small business outcomes when accounting for other observable traits using the SSBF, we estimate Equation (2) first for Hispanic-owned businesses and then for non-Hispanic-owned businesses. The statistical significance level of the education coefficients indicated whether firms with different schooling levels had different business outcomes, all else being equal.

Quantile Regression Analysis of Education and Earnings.   Similar to our quantile regression analysis of education and sales (described earlier in this appendix), we employ conditional quantile regression analysis to explore whether education mattered differently depending on where the self-employed worker was located in the earnings distribution in a given year, based on the PUMS and ACS data. To accomplish this, we estimate a series of earnings functions, based on Equation (4), for nine earnings deciles (using the "qreg" command in Stata), and we present the coefficients on the education variable in Figure 4.2.

Returns to Education.   We estimate the returns to education based on Equation (4) for the different demographic groups described in the chapter (e.g., self-employed Hispanics, other Hispanic workers). To determine whether these returns significantly differed between groups (e.g., between Hispanic entrepreneurs and other Hispanic workers), we pooled the two groups and reestimated a version of Equation (4) that further includes interaction terms between a binary variable identifying one of the groups (e.g., self-employed Hispanics) and all of the regressors. The *t*-statistic on the interaction term between education and this binary variable yields the statistical significance of the difference in education returns between the two groups.

A Closer Look at the Characteristics of the Newly Self-Employed.   To test whether education mattered for the likelihood of being newly self-employed, we focus exclusively on Hispanics between the ages of twenty-five and sixty-four who were not self-employed in the previous year in the CPS, and we estimate the following model using probit regression analysis:

(11)   *New Self* = *f(Education, V)*.

The binary variable *New Self* equals one for individuals who currently report being self-employed but who were not self-employed in the previous year (based on the previous year's worker classification variable). The vector *V* contains other characteristics presumably related to the odds of being self-employed, including gender, potential work experience (measured by age-education-5), U.S.- versus foreign-born birthplace, the amount of time immigrants lived in the country, family structure (marital status and the number of the worker's children residing at home), industry (described in the CPS section of Appendix A), and geographic region. The specific effects mentioned in the chapter refer to the marginal effects.

Chapter 5—Gender

Analyses of Gender for Sales and the Likelihood of Being an Employer.   Our investigation of the role of gender in the likelihood of being employer firms involves estimating the following probit model for Hispanic-owned firms (and then for non-Hispanic-owned firms) in the 2007 SBO PUMS:

(12)   *Employer* = *f(Owner, Firm, Industry, Region)*.

Employer equals one for employer firms and zero otherwise. The vectors include the same variables as those reported for Equation (1). The coefficient on the female-owned-firm variable is statistically significant for both groups. The likelihoods discussed in the chapter reflect the marginal effects.

When analyzing whether the sales of female-owned firms differed from those of their male counterparts, we estimate Equation (1) first for businesses owned by Hispanic men. We then use these estimates to predict the sales of Hispanic-female-owned firms. The difference between their actual sales and predicted sales represents the portion of the gender-related sales differential not explained by differences in observable characteristics. We repeat this exercise for non-Hispanics, as well as for employer versus nonemployer firms.

Analyses of Gender in Sales and Profits.   To test whether small businesses owned by Hispanic women had different sales and profit benchmarks than firms owned by their male counterparts using the SSBF, we estimate Equation (2) using the same methodologies for Hispanic male-owned small firms. We then used these estimates to impute what the sales and profit levels of small firms owned by Hispanic women would have been, had they faced the same sales and profit structures as their male counterparts. Taking the difference between their actual sales and profits provides the characteristics-adjusted male-female differentials for these metrics.

Relative Earnings of Self-Employed Hispanic Women.   We follow the empirical methodology outlined for Chapter 2 to estimate the relative earnings of self-employed Hispanic women in the ACS. In particular, we estimate Equations (3)–(6) for the unadjusted versus adjusted penalties, using the same control variables when separating Hispanic women from men. Similarly, we obtain the JMP estimates using Equations (7)–(9).

Gender and Returns to Education.   When estimating the returns to education, we use the same methodology described for Chapter 4. In this case, we separate the samples between Hispanic men and women in the ACS, first for the self-employed and then for the salaried sector. We further separate the samples according to birthplace (United States versus abroad).

Gender and the Newly Self-Employed.   To test whether observable characteristics played a role in the likelihood of being newly self-employed between men and women, we estimate Equation (11) separately for self-employed Hispanic men and women using the CPS. The specific numbers mentioned in the text based on this analysis pertain to the marginal effects.

Microentrepreneurship.   To test whether differences in observable characteristics affected the likelihood of being a microentrepreneur, we focus on workers in the CPS-IPUMS between the ages of twenty-five and sixty-four who were self-employed in the previous year. These data include the number

of paid employees the firm had in the previous year; this information is provided in categories, with the smallest one being zero to nine employees. Because this pertains to the previous year, to obtain the microentrepreneurship
rates for 2007, we use the 2008 survey.

The empirical results in the "Closer Examination" subsection are from
our estimation, using probit regression analysis, of the following model for
the self-employed:

(13) $Microentrepreneur = f(Education, V)$.

The *Microentrepreneur* variable equals one for the microentrepreneurs and
zero otherwise. The *Education* and vector *V* contain the same variables described for Equation (11).

Chapter 6—Credit Access

Analysis of the Inability to Access Credit for Expansionary Purposes.   Using
the 2007 SBO PUMS, we test whether Hispanic-owned firms had similar success rates in accessing credit as did their non-Hispanic-owned counterparts
for the purposes of expansion or making capital improvements, when controlling for other characteristics by estimating the following probit model:

(14) $Cannot\ Access = f(Owner, Firm, Industry, Region)$.

Cannot Access equals one for firms reporting being unable to access financial
capital to expand or improve in the past year and zero otherwise. The vectors include the same variables as those reported for Equation (1), with the
exception that the *Owner* vector also includes a binary variable equal to one
for Hispanic-owned firms, because Hispanic- and non-Hispanic-owned firms
are combined in this analysis. The statistical significance of this variable's coefficient indicates whether Hispanic entrepreneurs had different credit-access
rates from their otherwise similar non-Hispanic counterparts. The specific
likelihood mentioned in the chapter refers to the marginal effect. Firms that
did not report their expansionary capital access (as well as those that did not
need it) are excluded from this analysis.

For the relative success of Hispanic-owned businesses in different industries (as well as immigrants versus natives) with respect to accessing credit, we
estimate Equation (14) only for Hispanics. The coefficients (and their statisti-

cal significance) on the industry and foreign-born-owner variables yielded this information.

Analysis of the Loan Conditions in the SSBF.   To test whether Hispanic-owned small businesses had different loan conditions (i.e., loan amounts and interest rates) from their non-Hispanic counterparts in the SSBF, we estimate the following model using the method of ordinary least squares:

$$(15) \qquad\qquad Condition = f(Owner,\ Firm,\ Other),$$

where the *Owner* vector contains characteristics of the owners, including gender, highest education level (less than high school, high school but not a college graduate [base], college graduate), and age. The *Firm* vector has firm-level characteristics: assets, sales, number of workers employed, and binary variables for its credit rating: "safe" (Dun and Bradstreet score of up to 10), "medium" (base), and "risky" (Dun and Bradstreet score of 91–100). The *Other* vector contains additional variables conceivably related to conditions of loans, such as using collateral, having a guarantor, and geographic variables for region (North, South, and West) and a binary variable equal to one for cities in which the Herfindahl index for the concentration of banking markets exceeds 1,800 (and zero otherwise).

We first estimate Equation (15) for businesses owned by non-Hispanics and nonblacks. On the basis of these estimates, we impute the loan amounts and interest rates that Hispanic-owned businesses should have received, given their characteristics, if they faced the same lending structure as other firms. Taking the difference between their actual loan amounts (and interest rates) and these imputed conditions yields the ethnic-related differentials in the loan conditions.

Hispanic Concentration and Access to Credit in the SBO PUMS.   To test whether the share of Hispanics in a state related to the likelihood of accessing financial capital to expand or make physical capital improvements, we estimate an extended version of Equation (14) that further included the percentage of Hispanics in the state (based on our estimates using the 2007 ACS for the entire population) as well as an interaction term between Hispanic-owned businesses and this share. The coefficients on both variables were positive and statistically significant, which indicates that businesses, especially those owned by Hispanics, in states with a relatively large Hispanic presence were more likely than those in other areas to report being unable to access credit for expansionary or capital-improving purposes.

Chapter 7—Technology Usage

Estimating the Likelihood of Being Digitally Connected. To test whether Hispanic-owned firms differed in their propensity to be digitally connected when controlling for other characteristics using the SBO PUMS, we estimate the following probit model:

(16) $Connected = f(Owner, Firm, Industry, Region).$

The vectors include the same variables as those reported for Equation (1), with the exception that the *Owner* vector also includes a binary variable equal to one for Hispanic-owned firms because Hispanic- and non-Hispanic-owned firms are combined in this analysis. The statistical significance of this variable's coefficient indicates whether Hispanic entrepreneurs had a different likelihood of being digitally connected than otherwise similar non-Hispanics. The specific likelihoods mentioned in the chapter refer to the marginal effects. Firms that did not report their technology usage are excluded from this analysis.

Digital Technology and Sales in the SBO PUMS. To test whether digitally connected Hispanic-owned firms had different sales from their non-Hispanic-owned counterparts, we estimate Equation (1) solely for the connected, while further including in the *Owner* vector a binary variable equal to one for Hispanic-owned firms; Hispanic- and non-Hispanic-owned firms are combined in this analysis. The statistical significance of this variable's coefficient indicates whether the sales of Hispanic-owned connected firms differed from those of other connected firms. We repeat this exercise for the unconnected and then for samples partitioned by other demographic characteristics (including owner education).

Isolating Information Technology Effects. Our analysis of whether being digitally connected related to business outcomes differently for Hispanic versus non-Hispanic entrepreneurs is based on estimating the following using SSBF data:

(17) $Outcome = f(Connected, Race/Ethnicity, Race/Ethnicity$
$\times\ Connected, X).$

The *Connected* term equals one for digitally connected firms and zero otherwise. The *Race/Ethnicity* vector contains binary variables indicating Hispanic, black, and Asian ownership of the firm (defined in terms of businesses with at least half of owners from these groups), such that non-HBA-owned firms represent the base comparison group. The *Race/Ethnicity* × *Connected* term interacts all of the racial and ethnic variables with the connected binary variable to determine if significant racial and ethnic differences exist with respect to how being digitally connected relates to small business outcomes. The vector *X* is the same as in Equation (2) for Chapter 2.

We use the method of ordinary least squares to estimate Equation (17) for the outcomes of sales (in natural logs) and profits, and probit regression for the remaining business outcomes. We first estimate Equation (17) separately for the two years. However, to test whether the effects of being digitally connected significantly changed between the late 1990s and mid-2000s, we also estimate an additional set of regressions that combines the two samples and interacts all of the regressors with a binary variable equal to one for the 2003 sample; a *t*-test for sales and profits, and *z*-tests for the probit models on the *Connected* × *2003* interaction terms indicate that the coefficients on *Connected* did not significantly differ between the 1998 and 2003 samples.

As an additional test, we estimate Equation (17) for the natural logarithm of sales solely for connected businesses owned by non-Hispanics in each year. We then used these estimates to predict the sales (in natural logs) that unconnected other firms as well as connected and unconnected Hispanic-owned firms should have received, given their characteristics, if they faced the same determinants of sales as other firms. Taking the difference between their actual *ln*(sales) and the imputed values provides another measure of how Hispanic connected versus unconnected small businesses fared with respect to their success measures.

JMP Analysis of Sales.   We estimated our JMP results using the same methodology described for Chapter 2, with sales replacing earnings, and Equation (17) being used in place of Equation (7). The comparison group contains non-HBA-owned firms because black-owned firms had lower sales, and Asian-owned firms had higher sales than the non-HBA firms. We separately decomposed the sales of the connected and unconnected firms.

Chapter 8—Current Programs

Preferences of Hispanic Entrepreneurs.   We conduct our analysis of the likelihood that a firm used a government agency as one of its three main sources of financial services by estimating the following probit model:

(18) $Government\ Agency = f(Owner,\ Firm,\ Other).$

The *Government Agency* binary variable equals one for individuals who reported a government agency as one of their top three providers of financial services and zero otherwise. The *Owner* control variables include race and ethnicity, gender, education, and managerial experience. The *Firm* variables include firm assets, age, number of employees, whether it was a sole proprietorship, credit rating (risky, medium, or safe), and industry (construction and manufacturing, trade, transportation, or other). *Other* includes binary variables identifying geographic region, the concentration of the banking industry, and the 2003 versus the 1998 SSBF surveys. The latter is included because we combined the 1998 and 2003 surveys in this analysis given the small number of firms using a government agency (but this variable is not statistically significant).

REFERENCE MATTER

Notes

Chapter 1

1. Unless otherwise noted, the data used in this chapter come from the Public Use Microdata Sample (PUMS) of the 2000 decennial census and the 2001–10 American Community Surveys (ACS) from the Integrated Public Use Microdata Series (IPUMS); see Appendix A for the details, including the sample selection criteria.

2. For example, our estimates using the 2003 Survey of Small Business Finances (described in Appendix A) indicate that in the mid-2000s, incorporated small firms (including S corporations, C corporations, and limited-liability-partnership and limited-liability-company tax filers as corporations) had an average of 13.3 employees (including owners), $1.8 million in sales, $823,600 in assets, and $240,400 in profits. Other small firms had an average of 4.1 employees (including owners), $354,400 million in sales, $278,100 in assets, and $110,600 in profits.

Chapter 2

1. It should be noted the SBO estimates do not always align with other data sets used here (including the American Community Survey), such that readers should use caution in interpreting business growth rates solely on the basis of the SBO, especially for nonemployer firms. See Appendix A for more information.

2. The SBO PUMS provides sales information in $10,000 increments, such that firms with less than $5,000 in sales (which accounted for one-fifth of all firms in the SBO) are coded as having $0 in revenue. To avoid dropping these firms from the sample, we set their sales equal to the natural logarithm of $1,400, a figure that approximated the average sales of firms with less than $5,000 in revenue based on the 2003

Survey of Small Business Finances (see Appendix A for details). When setting this group's revenue equal to $1 (instead of $1,400), the sales differential between Hispanics and non-Hispanics narrows to 29.6 percent ($8.334 – $8.60).

3. Appendix B provides the details of the major empirical analyses throughout this book. For this particular test, our analysis focuses on a smaller sample of the SBO PUMS than the one used to estimate the sales differential between Hispanics and non-Hispanics because, as discussed in Appendix A, not all firms reported detailed demographic and firm-level data. Without controlling for other observable characteristics, focusing only on this subset yields a smaller revenue differential between Hispanic and non-Hispanic entreprenuers (of 27.8 percent) than the one obtained using the full sample. Our selection of control variables follows the ones commonly employed in the literature to analyze business success measures, such as those used in a series of studies by Robert Fairlie and Alicia Robb (e.g., 2009, 2007a, 2007b); see also Robb and Fairlie (2009, 2007).

4. See note 3 for examples. Fairlie and Robb's analyses of the profit level of $10,000 or more generally focused on a set of firms surveyed in 1992. When adjusting $10,000 for inflation using the Consumer Price Index, however, the basic findings we report here continue to hold.

5. At the same time, similar to the issue of sales distributions, recall the objection by Portes and Zhou that some information is lost when logarithmically transforming earnings.

Chapter 3

1. These estimates are based on the 2007 SBO PUMS. As discussed in Appendix A, not all survey respondents provided information on owner birthplace. When further including those that did not report birthplace, immigrants represented 40.5 percent of all Hispanic-owned businesses. This information indicates that, even if all Hispanic-owned companies that did not report birthplace had U.S.-born owners (which is unlikely), immigrants owned four out of ten Hispanic-owned firms in 2007.

2. We obtained these estimates using the PUMS and ACS data in the IPUMS. For details and the sample selection criteria, see Appendix A.

3. At the same time, recall that not all firms in the SBO PUMS reported information on owner birthplace. The sales of firms owned by U.S.-born Hispanics were 15.8 percent higher than those of businesses owned by immigrants plus businesses with owners with unreported birthplaces. This suggests that if immigrants owned all firms that did not report owner birthplace, U.S.-born Hispanics performed better than their foreign-born counterparts. While it is unlikely that immigrants owned all of the firms with missing birthplace, we cannot definitively say which group (natives versus immigrants) had higher sales because of this missing information.

4. When combining firms owned by the foreign born with those that did not report owner birthplace, the general pattern holds, in that U.S.-born Hispanics had

higher sales among employer firms than other Hispanic-owned businesses but lower sales among nonemployer companies.

5. We are unable to explore this relationship for 2002 because the data do not identify MSAs until 2005. Much has been written on how to define ethnic enclaves. The use of an MSA is fairly common (e.g., Fairchild 2010; Aguilera 2009; Davis 2004; Logan, Alba, and Stults 2003; Portes and Jensen 1989), although some researchers have identified enclaves on the basis of smaller geographic units, such as neighborhoods or common zip codes.

6. Examples of such policies include the Immigration Act of 1917 (which included a controversial literacy test), the Quota Law (popularly known as the Per Centum Limit Act) of 1921, and the Immigration Act of 1924. For discussions of these acts, see Carl Wittke (1949) and Thomas Curran (1975).

7. The sample sizes of self-employed U.S.-born Salvadorans in the cohort are too small to produce reliable estimates of the earnings of entrepreneurs from El Salvador, which limits this subgroup analysis to Mexicans and Cubans.

8. We obtained these estimates by calculating the total value of the sales and receipts of businesses owned by Hispanic immigrants (and then natives) in each state, and then multiplying those sales by the 2007 state sales tax. Because we cannot identify the cities or counties where the businesses were located, we could not estimate the additional sales-tax revenue generated in areas with additional sales taxes beyond the state rate.

Chapter 4

1. We estimate these education levels using the International IPUMS for individuals between the ages of twenty-five and sixty-four; see Appendix A for more details.

2. We obtained these estimates using conditional quantile regression analysis; as with the details for our other major empirical analyses, more information is provided in Appendix B. With respect to the terminology, a firm located in the thirtieth percentile (third decile) had higher sales than 30 percent of Hispanic-owned businesses and sales less than the other 70 percent. A business in the fiftieth sales percentile (fifth decile) had median sales.

3. These studies include the work of Rubén Rumbaut (e.g., 2004), Mark Ellis and Jamie Goodwin-White (2006), and B. Lindsey Lowell and Richard Fry (2006), among others.

4. One explanation may be specific industry or geographic effects, although our estimates of these returns already account for industry and regions. Another explanation relates to unobservable characteristics associated with schooling, such as the quality of education or coming from a relatively high socioeconomic status before migrating to the United States. Indeed, despite having fewer than ten years of education, the average Salvadoran entrepreneur in the United States has more schooling than nearly three-quarters of the adult population in El Salvador. Never-

theless, whatever skill-returns advantage these entrepreneurs might have had in 2002 seems to have vanished, as their schooling returns fell to the lowest of the four largest Hispanic ethnic subgroups later in the decade.

5. The average schooling levels of self-employed Hispanics in this age group are higher in the CPS than the ones observed in the 2002 ACS, discussed in the previous section. Part of the discrepancy may reflect seasonal effects in employment patterns, as the CPS surveys occurred at the same time of the year (in March), whereas the ACS surveys were conducted throughout the year. Such seasonal effects in the March CPS supplements versus other CPS data sets have been identified in a 2008 study by Fernando Lozano and Todd Sorensen. At the same time, the year 2002 might be an unusual case, as average education levels among Hispanic entrepreneurs in subsequent years of the CPS more closely match those in the ACS. Moreover, the average schooling of Hispanics in the paid-employment sector was the same (11.3 years) in both the CPS and the ACS.

6. Repeating this exercise for non-Hispanics, education also mattered in 2002 (but not in 2007 or 2010). In 2002, each year of education raised the odds of an individual joining the self-employment sector by 0.04 percent, when controlling for other characteristics. As such, it appears that Hispanics were not the only group with an education advantage among newly minted entrepreneurs at certain times in the decade.

Chapter 5

1. Unless otherwise noted, our estimates presented here are based on the PUMS and ACS in the IPUMS; see Appendix A for more information.

2. In fact, the share would even be closer, given that, to increase the sample size, we identify female-owned firms in the SSBF as those in which women represent at least half of the owners, whereas the SBO uses a female majority among the owners.

3. The observation that U.S.-born Hispanic women have a considerably larger self-employment earnings penalty than their foreign-born counterparts may explain their relatively low self-employment rates shown in Table 5.1. U.S.-born Hispanic men also have a larger self-employment penalty than immigrant men.

4. When considering additional years in the 2000s, we find that Hispanic women were not more or less likely than their male counterparts to have been newly self-employed in 2000, 2001, 2003, and 2004, all else being equal. Starting in 2005, however, female Hispanics were significantly less likely to be newly minted entrepreneurs every year in the rest of the decade.

Chapter 6

1. In contrast to the general assumption that borrowers are better informed than lender institutions, as discussed in a 1996 study by David de Meza and Clive Southey,

the theory of the optimistic borrower assumes that entrepreneurs have less information about their business prospects than do lending institutions.

2. Our results also indicate that firms owned by blacks were 2 percent more likely than otherwise similar firms owned by non-Hispanics and nonblacks to lack access to credit for purposes of expansion. We separated blacks from other business owners in this analysis in light of the wealth of studies showing that blacks (1) have lower loan-approval rates, (2) receive lower average loan amounts, and (3) face different loan-collateral requirements than their non-Hispanic white counterparts. Recent examples include Elizabeth Asiedu, James Freeman, and Akwasi Nti-Addae (2012); David Blanchflower (e.g., 2009); Blanchflower and his colleagues Phillip Levine and David Zimmerman (2003); Fairlie and Robb (2007a); Robb and Fairlie (2007); and Erika Mendez (2005); Ken Cavalluzzo, Linda Cavalluzzo, and J. Wolken (2002); among others. For a recent overview, see Timothy Bates (2011).

3. This difference is statistically significant. The estimates for the late 1990s are from the 1998 SSBF. It should be noted that credit information in the late 1990s refers to applications for new credit only, whereas data for the mid-2000s include applications for new credit as well as requests for extensions to existing credit. Nevertheless, when focusing only on small firms applying for new credit in the mid-2000s, those owned by Hispanics had statistically similar loan approval rates to those of other small businesses (71.3 percent among Hispanic new-loan applicants versus 78.0 percent among non-Hispanics). These rates were significantly higher than those in the late 1990s for both groups.

4. The SSBF provides firms' credit scores from Dun and Bradstreet; we define firms having the safest credit rating as those with credit scores of 10 or less, and scores between 91 and 100 indicate those with the riskiest credit rating.

5. In a 1998 study Cavalluzzo and Cavalluzzo defined concentrated banking markets as those metropolitan areas (or counties, in nonmetropolitan areas) with Herfindahl indexes for commercial bank deposits of at least 1800. We use this measure here.

6. We do not find a parallel pattern for black-owned small firms with respect to loan amount, as observable characteristics explain two-thirds of their credit differential with non-Hispanic and nonblack firms. This does not mean, however, that black entrepreneurs encounter few problems in accessing credit, as other credit-access barriers have been identified (see note 2). Moreover, we find that observable characteristics only explain a small portion (0.59 percentage points) of the 3.7-percentage-point interest-rate differential between black- and non-Hispanic and nonblack small firms, consistent with the possibility that financial institutions view certain firm and owner characteristics differently when structuring the conditions (prices) of loans to minority and nonminority entrepreneurs.

7. Not all of these entrepreneurs stayed outside of credit markets for the full three years, as some had applied for loans before forming expectations of rejection, and others overcame those expectations.

Chapter 7

1. We estimate this usage on the basis of the eight reported functions that computers served: the four categories we use to identify the digitally connected plus the utilization of computers for managing inventory, accounting purposes, administrative support tasks (e.g., word processing), and other functions.

2. Because we are considering the $10,000 in two different time periods, we adjust the $10,000 in the latter period for inflation.

Chapter 8

1. Community development financial institutions are private financial institutions that lend to community businesses and individuals in underserved communities at competitive rates, and they receive funds from a variety of sources, including the federal government. One such federal source is the CDFI Fund (established in 1994), housed in the Treasury Department.

2. The relatively large number of Hispanic-owned businesses in New Mexico is not a new phenomenon, given the state's history and demographics. It is therefore not surprising that the U.S. Hispanic Chamber of Commerce (described in the chapter appendix) was incorporated in New Mexico in 1979.

3. It should be noted that recent stimulus measures passed by the Obama administration eliminated fees on both SBA 7(a) and CDC/504 loans, and they raised the SBA guarantee on some loans to 90 percent, to encourage SBA lending partners to make small business loans.

4. Another nonprofit organization created to support economic development in the aftermath of the 1992 riots in Los Angeles is the nonprofit FAME Assistance Corporation (affiliated with the First African Methodist Episcopal Church of Los Angeles). Its Business Development Department (BDD) has as its mission "to revive low-income communities by promoting self-sufficiency through entrepreneurship." The BDD facilitates loans to minority- and female-owned small businesses in Los Angeles County, operates a business incubator program, and provides entrepreneurial training courses.

Chapter 9

1. Even policies and programs not directly aimed at fostering small business growth can affect Hispanic microentrepreneurs. For example, as Bárbara Robles discussed in a 2007 study, tax refund programs (e.g., the Earned Income Tax Credit) create capitalization opportunities for microbusinesses and stimulate asset building and economic stability in low-income communities.

References

ACCION USA. Accessed September 3, 2011. http://www.accionusa.org.

Aguilera, Michael Bernabé. "Ethnic Enclaves and the Earnings of Self-Employed Latinos." *Small Business Economics* 33 (2009): 413–25.

Asiedu, Elizabeth, James Freeman, and Akwasi Nti-Addae. "Access to Credit by Small Businesses: How Relevant Are Race, Ethnicity, and Gender?" *American Economic Review* 102 (2012): 532–37.

Batalova, Jeanne, and B. Lindsay Lowell. "Immigrant Professionals in the United States." *Society* 2 (2007): 26–31.

Bates, Timothy. "Minority Entrepreneurship." *Foundations and Trends in Entrepreneurship* 7 (2011): 151–311.

Bates, Timothy, and William D. Bradford. "Venture-Capital Investment in Minority Business." *Journal of Money, Credit, and Banking* 40 (2008): 489–504.

Bates, Timothy, and Alicia Robb. "Analysis of Young Neighborhood Firms Serving Urban Minority Clients." *Journal of Economics and Business* 60 (2008): 139–48.

Becker, Gary S. *The Economics of Discrimination.* 2nd ed. Chicago: University of Chicago Press, 1971.

Becker, Gary S. *Human Capital: A Theoretical and Empirical Analysis with a Special Reference to Education.* 3rd ed. Chicago: University of Chicago Press, 1993.

Berkowitz, Jeremy, and Michelle J. White. "Bankruptcy and Small Firms' Access to Credit." *RAND Journal of Economics* 35 (2004): 69–84.

Bilic, Ivana, Ante Prka, and Gaia Vidovic. "How Does Education Influence Entrepreneurial Orientation? A Case Study of Croatia." *Management* 16 (2011): 115–28.

Blanchflower, David G. "Minority Self-Employment in the United States and the Impact of Affirmative Action Programs." *Annals of Finance* 5 (2009): 361–96.

Blanchflower, David G., Phillip B. Levine, and David J. Zimmerman. "Discrimination in the Small-Business Credit Market." *Review of Economics and Statistics* 85 (2003): 930–43.

Bogan, Vicki, and William Darity Jr. "Culture and Entrepreneurship? African American and Immigrant Self-Employment in the United States." *Journal of Socio-Economics* 37 (2008): 1999–2019.

Borjas, George J. "Self Selection and the Earnings of Immigrants." *American Economic Review* 77 (1987): 531–53.

Burns, Renita. "Hispanic Firms Growing in S.C.: Businesses See Increased Popularity and Success." *Sun News* (Myrtle Beach, SC), July 9, 2006.

California Association for Micro Enterprise Opportunity (CAMEO). Accessed September 2, 2011. http://www.microbiz.org.

California Reinvestment Coalition. "Small Business Access to Credit: The Little Engine That Could." CRC Report (December 2010). Accessed August 25, 2011. http://www.calreinvest.org/publications/crc-reports.

Cavalluzzo, Ken S., and Linda C. Cavalluzzo. "Market Structure and Discrimination: The Case of Small Businesses." *Journal of Money, Credit, and Banking* 30 (1998): 772–92.

Cavalluzo, Ken, Linda Cavalluzzo, and J. Wolken. "Competition, Small Business Financing, and Discrimination: Evidence from a New Survey." *Journal of Business* 75 (2002): 641–79.

Chiquiar, Daniel, and Gordon Hanson. "International Migration, Self-Selection, and the Distribution of Wages: Evidence from Mexico and the United States." *Journal of Political Economy* 113 (2005): 239–81.

Chiswick, Barry R. "The Effect of Americanization on the Earnings of Foreign-Born Men." *Journal of Political Economy* 86 (1978): 897–921.

Clark, Kenneth, and Stephen Drinkwater. "Ethnicity and Self-Employment in Britain." *Oxford Bulletin of Economics and Statistics* 60 (1998): 383–407.

Curran, Thomas J. *Xenophobia and Immigration: 1820–1930.* Boston: Twayne Publishers, 1975.

Dalin, Shera. "St. Louis Technology Center to Help Small Businesses in Hispanic Community." *St. Louis-Post Dispatch*, November 19, 2004.

Darity, William, Jr. "Stratification Economics: The Role of Intergroup Inequality." *Journal of Economics and Finance* 29 (2005): 144–53.

Delgado, Melvin. *Latino Small Business and the American Dream: Community Social Work Practice and Economic and Social Development.* New York: Columbia University Press, 2011.

De Meza, David, and Clive Southey. "The Borrower's Curse: Optimism, Finance and Entrepreneurship." *Economic Journal* 106 (1996): 375–86.

Desai, Raj M., and Anders Olofsgard. "The Costs of Political Influence: Firm-Level Evidence from Developing Countries." *Quarterly Journal of Political Science* 6 (2011): 137–78.

Dickson, Pat H., George T. Solomon, and K. Mark Weaver. "Entrepreneurial Selection and Success: Does Education Matter?" *Journal of Small Business and Enterprise Development* 15 (2008): 239–58.

Ellis, Mark, and Jamie Goodwin-White. "1.5 Generation Internal Migration in the U.S.: Dispersion from States of Immigration?" *International Migration Review* 40 (2006): 899–926.

Ennis, Sharon R., Merarys Ríos-Vargas, and Nora G. Albert. *The U.S. Hispanic Population: 2010.* 2010 Census Briefs, May 2011. Washington, DC: U.S. Census Bureau.

Fairchild, Gregory B. "Intergenerational Ethnic Enclave Influences on the Likelihood of Being Self-Employed." *Journal of Business Venturing* 25 (May 2010): 290–304.

Fairlie, Robert W. "Recent Trends in Ethnic and Racial Business Ownership." *Small Business Economics* 23 (2004): 203–18.

Fairlie, Robert W., and Bruce D. Meyer. "The Effect of Immigration on Native Self-Employment." *Journal of Labor Economics* 21 (2003): 619–50.

Fairlie, Robert W., and Alicia M. Robb. "Families, Human Capital, and Small Business: Evidence from the Characteristics of Business Owners Survey." *Industrial and Labor Relations Review* 60 (2007b): 225–45.

Fairlie, Robert W., and Alicia M. Robb. "Gender Differences in Business Performance: Evidence from the Characteristics of Business Owners Survey." *Small Business Economics* 33 (2009): 375–95.

Fairlie, Robert W., and Alicia M. Robb. *Race and Entrepreneurial Success: Black-, Asian-, and White-Owned Businesses in the United States.* Cambridge, MA: MIT Press, 2008.

Fairlie, Robert W., and Alicia M. Robb. "Why Are Black-Owned Businesses Less Successful than White-Owned Businesses? The Role of Families, Inheritances, and Business Human Capital." *Journal of Labor Economics* 25 (2007a): 289–323.

FAME Corporations. Accessed September 3, 2011. www.famerenaissance.org/index.htm.

Fry, Richard, and B. Lindsay Lowell. "The Wage Structure of Latino-Origin Groups across Generations." *Industrial Relations* 45 (2006): 147–68.

Glaeser, Edward L. "Entrepreneurship and the City." In *Entrepreneurship and Openness: Theory and Evidence*, edited by David B. Audretsch, Robert E. Litan, and Robert J. Strom, 131–80. Northampton, MA: Edward Elgar Publishing, 2009.

Glaeser, Edward L., Stuart S. Rosenthal, and William S. Strange. "Urban Economics and Entrepreneurship." *Journal of Urban Economics* 67 (2010): 1–14.

Juhn, Chinhui, Kevin M. Murphy, and Brooks Pierce. "Wage Inequality and the Rise in the Returns to Skill." *Journal of Political Economy* 101 (1993): 410–42.

King, Miriam, Steven Ruggles, J. Trent Alexander, Sarah Flood, Katie Genadek, Matthew B. Schroeder, Brandon Trampe, and Rebecca Vick. *Integrated Public Use Microdata Series, Current Population Survey: Version 3.0* (Machine-readable database). Minneapolis: University of Minnesota, 2011. http://cps.ipums.org/cps.

Koenker, Roger, and Kevin F. Hallock. "Quantile Regression." *Journal of Economic Perspectives* 15 (2001): 143–56.

Kolenikov, Stanislav. "Resampling Variance Estimation for Complex Survey Data." *Stata Journal* 10 (2010): 165–99.

Lee, Jongho, Celina Torres, and Yin Wang. *Living in the Present, Hoping for the Future: Latinos and Insurance.* Los Angeles: Tomás Rivera Policy Institute, 2005.

Light, Ivan. "Asian Enterprise in America." In *Self-Help in America: Patterns of Minority Economic Development*, edited by Scott Cummings, 33–57. Port Washington, NY: Kennikat Press, 1980.

Light, Ivan. *Ethnic Enterprise in America: Business Welfare among Chinese, Japanese, and Blacks.* Berkeley: University of California Press, 1972.

Light, Ivan, Georges Sabagh, Mehdi Bozorgmehr, and Claudia Der Martirosian. "Beyond the Ethnic Enclave Economy." *Social Problems* 41 (1994): 65–80.

Loftstrom, Magnus, and Chunbei Wang. "Mexican-American Self-Employment: A Dynamic Analysis of Business Ownership." *Research in Labor Economics* 29: 197–227.

Logan, John R., Richard D. Alba, and Thomas L. McNulty. "Ethnic Economies in Metropolitan Regions: Miami and Beyond." *Social Forces* 72 (1994): 691–724.

Longhofer, S. D., and S. R. Peters. "Self-Selection and Discrimination in Credit Markets." *Real Estate Economics* 33 (2005): 237–68.

López, Mark Hugo, Gretchen Livingston, and Rakesh Kochhar. *Hispanics and the Economic Downturn: Housing Woes and Remittance Cuts.* Pew Hispanic Center Report, January 9, 2009. http://www.pewhispanic.org.

Lozano, Fernando, and Todd Sorensen. "Mexican Immigrants, the Labor Market and the Current Population Survey: Seasonality Effects, Framing Effects, and Sensitivity of Results." IZA Discussion Paper No. 3301, Forschungsinstitut zur Zukunft der Arbeit, Institute for the Study of Labor, Bonn, Germany, January 2008.

Mankiw, N. G. "The Allocation of Credit and Financial Collapse." *Quarterly Journal of Economics* 101 (1986): 455–70.

Mayorkas, Alejandro N. "Policy Memorandum Draft, Subject EB-5 Adjudications Policy." Draft Memo, U.S. Citizenship and Immigration Services, Office of the Director (MS 2000), PM-602-XXXX, January 11, 2012.

Medina, José F., Joel Saegert, and Alicia Gresham. "Comparison of Mexican-American and Anglo-American Attitudes toward Money." *Journal of Consumer Affairs* 30 (1996): 124–45.

Méndez, Erika. "An Investigation into the Loan Terms and Loan Approval Rates of International and Minority-Owned Small Firms in the U.S." PhD diss., University of Texas–Pan American, 2005.

Miao, Qingqing. "Chinese Entrepreneurs Respond to the U.S. EB-5 Immigrant Investor Pilot Program." *International Law News* 40 (2011): 6–9.

Minority Business Development Agency, accessed September 2, 2011. http://www.mbda.gov.

Mora, Marie T., and Alberto Dávila. "Mexican Immigrant Self-Employment along the U.S.-Mexico Border: An Analysis of 2000 Census Data." *Social Science Quarterly* 87 (2006): 91–109.

Mora, Marie T., Alberto Dávila, and Erika M. Garza. "Self-Selection and the Loan Approval Rates of Minority-Owned Small Businesses in the U.S.: Evidence Using 2003 SSBF Data." Unpublished manuscript, University of Texas–Pan American, 2011.

National Minority Supplier Development Council. Accessed October 22, 2012. http://www.nmsdc.org/nmsdc.

National Urban League. Accessed October 22, 2012. http://www.nul.org.

New York Business Development Corporation. Accessed October 21, 2012. http://www.nybdc.com.

Oaxaca, Ronald. "Male-Female Wage Differentials in Urban Labor Markets." *International Economic Review* 14 (1973): 693–709.

Olkon, Sara. "Riding Wave of Growth: After Starting Out as a Teenage Dishwasher, Mexican Immigrant Built His Career—and Helped Resurrect a Cicero 'Hellhole'—by Capitalizing on a Surge in the Hispanic Population." *Chicago Tribune*, August 7, 2006.

Operation Hope. Accessed October 22, 2012. http://www.operationhope.org.

Orrenius, Pia M., and Madeline Zavodny. "The Effects of Tougher Enforcement on the Job Prospects of Recent Latin American Immigrants." *Journal of Policy Analysis and Management* 28 (2009): 239–57.

Orrenius, Pia M., and Madeline Zavodny. "Self-Selection among Undocumented Immigrants from Mexico." *Journal of Development Economics* 78 (2005): 215–40.

Palomares, Javier. Comments at the Public and Nonprofit Sector Small Business Finance Panel, at Addressing the Financing Needs of Small Businesses: A Capstone Forum Highlighting Findings from the Federal Reserve System Series, July 12, 2010. http://www.federalreserve.gov/events/conferences/2010/sbc/downloads/sbc_panel2.pdf.

Passel, Jeffrey, D'Vera Cohn, and Ana González-Barrera. *Net Migration from Mexico Falls to Zero—and Perhaps Less*. Washington, DC: Pew Hispanic Center, April 23, 2012. http://www.pewhispanic.org.

Passel, Jeffrey, D'Vera Cohn, and Mark Hugo López. *Census 2010: 50 Million Latinos Hispanics Account for More Than Half of Nation's Growth in Past Decade*. Washington, DC: Pew Hispanic Center, March 24, 2011. http:// www.pewhispanic.org.

Pew Hispanic Center. *Statistical Portrait of the Foreign-Born Population in the United States, 2009*. Accessed April 4, 2011. http://www.pewhispanic.org.

Portes, Alejandro, and Rubén G. Rumbaut. *Immigrant America: A Portrait*. 2nd ed. Berkeley: University of California Press, 1996.

Portes, Alejandro, and Min Zhou. "Self-Employment and the Earnings of Immigrants." *American Sociological Review* 61 (1996): 219–30.

Raijman, Rebeca, and Marta Tienda. "Pathways to Business Ownership among Immigrants to Chicago: A Comparative Ethnic Perspective." *International Migration Review* 34 (2000): 681–705.

Robb, Alicia M., and Robert W. Fairlie. "Access to Financial Capital among U.S. Businesses: The Case of African American Firms." *Annals of the American Academy of Political and Social Science* 613 (2007): 47–72.

Robb, Alicia M., and Robert W. Fairlie. "Determinants of Business Success: An Examination of Asian-Owned Businesses in the USA." *Journal of Population Economics* 22 (2009): 827–58.

Roberts, Peter. *The New Immigration: A Study of the Industrial and Social Life of Southeastern Europeans in America.* New York: Macmillan Company, 1914.

Robles, Bárbara J. "Tax Refunds and Microbusinesses: Expanding Family and Community Wealth Building in the Borderlands." *Annals of the American Academy of Political and Social Science* 613 (2007): 178–91.

Roy, A. D. "Some Thoughts on the Distribution of Earnings." *Oxford Economic Papers* 3 (1951): 135–46.

Ruggles, Steven, et al. *Integrated Public Use Microdata Series: Version 5.0* (machine-readable database). Minneapolis: University of Minnesota, 2011. http://www.ipums.org.

Rumbaut, Rubén G. "Ages, Life Stages, and Generational Cohorts: Decomposing the Immigrant First and Second Generations in the United States." *International Migration Review* 38 (2004): 1160–1205.

Sanders, Jimy M., and Victor Nee. "Immigrant Self-Employment: The Family as Social Capital and the Value of Human Capital." *American Sociological Review* 61 (1996): 231–49.

Shao, Jun. "Resampling Methods in Sample Surveys (with Discussion)." *Statistics* 27 (1996): 203–54.

Simpson, Mike, Niki Tuck, and Sarah Bellamy. "Small Business Success Factors: The Role of Education and Training." *Education and Training* 46 (2004): 481–91.

Stevenson, Thomas H., and D. Anthony Plath. "Marketing Financial Services to Hispanic American Consumers." *Journal of Services Marketing* 20 (2006): 37–50.

Stiglitz, J. E., and A. Weiss. "Credit Rationing in Markets with Imperfect Information." *American Economic Review* 73 (1981): 393–409.

Trejo, Stephen J. "Intergenerational Progress of Mexican-Origin Workers in the U.S. Labor Market." *Journal of Human Resources* 38 (2003): 467–89.

U.S. Bureau of Economic Analysis. *Percent Change from Preceding Period in Real Gross Domestic Product.* Last updated September 27, 2011. http://www.bea.gov.

U.S. Bureau of Labor Statistics. *Labor Force Statistics, Current Population Survey.* Accessed October 3, 2011. http://www.bls.gov.

U.S. Department of Agriculture. *Small Socially Disadvantaged Producer Grants Program.* Last modified October 18, 2012. http://www.rurdev.usda.gov/rbs/coops/ssdpg/ssdpg.htm.

U.S. Small Business Administration. Accessed October 22, 2012. http://www.sba.gov.

U.S. Small Business Administration. *SBA—Business Loan Approval (Gross $) FY 2006– FY 2010 (YTD), Month Ending 09/30/10*. Accessed August 26, 2011. http://archive. sba.gov/idc/groups/public/documents/sba_homepage/serv_fa_lending_major _progs.pdf.

Valdez, Zulema. *The New Entrepreneurs: How Race, Class, and Gender Shape American Enterprise*. Palo Alto, CA: Stanford University Press, 2011.

Van der Sluis, Justin, Mirjam van Praag, and Wim Vijverberg. "Education and Entrepreneurship Selection and Performance: A Review of the Empirical Literature." *Journal of Economic Surveys* 22 (2008): 795–841.

Waldinger, Robert. "Immigrant Enterprise: A Critique and Reformulation." *Theory and Society* 15 (1986): 249–85.

Wickham, DeWayne. "Urban League's New Mantra: Economic Development." *USA Today*, November 8, 2005.

Wilson Kenneth L., and Alejandro Portes. "Immigrant Enclaves: An Analysis of the Labor Market Experience of Cubans in Miami." *American Journal of Sociology* 86 (1980): 295–319.

Witko, Christopher, and Adam J. Newmark. "Business Mobilization and Public Policy in the U.S. States." *Social Science Quarterly* 86 (2005): 356–67.

Wittke, Carl. "Immigration Policy Prior to World War I." *Annals of the American Academy of Political and Social Science* 262 (1949): 5–14.

Wolter, K. *Introduction to Variance Estimation*. 2nd ed. New York: Springer, 2007.

Index

Page numbers with "t" or "f" indicate material in tables or figures.